Flavell Edmunds

Traces of History in the Names of Places

With a Vocabulary of the Roots out of which Names of Places in England

Flavell Edmunds

Traces of History in the Names of Places
With a Vocabulary of the Roots out of which Names of Places in England

ISBN/EAN: 9783337203801

Printed in Europe, USA, Canada, Australia, Japan

Cover: Foto ©ninafisch / pixelio.de

More available books at **www.hansebooks.com**

TRACES OF HISTORY

IN THE

NAMES OF PLACES.

LONDON: PRINTED BY
SPOTTISWOODE AND CO., NEW-STREET SQUARE
AND PARLIAMENT STREET

TRACES OF HISTORY

IN THE

NAMES OF PLACES.

WITH

A VOCABULARY OF THE ROOTS OUT OF WHICH

NAMES OF PLACES IN ENGLAND AND WALES ARE FORMED.

BY

FLAVELL EDMUNDS.

'The best and most forcible sense of a word is often that which is contained in its etymology.'—COLERIDGE.

LONDON:

LONGMANS, GREEN, AND CO.

1869.

PREFACE.

In this book, the result of many years' reading and study, I have aimed to do, for names of places in England and Wales, something like what has been done for the ordinary words of our language by the Archbishop of Dublin and other writers. In defence of my choice of this neglected branch of antiquarian lore, I feel that nothing in the way of apology is necessary: a knowledge of place-names seems to me to be essential to a right understanding of the history, topography, and antiquities of a country. The place-names of any land are the footmarks of the races which have inhabited it, and are numerous and important in proportion to the length of the stay and the numerical strength of each race. Thus the map supplies a clue to the history, and the history explains and confirms the hints of the map. While the latter gives us dates and details, leading incidents, and sketches of character, the former gives localities, preserves names of persons and forgotten episodes, and sometimes explains obscure allusions. Each is thus incomplete without the other, and together they form an essential part of a good education. In some cases important gaps in history are thus supplied, while in a still greater number the statements of historians receive valuable corroboration. It is certain that the nomenclature of a country reflects the fortunes of the people; and in this work I have taken pains to show that it not only preserves distinct records of the successive immigrations of races, but reveals with unerring accuracy the order in which they occurred, and the extent of the influence exercised by each upon the process of building up the people as we now find them.

Of late years, a perception of the importance of local nomenclature to history has begun to show itself, but hitherto it has not been recognised to any great extent. Historians generally have contented themselves with brief passing references, leaving the systematic pursuit of this branch of their subject to the philologists. The consequence of this neglect has been that we rarely find a person of ordinary education who has any idea of the rich store of interesting information which thus lies all around him. Occasionally a name strikes the mind from its oddity, and reference is made to the local or county history, or to the gazetteer, but the information there given is always scanty and often erroneous. Out of many thousand place-names in England and Wales, not a tithe of the number are explained by gazetteers or county histories; and the explanations given are founded on no principles. Above all, no rules are given for the interpretation of similar cases. I have aimed to supply these defects, and to do so in a manner which may enable the student to pursue the study for himself.

A word or two as to the mode of inquiry may here be fitly introduced. My process has been strictly inductive. Taking any given word, the first question is, does any part of it belong to a known language? If so, the next step is to interpret that part. The remainder of the word is then to be traced *first* in the same language, and afterwards in the other languages of races known to have inhabited the country. The information thus obtained will be either descriptive or historical. If descriptive, the next step is to inquire whether it accords with the present features of the locality, or with what may be fairly presumed to have been its features in the period when the language to which the word belongs was spoken there. If the word or any part of it be a proper name, the next step is to ascertain whether history records the existence of any person so named as connected with the place, or any memorable action performed there by him. Where the place-name consists—as in most instances—of a proper name and a descriptive word, we have thus gained a clue to a class of names. In all cases, it is desirable to consider the most ancient form of the name, which often contains the right clue to the derivation and the meaning. Amesbury (Wilts) may be taken as an example. In its present form, it means the *burh* or fortified town of Ame; but as there is no such personal name known as Ame, we conclude that this part of the word is corrupted. The ancient name solves the difficulty. The town was called 'Ambrose-byrig,' and the repeated allusions of old historians to the place and the district in connection with the British king Aurelius Ambrosius indicate at once the reason of the name. It is observable, too, that the descriptive word in the old historians is *byrig*, not *burh*; and this use of the dative case instead of the nominative is a fact of very frequent recurrence. Probably it was an idiom of the dialects spoken in the southern and midland parts of England. North of the Trent and the Humber, with the single exception of Bury (Lancashire), the word used is *borough*; and in the Anglian and the Norse districts of Northumberland, part of Cumberland, and the eastern part of South Scotland, the word appears more purely as *burgh*. All the three words, *bury*, *borough*, and *burgh*, however, have the same meaning—a fortified town.

The terminology used in the subsequent pages is open to differences of opinion, but is, I think, justifiable on historical grounds. The word British, for example, I have used invariably to designate the people whom the Romans found in this country, without attempting to discriminate the Pictish, Gwyddelian, and Belgic elements—an inquiry into which would have been beyond the range of the subject. So, too, with the terms Norse and Old Danish, between which I see no diversity worth mention in this inquiry. I have indeed used the latter term chiefly in a negative sense, *i. e.* to mark the fact that certain words are not part of the present Danske tongue, although certainly used by the Danes who conquered a part of England at the close of the tenth century.

On the 'vexed question' as to the proper word to

apply to the speech of the people in the four centuries preceding the Danish conquest, I have accepted the conclusion of Sir Francis Palgrave, and have given at some length the reasons which seem to me to justify that conclusion. It is certain that the Teutonic invaders were of three stocks, all speaking the same language and forming part of the same great migratory horde, but distinguished to us according to the parts of Europe from which they came to this country. Of these, the Angles seem to have been by far the most numerous as well as the earliest in their arrival, as shown by the fact that the country finally received its name from them. The Jutes were next in order of time, but fewest in number, and were soon swallowed up in the streams of immigrants from the Saxon part of Europe. The Saxons, however, previous to the commencement of the ninth century, held only the three kingdoms of Essex, Sussex, and Wessex, including altogether not more than one-fourth part of England. After that time they gradually advanced in political importance until, in the first half of the tenth century, they became supreme. We find the terms Seaxnaland and Saxony in the writers of those times, but they are always applied to the Saxon kingdoms proper, and never to the whole country. The term first used to designate the whole people living east of the Dee, the Severn, and Devonshire, is 'English,' and the earliest designation of the country which they occupied is 'England.' In writing of the people of the pre-Danish era, I have discriminated them as Angles or Saxons or Jutes, according to the evidence in each case; and their language I have styled 'Old English,' as being a nearer approach to historical accuracy than either of the terms usually employed. 'Saxon' is objectionable, as ignoring two out of the three bodies of immigrants; 'Anglo-Saxon' is historically incorrect, as implying that the Angles were the later in arrival, and were predominant over the Saxons, which is the exact reverse of the truth; while, as I have shown, neither term was ever applied by the people to themselves.

CONTENTS.

ERRATUM.

In page 44, *for* 'Cae Oswyth, St. Oswyth's meadow,' *read* 'Cae-yswydd, the meadow of the privet bushes.' The error is due to mis-spelling in a legal document. It is an example of the results of the prevalent practice of spelling British words according to English rules of pronunciation.

TRACES OF HISTORY

IN THE

NAMES OF PLACES.

The name—the first item of our knowledge of any place—is usually the last to excite any thought. To most persons, even among the intelligent, the name of the town or the village in which they live conveys no meaning, and suggests no inquiry. 'I suppose that every place must have a name, but I never thought there was any reason for the names of places,' is the sentiment of people who are otherwise well informed. There are of course exceptions; a lingering tradition, or the discussions of local antiquaries, may have fixed in the minds of the inhabitants the idea that the names of some few places embody facts of their history. The information thus obtainable by ordinary readers is, however, always scanty, often erroneous, and at best founded on no exposition of principles. It is, therefore, useless beyond the individual case. Local histories rarely command more than a local circulation: the repulsive dryness of treatment, which seems to have been cultivated by antiquaries as necessary to truth, repels the ordinary reader from their writings, and thus one of the commonest of all 'common things' is one of which less is known than of almost any other.

Thanks to the labours of my lamented friend, the late Dean of Hereford, the Earl of Ashburton, and other practical educationists, education is now made more practically useful by the introduction of many of the 'common things' of which our fathers were content to remain ignorant; and the aim of the present writer is to add another to the list. The principle may with advantage be carried much farther than it has hitherto been. The time when every schoolboy shall be taught to know the nature of the soil upon which he plays, the stone which he throws from his sling, the wild-flower which he plucks from the hedge-bottom, or the clouds which in infinite variety of form float over his head, is probably not far distant. Why should he not add to that knowledge the history of his own native town, of which its name is often not the least interesting part? Perhaps a part of the time which is now spent in teaching him the geography of Tibet or of South America, might be as usefully employed in giving him correct ideas of the county in which he was born, and in which—taking the average of English boys, from the facts of the last census—he will probably spend his whole life.

The addition of nomenclature to the 'common things' of education may perhaps be opposed by two different classes of objectors. To the happily diminishing few who think that the people have too much education already, it is not necessary to say much: the spirit of the objectors is a sufficient evidence that *they* are not among the too highly educated class. When they have ascertained the real extent of the education which the poor now receive, they will see little reason for apprehending any excess at present; and when they have mastered the facts which prove the close connection between improved education and an improved social and moral condition, they will see as little cause to dread over-education for the future. Friends of education, however, may be among the objectors; and their objection deserves a different treatment. They will probably plead that the study of names of places must necessarily be an abstruse one, requiring lingual and other previous knowledge which is beyond the range of ordinary education; and the objection would be a sound one if I proposed to make every pupil a philologist. On the contrary, I merely wish to subject nomenclature to the treatment which astronomy or chymistry now receives from the skilful teacher. He teaches his pupil the distances and magnitudes of the planets, without troubling him with the process of calculation by which those facts are proved: he inculcates the general facts of chymistry, without teaching either qualitative or quantitative analysis. In like manner, I wish merely to place in the pupil's hands the results of my own inquiries, and to indicate the principles which I have thought out. The objection itself is, indeed, an argument in favour of the study. The difficulty alluded to is the practical side of a historical truth, which, were there no other evidence of it, we could ascertain from the names of places.

Why is it that some knowledge of other languages, dead as well as living, is needed ere we can interpret the names of places in our own land? Simply because different races of men have successively inhabited it. The kindred truth, that we are a mixed people, is established in like manner by the frequent occurrence of hybrid names; while the positions of the particles which form those hybrids explain the order of succession. When we find a name belonging to one language modified according to the usages of another, that modification shows that the people who spoke the former language were conquered by those who spoke the latter.

In the names of places, we thus read the elementary facts of the history of the country. For example, in the mountain districts west of the Severn and the Dee, we find British names pure, or, if modified, merely Romanized, while on the sea-coast and in the lowlands the British names of places are only to be found here and there, hidden beneath an overgrowth of Saxon and Norse. From those facts we infer that the Britons were the aborigines, that they were worsted by the invaders, that the Romans followed them into their mountain fortresses, but that the after-coming Northman or Angle was never able to do more than hold a divided sway with the Briton over the marches, and that the Norse rover made good his footing only on the sea-coast, and on the banks of the larger rivers. History justifies these inferences in the case of our own country; and there seems no reason to doubt that the method of inquiry is applicable to other countries, at least in Europe.

The names of places in the lowlands, taken by themselves, are equally instructive. The English descent of the great body of the people is shown in the great preponderance of names belonging to the pre-Conquest period;* while the frequency of double names—the second being usually a personal name—indicates the

* 'In England, although the names of the towns and villages are almost universally of Anglo-Saxon derivation, yet hills, forests, rivers, &c., have generally preserved their old Celtic names.'—Bishop Percy.

prevalence of the feudal system. If we did not know that there had been a Norman Conquest, which changed the ruling class without making much impression upon the great body of the people, we could read the event in such names as Stoke Say or Brampton Bryan, where the Norman lord's name is appended to the English appellative; and in the fact that it is appended, we see the effect of French habits of speech upon the grandsons of the Northmen. The Angle puts his name first, as in Child's Ercall, or Tewkesbury; just as his Norse visitor Hubba or Sweyn prefixes his name to the '*ton*' or the '*ea*,' which thenceforth became Hubberston—i.e. Hubba's town, or Swansea. Another class of double names, usually to be found in couplets or triplets, indicates the division of the soil between king, lord, and church. Thus, in Herefordshire, King's Pyon answers to the neighbouring Canon Pyon, and the triplet Bishop's Froome, Canon Froome, and Castle Froome, is equally significant; while Prieststown, now Preston, contrasted with Eaton Bishop, shows the existence of priests and bishops among the landlords of pre-Conquest times. The vast power of a single baronial family we read as clearly in the frequent recurrence of a name. Taking the Lacy as an example, we find in the Welsh marches one hundred, and four parishes not within its bounds, all bearing 'Lacy' as affix to the English or British root-name.

That the Norman was the last invader of this island, and that his posterity gradually melted down into the mass of the conquered people, are facts which are indicated in the modifications which Norman names have undergone. These modifications are usually abbreviations or mutations of consonants, in accordance with the tendencies of English speech even in our own day.

The thoughtful man will not be surprised to find the facts of British History thus fossilized in British names, for he knows that place-naming is the earliest form of history. The early annals of mankind, as recorded by the sacred writers, abound with illustrations of this truth. The first city of which we have any record was named by the founder in order to commemorate his infant son;* and down throughout the patriarchal ages extends the practice of affixing memorials of events and of men, in the shape of names, to the places wherewith they were connected. The *jegar-sahadutha*, or 'heap of witness,' erected by the Israelites on the western bank of the Jordan, was so named that it might be a witness to all future ages of the historical fact that the dwellers on the eastern shore were Israelites, not less than the men of Shechem or of Ephratah. Names thus composed became the landmarks of oral tradition, and gradually passed into the corroboratives of written history. In this, as well as in other particulars, the history of the Jewish nation was a type of the histories of all other nations.

Before I proceed to consider place-names in detail, there are some general considerations which must not be overlooked. In several particulars, all the place-names which come from either British, Saxon, or Norse, have a family likeness, which is interesting as a confirmation of one of the leading maxims of ethnology. We are taught that the affinity of languages must be decided, not by mere resemblances of words, which are often accidental, but by similarity of inflections and modes of combination.

Such a similarity is to be found in the leading ideas

* 'And Cain builded a city, and called the name of the city after the name of his son Enoch.'—Gen. iv. 17.

of the place-names in the two families of Celtic and Gothic languages, while the idiom shows itself in the mode in which the different words are combined to form the name. In both, the place-name is most frequently composed of a specific and a general appellation, but the positions vary according to the idiom of the language. In the British names, the general descriptive word is placed first, the personal or specific word being treated as an adjective, and therefore postponed in compliance with the rule of construction in the Celtic tongues. Thus we find the descriptive word *llan* preceding the name of the saint to whom the church is dedicated, as Llanharmon, St. Germanus's church; *ty* in like manner precedes the name of the owner, or the specific word describing its appearance, as Ty-coch, red-house; and *tref* or *afon* is followed by some word which stands for the proper name of the village or river.

In Saxon and Norse, on the contrary, the general descriptive word is placed last, according to the law of the Gothic tongues. Thus, we have from the Saxon Eddis-burh, now Eddisbury, indicating the fortified town of Ead, and Har-burh, now Harborough, designating the hoar or ancient fortification.

From the Norse, we have such names as Gamelthorp and Ingoldsby, marking the dwelling of Ingold and the farm of Gamel. The few names for which we are indebted to the Norman-French show the Norse origin of the people in the identity of the ideas out of which the name arose, and their French training in the position of the word, which is appended like an adjective to the original name. Thus, we have three of the sixty-five Stokes which bear evidence of Norman ownership in the names Say, Lacy, and D'Abernon being added to the word 'Stoke;' while Alverstoke, Maxstoke, Basingstoke, and other names, by the positions of the general descriptive word and the owner's name, show that they remained unaffected by the Norman conquest.

In the British tongue, the adjective *hên*, old, is an exception to the rule which postpones the adjective, as in Hên-ffordd, old road; Hên-cwrt, old court; and Hênllys, old palace. In some cases, *gwyn*, white, is found preceding the specific or root-name, but these are rare exceptions to the almost universal rule. In Saxon and Norse place-names, the only exceptions to the rule are the few easily distinguished cases in which a second descriptive word is prefixed to identify different places bearing the same general name, as in Stony and Fenny Stratford, Hook and Chipping (i.e. market) Norton, &c.

For all practical purposes, the rule may be taken as invariable, that the position of the descriptive word indicates the family of languages to which the place-name belongs.

The accentuation, too, although at first sight a mark of diversity, becomes when examined an evidence of affinity. The majority of names of places in this country is composed of words of three or four syllables: when British, accented usually on the penult, but in some few instances on the ultimate; when Saxon or Norse, accented usually on the antepenult. As already explained, the place-name is composed of a general descriptive word and a specific term. This latter is in most cases the name of the owner, and is a word of two syllables. Being the distinction of the place, the word is emphasized; and the first syllable, being usually the root of the word, carries the accent. Thus Wib, a web, is the root of Wiba, the *a* marking the agent by whom the web is produced, as the syllable *er* does in modern English. Wiba having been adopted as a name, the bearer of which wished to mark out the *lege* or land which he had acquired, the place was called Wiba-lege (now Weobley). In this case the general descriptive word has been corrupted by being shortened; but the accent still remains on the first syllable.

Thus Gorham-burh and Payham-burh have been lengthened by usage into Gorhambury and Payhambury, while Cholmondeley has been shortened into Chumley. Norse names, when adopted into English usage, follow the same rule.

The accent in British place-names in like manner falls upon the first syllable of the specific name, which, as in the Gothic tongues, is usually a word of two syllables, but as the general descriptive word precedes it, the accent therefore falls upon the penult. In the words Llan-egwad and Llan-gynog, Egwad and Gynog are the specific words, being the names of the saints to whom the churches are dedicated, and the accent therefore falls upon the first syllable of each of those saints' names. Sometimes the general descriptive word is of two syllables, as *aber*, while the specific word is only of one syllable, as in Aberffraw, and there the latter takes the accent; in other cases, as in Pwll-laith, the bloody pool, the words are each of one syllable; and in a few cases a second specific word, intended to distinguish one place from another of the same general name, has become by corruption a part of the word, and then it comes last and takes the chief accent, while the first syllable of the original specific word takes a subordinate accent.

The word Llanddewifach, as commonly mis-written, is a case in point. Here the descriptive word *llan* is joined with the specific word Dewi (St. David), the first syllable of which took the accent, but when the word *fach* (little) was added to distinguish it from some larger church in the district named from the same saint, it became the emphatic word, and took the principal accent. Llanbadarnfawr is another example of the same apparent anomaly, which proceeds in all such cases from the corrupt habit of writing as one word what is really two. When they are correctly written as Llanbadarn-fawr and Llanddewi-fach, the apparent anomaly vanishes; and the student sees at once that the rule as to the accentuation of the antepenult is not affected, while the first syllable of the specific word Badarn or Dewi is in each case marked by the accent.

Out of the whole hundred saints who are commemorated in British place-names, there are only thirteen which are composed of more than two syllables; and of these nearly all are explicable on various grounds, which show that the anomaly is only apparent. In Deiniol, Elian, and Trinio, it is probable that the last two vowels form a diphthong; and in the words Tygonwy, Tyfodwg, Tyfryddwg, and Tysilio—as will be hereafter shown—the syllable *ty*, meaning a house, really belongs to the preceding word *llan*, making with it the compound 'church-house.' Of the remaining six, Gwyddelan and Gwinifor are of comparatively modern origin, leaving only four (Dinebo, Eliw, Gwstenin, and Llwchaern) as absolute exceptions to the rule that ancient British names are composed of not more than two syllables. One of these four, Eliw, is a Hebrew name, and Dinebo is of doubtful etymology, and occurs only in the name of a church in Herefordshire. *Din* means a fortification, and *abo* is a dead body, but I find no such word as *ebo* anywhere but in that one instance. It may be a form of Ebbw, the name of a river in the adjoining county of Monmouth; or the etymon may be *ebol*, a young horse, the adoption of names of animals by human beings having been a common practice in early times.

Before entering into the details of the inquiry, a word of explanation as to the terminology used may here be fitly inserted. Sir F. Palgrave has shown that historical accuracy requires us to reject the terms Saxon and Anglo-Saxon as too narrow to include the inhabitants of this country in the period between the departure of the Romans and the Danish conquest under Canute; and the only question which remains is as to the term which ought to be substituted. A brief review of the history of that period will show that there is but one term which meets the requirements of the case.

The history of the Teutonic and Scandinavian immigration begins among the mists which envelope the later years of the Roman period. In the reign of Diocletian, A.D. 288, we find Scandinavian and Saxon pirates ravaging the British coast, and soon afterwards Allectus, in overthrowing the island emperor Carausius, is said to have had an army chiefly composed of Franks and Saxons. In the course of the next forty years, there seems to have been an officer of high rank specially appointed to protect the coast, whose title, 'Comes Saxonici Littoris,' sufficiently indicates the constant flow of a stream of immigrants from the Continent. The close affinity between the dialects of Yorkshire and those of Friesland, as shown by Mr. Halliwell, renders it probable that many of these early immigrants were Frisians, but we have no data which enable us to fix the localities in this country in which they established themselves. The histories of Gildas and Nennius afford us the first clear traces of the Teutonic immigration, or, to speak more precisely, indicate the first time at which the immigrants were called in as auxiliaries by British chiefs; and the Saxon Chronicle gives us the precise dates. From those writers we learn that in 449, Vortigern—a Latinised form of the British Gwrtheyrn, 'Prince of Men'—being pressed by the Picts, or Britons of East Scotland, sought the aid of two chiefs of the Jutes, named Hengist and Horsa; that they accepted the invitation, and received the Isle of Thanet in payment for their services; and that, having conquered the enemies of their host, they afterwards conquered him in his turn. The Saxon Chronicle says, under the date of 449:—'They (Hengist and Horsa) fought against the Picts, and had the victory wheresoever they came. They then sent to the Angles, desired a larger force to be sent, and caused them to be told the worthlessness of the Britons, and the excellence of the land. Then they soon sent thither a large force in aid of the others. At that time there came men from those tribes in Germany; from the Old Saxons, from the Angles, from the Jutes.' * From Thanet, the Jutes gradually extended their sway over the adjoining country, until their authority was consolidated as the kingdom of Kent. About the same time other Jutes conquered the Isle of Wight and part of the neighbouring coast of Gwent, now known as Hants. Fifty years later, Ælla, a Saxon chief, landed on the south-east coast, destroyed the Romano-British city of Anderida, conquered the district around it, and founded the kingdom of the South Saxons. About 519, another Saxon chief, named Cerdic, carved out for himself a kingdom, afterwards

* Dr. Giles' *Translation*, p. 309.

called Wessex, amid the Britons who lived westward of Sussex; and in 527, Ercenwin, also a Saxon adventurer, founded the kingdom of Essex, which gradually extended itself over the adjoining districts now known as Middlesex and Hertfordshire. Fifty years later, Uffa erected the East Anglian kingdom; and about fifteen years after that event, viz. in 586, Crioda or Crida, an Anglian chief, made his way across the Severn, overthrew the British chiefs of the district between that river and the Wye, and founded the kingdom of the Myrcna-ric (or Marches), which is known to history under the Latinised disguise of Mercia. While these events were going on in the south, the British princes who ruled between the Humber and the Forth—there was no Scotland for ages afterwards—were subdued by two Anglian chiefs, Ida 'the flame-bearer,' and Ella the terrible, the former ruling Bryneich from Tyne to Forth under the name of Bernicia, and the latter founding in the British Deifyr, between *the two waters*, Tees and Humber, the kingdom of Deira. The dates assigned for the foundation of these two little kingdoms are 547 and 560. They remained independent for only eighty years, when they were united into the kingdom of Northumbria. For many years, the Angles of Northumbria laboured to extend their sway to the southward, but had made only transitory conquests when they were met by the Angles of Mercia advancing to the northward, and were driven back across the Humber, which became the boundary between the two kingdoms.

The kingdoms thus enumerated were successively obliterated. Mercia, under the fierce Penda, conquered part of Northumbria, and under Offa annexed East Anglia, Essex, and Kent; Sussex was in 728 absorbed into Wessex; and by the end of the eighth century the Octarchy was reduced to three kingdoms, Wessex, Mercia, and Northumbria. Soon after the year 800, Egbert of Wessex conquered Mercia, and soon afterwards reduced the king of Northumbria to a condition of vassalage. A century later, these tributary kings were suppressed by Æthelstan, who became in name as well as in fact monarch of the whole country which had been divided among the Octarchy. The sovereignty of Æthelstan may be said to have been completed as to the southern part of the island by the battle of Malvern, in 924, when he defeated the British prince and finally crushed the Britons, so that (as the Chronicle of Brut says) 'they possessed not Wye afterwards.' As to the north, the great controversy was settled at the battle of Brunanburgh, fought in 937, in which the mixed force of Britons, Danes, and Angles was overthrown beyond recovery.*

It is recorded that Egbert was the first of the Teutonic invaders who gave a collective name to the kingdoms under his sway. Caradocus of Llancarfan thus describes the name-giving:—

'All these were brought under subjection by Egbert, king of West Saxons, and this realm called England, 149 years after the departure of Cadwalader; 680 plus 149 = 829. In this year Egbert subdued Wihtlafe, king of Mercia.'

Egbert, however, continued to be called merely king of Wessex, and his successors seem to have followed

* 'From the Jutes came the Kentishmen and the Wightwarians, that is, the tribe which now dwells in Wight, and that race among the West Saxons which is still called the race of Jutes. From the old Saxons came the men of Essex and Sussex and Wessex. From Anglia, which has ever since remained waste betwixt the Jutes and Saxons, came the men of East Anglia, Middle Anglia, Mercia, and all North-Humbria.'—*Anglo-Saxon Chronicle*, 449.

his example, until the crown fell to Æthelstan, the grandson of Alfred. He not only completed the subjugation of all his rivals, but gave a collective designation to the people, by styling himself king of the English.

From this sketch of the post-Roman and pre-Danish period, several conclusions follow. First, it appears that the Saxons really formed but a small part of the immigrants, who themselves were but few in comparison with the Romano-British population, and that their ultimate supremacy was political, not numerical. The greater part of the island was conquered by the Angles, who founded four out of the eight kingdoms, viz. East Anglia, Mercia, Deira, and Bernicia, whereas the Saxons merely founded the three small kingdoms of Sussex, Essex, and Wessex. Neither the people nor the country beyond the limits of these kingdoms were ever called Saxons; in fact, after the disuse of the British name Prydain and the Roman Britannia, the only name ever given to the country east of the Wye was England, and the only designation adopted by the people was English. The first time the Anglo-Saxon Chronicle speaks of the 'nation,' it styles them 'English.' (Anglo-Saxon Chronicle, 895.)

I conclude, therefore, that the correct term for the people of this country during the period preceding the Danish conquest in 1016, must be the proper term for their language also. To that period the vast majority of place-names in this country must be assigned. To avoid ambiguity, however, I have prefixed to 'English' the adjective 'Old,' as distinguishing the first English people from the modern English natiou—the result of the fusion of all the different races and peoples which have successively settled in this island. The modern English nation, properly speaking, can scarcely be said to have begun to exist until the latter half of the fourteenth century; when Norman-French finally ceased to be the language of the court. This great change was marked, among other things, by the disuse of the Lombardic character along with the Norman-French language, in the inscriptions on tombs; and as we can fix with tolerable exactness the date when Latin and black-letter took their places, viz. between 1360 and 1377, we shall not err greatly if we regard that period as the final close of the Norman era.*

I have not attempted to distinguish between Saxon, Jutish, Frisian, and Anglian names, for the sufficient reason that any such distinction is impracticable. There is good ground for supposing that all those bodies of immigrants spoke the same language, with slight differences, out of which have sprung the provincial dialects which still exist.

The historical facts which are preserved in the place-names of England and Wales may be, for convenience, arranged in thirteen classes.

* The latest instances of the use of Lombardic characters are assigned to 1361: the earliest use of black letter—viz. on the tomb of Edward III.—to 1377.

I.

NAMES WHICH RECORD THE PHYSICAL CONDITION OF THE COUNTRY IN EARLY TIMES.

In this class is included the large number of names which are wholly or in part descriptive. Their origin is not a difficult problem. The distribution of land and water, marsh and rock, hill and plain, naturally attracts the attention of immigrants to an unsettled country; and their observation is condensed into the names which they bestow. It evidently was so with the Britons; since we find the following words belonging to their tongue forming parts of the names of places and natural objects:

Wy and *Usk*, meaning water.
Taf, a river.
Morfa, a marsh.
Cors, a bog.
Rhos, a moist plain or boggy piece of mountain land.
Aber, an estuary, or the place where a small stream falls into a larger one.
Cymmar, the confluence of two equal or nearly equal streams.
Nant, a brook.
Afon, a river.
Bettws, a piece of fertile land between a river and a hill.
Dyffryn, a river valley.
Ynys, answering to *Inch* in Scotland and *Innis* in Ireland, meaning an island.
Waun, a moor.
Cwm (corrupted into comb), a hollow.
Allt, a hanging grove or a steep place.
Bron, a pointed or breast-shaped hill.

Bryn, a hill of any other form.
Bro, *Bre*, a promontory.
Crûg, a heap or a broad hill.
Cefn, a ridge, shaped like the backbone of an animal.
Cnwc (corrupted into knock), a boss or knob of rock.
Genau, the mouth or entrance of a pass.
Pant, a broad valley or vale.
Glynn, a valley.
Hope, a sloping plain between hills.
Pen, a headland.

The Saxons, Angles, and Jutes, have also left descriptive words belonging to their tongue, which have in like manner survived in place-names:

Ea, *Ey*, *I*, *Ig*, meaning water or an island.
Bourn, a brook.
Chesil, a sandbank.
Edge, a ridge, answering to the British *Cefn*.
Hat, a heath.
Hurst, or *Hyrst*, a wood.
Holt, a hold or haunt of wild animals.
Stan, a rock.
Wold, *Weald*, or *Wood*, a wild or uncultivated place.
Worth, an estate which is well watered.
Well, answering to the British *Ffynnon*, a well or spring.
Head, answering to the British *Blaen*, the source of a stream, or the point or summit of a hill.
Mere, a pool or lake.
Flad, *Flede*, a place liable to be flooded.
Fleet, a harbour.
Shal, a flat place or shoal.
Worldsend, or simply *End*, the extremity of the cultivated land.
Nomansland, a settlement on waste land.
Car, a pool.
Carse, flat, moist land.

Some Norse descriptive words have been preserved in the same way, e.g.:

By, an abode.
Holm, a grassy bank near water, or an island.

Haugh, a green hill or declivity.
Tofte, a grove.
Beck, a brook.
Hoe, a hill.
Fors, or *Force*, a waterfall.
Thwaite, a cleared spot, answering to the Saxon *Clere* and the British *Llannerch*.
Fell (a form of *fjeld*), a range of lofty hills.
Thorp, a farm-house.
Topping, a hill.
Scaur, a precipice or rugged hill, from whence comes our word *scar*, a roughness on the skin.
Ness, *Naze*, *Nash*, a headland.
Yar, a river.
Dale, a broad valley, answering to the Saxon *Vale*, and to the British *Pant*.
Field, open land.
Ing, a field near water.

Such names need little assistance from the imagination to enable us to picture a country covered in the most part with ancient forests, here and there a cleared spot showing itself, in which man wrestled with the wild beasts for a habitation. The choice of islands, and of tongues of land, amid the reedy pools, indicates a necessity for defence; and the occurrence of name-words signifying rude fortifications suggests that men had to defend their abodes, not merely against wolves, but also against each other. This fact appears in the frequency of *din* (British for camp), and of *tun* * (Saxon), a word which originally bore the same meaning, i.e. a place enclosed by some kind of fortification. Most of these fortifications were probably mere ridges of earth, or walls of loose stone, like the 'dry stone dikes' of Scotland, but some were more elaborately constructed.

* A churchyard is called *ciric-tun*, church-town, by some Saxon authors.

In the words *stoke* and *stow*, I think we can trace the use of *stakes* of wood driven into the ground, forming what we designate by a word of the same derivation—a *stockade*. The words *wattle*, as in Wattleborough (Sussex) and *Watling* (Watling Street), seem to indicate that these stakes were sometimes wattled, i.e. interwoven with branches of trees, and the interstices filled with mud or clay.

In the frequent occurrence of the names of particular species of trees, we see the composition of the woods of ancient times, and we recognise in them the most prevalent arboreal forms of the present day. The species perpetuated by British name-words are—

Deru, now corrupted into derry, the oak.
Fedw or *Bedu*, birch.
Onw or *onn*, the ash.
Coll or *celle*, the hazel.
Wern, the alder.
Celyn, the holly.
Helygen, the willow.
Afal, the apple.
Ffawydd, the beech.

These words seem to create anew to the imagination the awful forests where dwelt the white-robed *derwyddon* or oak-priest, whose title is still preserved to us in the slightly altered form of Druid. Then, as now, the *afal* was cherished for the sake of its fruit; then, as now, the nut-bearing hazel fringed the path, or dipped into the brook its tassel-shaped flowers; the scarlet-berried holly was then the adornment of the *ïol* as now of Christmas festivities; then, as now, the alder waved beside the rivers, and the willow's golden buds were the amusement of the Briton's child, amid the keen winds of March and the fitful smiles of April.

The Saxons, Angles, and Jutes, too, have perpetuated

in their tongue the names of the trees which they found common in the pleasant land which they seized. In such names as Withington, a corruption of *withig-tun,* we see the town among the willows; the oak survives in many an Acton (*aec-tun*); the ash (*aesc* or *aecs*) in the Ashtons, Assan-dun, Axe-minster, and Ask-ham; the birch in Birk-land and Birch-hill; the beech in Bocking* and Bucking-ham; the elm in Elm-ley; and the alder or orle in Orle-ton. The lesser forms of vegetation are also recorded. The yarrow and the fern may be traced in the names of many a place where, doubtless, they grew for ages. The commonness of the Genista, or common broom, in those early times, is testified by the many places in the names of which *brom* or *broom* is found. Probably Docklow (Herefordshire) is so named from the Rumex, and means the *low* or hill on which the *dock* grew. Thus also Sugwas, on the Wye, records the fact that the sedges (*segga*) grew in the *waes* or moist place beside the stream, when the Angle first plashed his oars in Silurian waters.

* From *boc* comes book, the earliest Saxon books being made of beech bark. So the Latins got their *liber*.

II.

NAMES WHICH INDICATE THE FAUNA.

THE names of the wild animals which were found in the country are also preserved in the place-names, although less frequently in British than in English and Norse names. The presence of the eagle on Snowdon is recorded in its British name, Creigiau-yr-eryri, the eagles' rocks; but grand as such a name is, there is something grander still in the title of the highest peak of the same range. *Y Wyddfa*, the presence, is perhaps the most sublime name that mountain ever received. It is a poem in two words.

The less poetical mind of the Saxon was not an unobservant one. He seems to have been particularly fond of adopting the name of some wild animal as his own, or giving it to his child, thus laying the foundation of that science of heraldry which the Normans afterwards treated as a part of their feudal system. In that way, I think, came the great variety of names of animals which we find included in the place-names of the pre-Norman era. Here is a list of some of them:

Adder, *Adding*, from *aetor*, an adder.
Bever, from *beofor*, a beaver.
Brock, from *broc*, a badger.
Buck, a male deer.
Buzzard, a buzzard.
Caven, from *cheven*, a chub.
Cran, from *cran*, a crane.
Craw, *Crow*, from *craw*, a crow.
Deer, from *deor*, a deer.
Doe, a doe.

Eagle, Ern, Ayl, from *aern, aegl*, an eagle.
Finch from *finc*, a linnet.
Hare, from *hara*, a hare.
Hart from *heorot*, a hart.
Hawk, a hawk.
Hearn, a heron.
Ted, Tad, Tod, tod, a fox.
Wulf, Wolv, from *wulf*, a wolf.

The prevalence among the Teutonic nations of this custom of naming men from the cognizance on their shields, is remarked by Carlyle, in the introduction to his 'Life of Friedrich II.,' e.g.:—'Albrecht der Bär, Albert the Bear. That name he got not from his looks or qualities, but merely from the heraldic cognizance on his shield, as was then the mode of names.' This remark refers to the eleventh century, but the practice was then an ancient one.

Hunting being a favourite diversion among the old English as well as among the Normans, we have frequent traces of animals of the chase. Harrow, Harewood, and Haran-ey (now Hornsea, Middlesex), are named from the hare; Tedstone and Todmorden from the *tod*, or fox; Deoraby (now Derby), Deerhurst, etc., from the deer; Roe-hampton, from the roe; Hind-well and Hindmarsh from the hind; Otterbourn and Ottercliffe from the otter, etc.

That cats were kept in the pre-Norman period is shown by such names as Cates-by, Cat-thorp, and Cater-ham. The cat was also a heraldic symbol, and its name was a personal designation in Scotland as well as in England, being the cognizance of the great clan Chattan.

Ferocious animals, as well as the hardly less ferocious men who chose them as their symbols, may be traced in the names of places which they probably once haunted.

A group of places on the Wye, between Hereford and Ross, records in its nomenclature the presence of some terrible wild beast, perhaps the sole survivor of a race of Saurians. *Ffau,* the British term for a wild beast's den, forms part of the names of three places, situated within a short compass, among the hills of that district: Ffauenhwpp, now Fownhope, the slope of the den; Ffau-wy, now Foy, the water near the den; and Ffau-lle (now Fawley),* the place of the den. The legend of the Dragon of Mordiford belongs to the same neighbourhood, and may refer to the monster whose 'den' is commemorated in those names. The late eminent archæologist, Sir S. R. Meyrick, explained the word Mordiford as the *ffordd* (way) to the *wy* (water), in which the dragon met his *mord* (death); but there is a serious objection to this etymology, which that distinguished antiquary seems to have overlooked. The word *mord*, the root of our word murder, is Teutonic, while the rest of the word Mordiford is admitted by him to be British. But the majority of the names in the vicinity are British, and hence it seems probable that the whole of the word Mordiford belongs to the same language. This derivation is strengthened by the circumstance that, taken as a British word, it falls into a large class of place-names which accurately describe the position. Mae-'r-dwy-ffordd, i.e. the place on the road by the two waters, is a name which would naturally be given to a spot lying between the confluent streams of the Wye and the Lugg.

The same legendary allusion, as in the *Ffau* group of names, is curiously reflected in the English names of a similar group of places lying not many miles to the westward: the river Worm, and the villages of Worm-

* Hence perhaps the baronial name Foley.

bridge, Worms-ley, Wormside, Wormhill, and Wormhlaew (now Wormelow). The word *worm*, although cognate with *ormr* (N.), a serpent, seems in early and mediæval times to have meant a reptile of almost any kind, doubtless from the kind of motion common to most animals of that class. It needs not to be said that precision in the names of animals, as in those of plants, is an improvement of very recent times, as every old herbal or book of natural history shows. The real serpent and the legendary dragon were, until the revival of classical knowledge, included under the phrase 'the cruelle worme,' as our ancient English ballads show. These creatures were afterwards distinguished by the words *serpens* and *δράκων*, which were transplanted from the Latin and Greek tongues.

Taken in connection with this part of the inquiry, the use of the red dragon, *y ddraig coch*, as the armorial bearing or standard of the Britons, is not devoid of interest. Whether that standard was a relic of the widely-spread worship of the serpent, as some eminent writers argue, or had a local origin, like the place-names quoted above, is a question into which it is unnecessary to enter here.

From these dim vestiges of the pre-historic times, we advance to more certain traces when we notice—

III.

NAMES WHICH INDICATE THE OCCUPATION AND MILITARY ORGANIZATION OF THE PEOPLE.

THE frequency of place-names derived from agriculture carries its own lesson with it. We see that the great body of the people, in British as well as in early English times, gained their subsistence from the cultivation of the soil. The pastoral occupation of one part of the British people is indicated by place-names which include the words *bu* (cow), and *bwla* (bull); while the occurrence of *ar* (ploughed land), *garth* (farm), etc., show that tillage was the pursuit followed by others. That much of the land was common, may be seen in the number of names of which *cyd* (common) forms part, as in *Cymin*, 'common hill,' near Monmouth.* A large part of the land, however, was appropriated, as shown in the frequency of the word *tir* (an estate), and *manor* (*maen-or*, i.e. stone boundary). The latter word indicates, too, that the use of stone walls as fences is a very ancient practice.

In the occurrence of the words *llan* and *llain*, the same practice of enclosing land is indicated, although the former word will more properly fall under notice when we come to treat of the traces of the religion of our forefathers.

The Teutonic branch of our ancestry have, in like manner, recorded the pastoral employment of many among them, by such names as Cow Honeybourne,

* *Min*, a brow. *Minax*, Latin, is derived from the same root, and means literally brow-beating.

Neat-hill, Net-ley, Ship-ton, i.e. sheep-town, and Cottes-wold, the 'cot' being the shepherd's hut. As all the more fertile parts of the island had fallen into English hands, we are not surprised to find the world Carl or Charl, a corruption of *ceorl*, a husbandman, forming part of the names of 38 places in the midland and southern counties. The frequency of the word Bar-ton shows that bere, a denomination which perhaps included rye as well as barley, was very commonly cultivated, although such words as Wheat-hill and Wheaten-hurst show that the more valuable kind of corn was also raised.

Horses were bred to a great extent among the Britons, as we gather from Cæsar's Commentaries; and it would seem, from the occurrence of such names as Trefil, Herefordshire and Breconshire, i.e. Horse-town, and Rhyd-y-meirch (Mon.), the stallions' ford, that the Britons had stud-farms. The word Hors occurs in some English place-names, but there it seems to be a half mythologic reminiscence. The names of Hengist (stallion) and Horsa (mare) are stated to be those of the Saxon chiefs invited into the island by Vortigern, and the white horse was a favourite symbol among the Saxon part of the English people. Hence the gigantic 'white horses' cut on the sides of the chalk hills in Wilts and other counties. To this day, the white horse is the armorial bearing of the German Saxon.

Next to agriculture, the trade of the smith, as the forger of weapons of war, stands highest among a rude people, but it has left fewer traces than we might have expected. Smith-wick, Smithy, Smith-field, may serve as specimens of this class.

The dyeing and fulling of cloth seem to have been carried on to a considerable extent, although there are but doubtful traces of the weavers. It may be that some of the names beginning with Wad indicate places where the woad (*Isatis tinctoria*) was cultivated for the sake of the blue dye, which was obtained from it as far back as the times when British warriors used it to paint their bodies for battle. In Herts, Notts, and Yorks., we have place-names of which Wilk, Walk, and Walker, from *wealcere*, a fuller of cloth, form part; and in Herefordshire and Wales the word *Pandy*, a fulling-mill, is equally significant as to the existence of that trade among the Britons.

The military organisation and self-government in which British and Teutonic institutions were so much alike, are also handed down to us in the names of places. Cantred and commot are alike in meaning to Hundred and Division; while the tithing, the unit of the Saxon system, is preserved in the names beginning with Tat, Tath, Tatten, Tatter, Toot, Totten, and Tattings, all which seem to be derived from *teotha*, a tithing, or group of ten families, who were responsible for the good order of their little district, and for the payment of the *bot* or fine leviable in the case of a homicide or other offence of which the perpetrator could not be ascertained. In some parts of England, the places where the men of a given district assembled together in arms are indicated by the word Wap, Wapper, or Wappen, and the district is still called a wapontake, the place where the people 'took weapons' together.

IV.

NAMES WHICH INDICATE THE RELIGION OF THE PEOPLE.

The indications of the religion of the ancient Britons are in keeping with the subject; dim, shadowy, uncertain; names of things more frequently than names of places. The *crom-lech* (crooked or covering stone), the *llech-faen* (broad, flat, altar-like stone), and the *maen-hir* (tall, upright stone, like the Roman god Terminus), designate rude structures or natural masses of rock, whether sacrificial, sepulchral, or memorial the learned have not agreed. The names of Ave-bury, Aven-bury, Aw-bury, and the like—in the British half of the word—may perhaps contain an allusion to the *awen* or sacred frenzy, which was supposed to make the priesthood prescient; an inspiration resembling that of the Pythoness of Greece. This conjecture is to some extent strengthened by the fact that Ave-bury is the name of one of the greatest of the Druidic temples, but it is only as a conjecture that I offer it.

About the traces of Teutonic and Norse paganism, there can be little doubt. The Erming Street—as the Saxon Chronicle tells us—is clearly the street named from the *Er-mund-sul*, or image of the war-god; whose worship is also recorded in the word *wig* (as in Wig-stone), meaning both war and the idol which personified it; Tiw or Tuisco, from whom Tuesday is named; Thor, the hammer wielder and thunder god; Freya, the Northmen's Venus; Seater, whose *daeg* is still called Saturday; Woden, the deified warrior; Loki, the mischief-making deity; and Balda, or Baldur, the sun-god, whom he is said to have slain with an arrow of mistletoe, still survive in such names as Tew (Herts), Thores-by (Linc.), Friday-thorpe (Yorks.), Satter-thwaite (Camb.), Wednes-bury (Staff.), Lox-ley (Yorks.), and Bald-ock (Herts). In words like Wickers-ley (Yorks.), we recognise the *wicca's* (witch's) abode; and in Ais-thorp and Ais-monder-ley, the farm and mound-protected place, named from the Northman's paradise, As-gard. That the Northmen of both races had temples, and offered up sacrifices, is shown by the existence of several groups of names, in different parts of the island. Tib-shelf (Derbyshire), Tib-burton (Glouc.), Tibrintin-tun, now Tiberton (Herefords.), and Tiverton (Devon.), like Tiben-ham (Norf.), all seem to come from the root of *tiber* in Saxon and *tivor* in Norse, meaning a victim. In the ancient Norse poem entitled, 'The Völuspâ,' is the line—

'Ek sâ Baldri blôdgum tivor,'
I foresaw for Baldur, that bloody victim.

Other evidence of this fact will come under notice when we have to treat of the tribal settlements (*ingaham*, etc.) of the Saxons and Norsemen.

When we come to traces of early Christianity, we are struck by the frequency of the word *Llan.* Three-fourths of the names of the parishes of Wales and the Marches begin with this word, which has come to signify a church and its grave-yard.

Anciently, however, it meant an enclosure for any purpose. The well-known practice of the early Christian missionaries, in transferring heathen temples, festivals, sacred wells, &c., to the purposes of the new religion, may help us to see how the meaning of the word *llan* became restricted. The sacred enclosures of paganism, as enclosures, would be called by this name, just as an orchard is still called *ber-llan*, and a sheep-fold *corph-llan*; and when the Christian Church supplanted the temple, the word was still retained to designate the enclosure, while its general meaning was in course of time forgotten. In such a word as Leintwardin (Heref.), we seem to see a trace of the extended meaning. Llain-dwr-din is 'the water-camp of the strip' or patch of land; and a reference to the map will show that the village is seated on a piece of land lying between the Teme and the hills, and thus separated from the rest of the champaign country. The word Eglwys (from the Greek ἐκκλησία) seems to distinguish a church founded in later times, on a site *not* sacred to heathenism.

It may be interesting to note by the way how strongly the nationality of the Briton comes out in the names appended to the word *llan*. With a few scriptural exceptions, such as Llan-stephen and Llan-silo (the churches of St. Stephen and St. Silas), the dedication of churches in Wales is mostly to British saints, of whom the only records are hidden in the Welsh hagiology. We all know that Wales had its St. David, whose name is irreverently shortened into Taffy; but very few men born to the eastward of the Severn have learned to see, in the frequency of the name Llanddewi, the affectionate remembrance in which the British race for long ages held their greatest missionary. The very names of the British saints, about one hundred of which still survive in those of the churches dedicated to them, have to us a strange, uncouth sound.

The names of British saints which are thus preserved may in most cases be identified from the 'Lives of British Saints,' and similar works. It is interesting to note the fate which has befallen them in different parts of Britain. Only three of them remain in the appellations of places east of the Severn, viz. St. Lefan, in Lavington, St. Cewydd, in Kew, and St. Tangwn, in Tangwn-town, now Taunton. In the district lying between the Severn and the Wye, we find St. Briafel, St. Clydawc, St. Cain, and St. Idloes, commemorated in St. Briavels (Glouces.), Clodock (Heref.), and Cainham (Heref.). Devon retains St. Petrox, who appears also in Pembrokeshire as Petros. St. Cain is still known in Cornwall, under the scarcely altered name of Keyne, whose famous 'well' is familiar to readers of poetry by means of Southey's amusing ballad. Probably the good saint herself, who was the daughter of a British king, and was one of the early Christian martyrs, would have been somewhat surprised, if not disgusted, if she could have foreseen the ludicrous superstition which is connected with her name. 'Welweorthunga,' as the Saxons called it, or well-worship as modern English renders the word, was a form of paganism which survived all down through early English times, in spite of the adroitness of the monks in naming the holy wells from St. Bride and other heroines of Christianity; and in spite, too, of the punishments denounced against it in the Anglo-Saxon laws. It scarcely can be said to have died out until some time after the Reformation. The Derbyshire custom of well-dressing is, however, the only trace—and that a picturesque and harmless one—which survives at the present time.

Besides St. Cain and St. Budda or Badawc, which it shares with the Welsh, Cornwall has some saints of its own, whose names are still preserved in its nomenclature, viz. Dilpa, Hydrock, Ives, Morran, Madion, Maela, Merther, Piran, Ruth, Sennen, and Zeal.

The saints' names which occur in the Welsh counties only are the following:

Aedan
Afan
Anno
Arthan
Asaf
Badrig
Bayham
Beuno
Brân
Brochmael
Brynach
Cadfan
Caedwyn
Cammarch
Canten
Carfan
Cathan
Cattwg
Cenau
Cenydd
Crannog
Cybi
Cynllo
Cynog
Cyntaf
Cynwyd
Degai
Dewi
Dinebo
Deiniol
Dogmael
Dogo (Oudoceus)
Dyfan
Eadwen
Egwad
Elen
Elian
Eliw
Elli
Elwedd
Ffili
Fwyst
Gafo
Garmon
Glewis
Gulan
Gwerydd
Gwfor
Gwinifor or Winifred
Gwladys
Gwnog (perhaps only a form of Cynog)
Gwrda
Gwstenin
Gwyddelan
Heinwyn
Hetty
Idan
Idloes
Ilan
Ilar
Ilid
Illtyd
Llechyd
Llowell
Llwchaern
Mabli
Mabon
Madawc
Maelog
Mathaern
Medwg
Meurig
Milo
Moel
Nam
Niddan
Nietan
Nonn
Oswal
Padarn
Peblig
Petros
Rhwst
Sannea
Sannor
Seiriol
Tanwg
Tegfan
Tegonwy (probably a corruption of Tygonwy)
Tegwen
Teilo
Trillo
Trinio
Tudnof
Twrwg
Tydfil
Tyfodwg
Tyfryddwg
Tygai
Tyssilio
Tyssul
Wenarth
Wonno
Wrda
Wrtyd

The word Llan-dy-faelog, the church-house of Maelwg, taken with the occurrence of *dy*, the feminine form of the word *ty*, as a prefix to the names of Fodwg, Fryddwg, Gai, Gwen, Silio, Conwy, Nam, and Sul, seems to point to a fact which is still traceable in the structure of some of the ancient churches of Ireland and Wales. In those cases a part of the church was fitted up as a house for the clergy who ministered within its walls; and the same practice seems to have continued down far into mediæval times. The parish church of Kingsland (Heref.), and many of our cathedrals, have chambers over or adjoining the porches, cloisters, and other parts of the structure, which seem to have been the abode of devotees or of functionaries connected with the service of the church. In Cornwall, we have similar cases in Lan-ty-Hydrock, Lan-ty-Dilpa, &c.

Of most of the personages commemorated in the names given *ante* we know very little. Badrig is a Welsh disguise for St. Patrick, whose missionary journeyings in the former half of the fifth century included Wales. Brân, whom the Triads style 'Fendigaid' or 'the blessed,' is stated to have been the father of Caractacus. Tydfil, one of the early martyrs, was one of the twenty-five daughters of King Brychan, of Brycheiniwg or Breconshire. Garmon is a form of the name of Germanus, the famous bishop of Troyes, in France, whose exertions in combating the Pelagian heresy fill a large space in the history of his time. Illtyd, surnamed 'the blameless,' the Iltutus of monkish Latin writers, was a knight before he became a Christian missionary; a true Bayard, who lived a thousand years before the *chevalier sans peur et sans reproche*.

Cai or Gai is the name of one of the knights of Arthur's court; and Teyrn, whose name, Latinised into

Tegernacus, remains upon an incised stone at Capel Brithdir (Glam.), was one of the grandsons of Gwladys, a sainted daughter of King Brychan Brycheiniwg, but whether he was the patron saint after whom Tintern (Din-teyrn) was named, is not certain, although highly probable.

Gwladys, whose name often re-appears in mediæval times in the Anglicised form of Gladdice, was a sister of the martyr Tydfil (who was murdered by the Picts, A.D. 400); and Brynach was one of her twenty-five brothers, all (so says the legend) being like herself saints and most of them martyrs.

A pretty legend of the wooing and wedding of this royal lady is told in the 'Lives of British Saints.' King Gwynllin loved her, was repulsed by her father King Brychan, and carried her off. The angry father pursued, slew many of the lover's followers, but was finally beaten off by King Arthur, who came to the rescue of the lovers. A successful elopement does not seem to make out a valid claim to saintship, but sainted the lady certainly was, for some reason which satisfied her compatriots, although it eludes our search.

Nonn is remembered as the mother of St. Dewi or David. Ilar is Hilary bishop of Poictiers. Meurig wears in Welsh hagiology the triple crown of king, saint, and martyr, but we have no facts to justify the honours thus heaped upon his memory, save that he died in battle at Pwll-meurig in Monmouthshire, in the later days of the unavailing struggle against the Saxons. Maelog was brother of Gildas the historian, and is recorded to have retired to a cell at Gelly-faelog (Glam.), in 603. The existence of Cattwg rests on the sure evidence of the incised stone bearing his name, which was dug up some twenty years ago in

Breconshire, and is preserved by being built into one of the buttresses of the church of Llanfihangel Cwm-dû, near Crickhowell. Of Llwchaiarn, the oddly named —the word meaning 'iron-dust'—we know nothing; and many others in the list are to us mere shadows, good and useful men and women as we believe them to have been.

Cybi is memorable for his connection with the Roman pharos or lighthouse on Holyhead mountain. On that bleak spot he fixed his abode for many years, and it may be believed that he humanely performed the duties of light-house keeper. The saints of the Romano-British age were no mere idle dreamers, but true hard-working Christians; and we can well believe that St. Cybi, while striving to enlighten the minds of his countrymen, did not forget to supply such of them as voyaged by sea with the material enlightenment so necessary for their safety at night when passing the rocky promontory named from him Caer-gybi, or Cybi's Roman camp.

Brochwel is somewhat grotesquely portrayed for us in the uncomplimentary addition of Ysgithrog, or 'long-toothed.' He is said to have been a king of the district now called Breconshire, A.D. 617; but his 'long tooth' remains the only distinct fact by which he is remembered.

St. Badarn, whose name appears in Latin writers as Patarnus, is recorded in ancient writings (Myfyrian Archæology, vol. ii. p. 50) as having come over with St. Cadfan from Britanny in A.D. 524, at the head of a somewhat inconveniently large band of monks. We may suspect that a figure, perhaps two, have crept into the text in the course of ages, but there the number stands, just 847—enough to fill a squadron of the ships of the sixth century. At Llanbadarn, near the spot where now the pretty bathing-town of Aber-ystwyth stretches along the shore, St. Badarn founded a college, which became famous.

Gwynifer, a saint of the seventh century, better known by the English softening of her name into Winifred, is the best known of all the hundred to general readers. St. Winifred's well was for many ages a great place for pilgrimages and for miracles of the most astounding nature, and its legendary history is familiar to everybody. The fair saint's walk down the hill at the place now called Holy-well, bearing in her hands the head which a ruthless wooer, Prince Caradoc, had just struck off with his sword, has been painted and sung a thousand times.

It is curious that a similar miracle is told of an Anglian royal lady, Osyth or Oswyth, the daughter of Redwald King of East Anglia, with this difference, that she is said to have been beheaded by the Danes, when they destroyed the church and nunnery in Essex which she founded and at which she lived. The ghastly promenade, the headless body carrying in its hands the severed head, is recorded in both legends, and seems to have been equally purposeless and resultless in both cases.

St. Peblig, in which name we recognise the common Roman name Publius, is recorded to have been a son of the Emperor Maxentius, who figures in British legends under the name of Maxen Wledig. The contrast between father and son, the cruel heathen tyrant and the Christian missionary and martyr, is striking and instructive, although but one of many such which the end of the third century presents to any one who knows the history of the time.

St. Beuno, who is said to have restored St. Winifred to life, after her headless promenade, is memorable for a posthumous miracle equally wonderful and true with that of which the fair princess was the subject. As with St. Teilo, after his death three churches claimed his body, which obligingly multiplied itself by three, so as to gratify them all.

St. Asaf is one of the names which connect the religious history of Wales with that of Scotland. St. Kentigern or Mungo founded a Christian community on the spot now called St. Asaph's, and on his departure left Asaf as his successor in the government of the 365 brethren who kept up daily worship where the cathedral now stands.

St. Bridget, a king's daughter, is the only native Irish saint whom we can trace in the place-names of this country; and she seems to have been almost equally popular with Britons and English. The latter softened and shortened her name to Bride, and dedicated to her many wells in different parts of the kingdom, as shown by the frequency of the phrase St. Bride's-well. A royal palace, built near the well of St. Bride in London, was thence named Bridewell; and, having been given up by one of the Edwards to the citizens of London, was by them converted into a prison, and thus the name of a holy well has become a common term for a gaol. Among the Britons, the fair saint's name seems to have been put only to a strictly religious use.

Although disguised to any but Welsh and antiquarian eyes under the form of Ffread or Ffraed, the name of St. Bridget is the designation of several churches in Monmouthshire, Herefordshire, and Radnorshire. The Herefordshire church has been still further disguised by the translation of the saint's name into the Saxon form, and its combination with the word *stow* (station); but in the Liber Landavensis we find the place now called Bridstow designated by its original name of Llansanffread.

St. Elian, who is commemorated in an out-of-the-way spot of Anglesea, is known in these days only by the odd superstition which clings around the little closet called his chamber. It has a narrow doorway, so small that few persons of average bulk can squeeze themselves through it; yet at the annual wake people of all magnitudes attempt the difficult feat, in the firm belief that he or she who succeeds will thereby be rendered lucky. When a betrothed couple make their way through the narrow entrance, they are supposed to be thus made certain of happiness for life.

The existence of St. Cadfan, a native of Britanny, who, like Germanus, came to Wales to preach against Pelagianism, is established by the inscription on the stone near the holy well dedicated to him, at Towyn, in Merionethshire. It is believed to be a genuine memorial of his time, the sixth century, and is the oldest inscribed stone in Wales.

Llan-sior (Denb.) is the only church in Wales named from the English patron St. George.

The names of Milo and Oswal are worthy of note, as the only English saints who seem to have been admitted by the Britons to like honour in their saint roll. Milo is a contraction of Milburgha, the name of a Mercian princess, who, like Frideswide and many other kings' daughters, became a nun, and was afterwards canonised. She is commemorated at Llanfilo (Brecon.), and at Stoke St. Milborough (Salop). 'Oswal' was the pious king of Northumbria, who on August 5, 642, lost both throne and life for the sake of his faith; and as his death occurred on the spot in Salop afterwards named from him Oswaldestref, which was then included in the British princedom of Powys, it is not surprising that the hearts of the Christian Britons warmed to the young martyr king, Angle as he was. Perhaps the brutal savagery of Penda, wreaked even on the dead body of the Christian king—which he ordered to be cut in pieces, and to be suspended thus piece-meal on three crosses, in derision of Oswald's faith—had the usual effect of like exhibitions, in endearing the victim to the silent spectators. There was, however, another reason for the bond of fellowship. Oswald, when a youth, was for some years an exile in Scotland, and while there he was taught the Christian verity by the Culdees, who like the Britons denied the authority of the Pope and rejected Rome's distinctive dogmas.

To the British Christian, who had been smarting for centuries from the vengeance denounced against his race by the Roman missionary Augustin, Oswald was a brother at once in his faith and in his sufferings.

Our idea of a martyr is somewhat rudely disturbed when we learn that Oswald died in battle against the heathen king Penda, but the Christians of his age—at least those of British race—saw no incongruity in the union of the two characters in the same person. They were in truth somewhat too combative at all times, and when Roman Christianity and Saxon Paganism combined to harass and slaughter them, the provocation seems to have become too strong for the Briton's Christian principles. The old warlike spirit of the race blazed out again;

> Even in their ashes lived the wonted fires.

This combative spirit is curiously exemplified in the

fondness of the Britons for the name of Michael, the warrior archangel. Of all the so-called saints' names which are not those of British men and women, this is the most frequent in its occurrence. Under the form of *fihangel,* it occurs in the names of thirty-seven parishes in the thirteen Welsh counties, while there are no Llanfihangels in any other part of the kingdom. In two cases in Herefordshire the name is translated, and appears as Michaelchurch, but both are near the Welsh border.

Of places in Britain named from the Virgin Mary there are only twenty, one of which (Llanfairwaterdin) is in Salop, three are in Monmouthshire, and the rest in Wales. It would seem that the Roman doctrine in reference to the Mother of our Lord did not reach Wales very early.

Closely connected with religion are the funeral observances of a people; and the frequency of the words *carn, carnedd,* and the plural *carneddau,* may be held as indicating the habit of erecting a tumulus over the grave of an eminent person. Unless, indeed, the reader should prefer the explanation which treats the *carn* as a memorial or a beacon, or both in succession. Sacred history affords frequent instances of the erection of memorial heaps: Joshua's carn of twelve stones to commemorate the passing of the Jordan will at once recur to the reader's memory. The position of many of these carneddau, on the summit of lofty hills, is equally favourable to the belief that they were used as beacons to announce the approach of an invader. The word *tump* (from *twmpath,* any artificial mound of earth) may show that the Britons sometimes, if not always, raised that kind of sepulchral memorial.

Like the Saxon *baerw,* barrow, the tump was an

artificial hill raised over a grave, either circular, oblong, or square in form. The sepulchral object of the heap has been sufficiently proved by the abundance of human and other remains which have been disinterred in the excavation of this class of mounds. In the Welsh marches, the word tump is still in common use to designate an artificial hill or mound.

That the Teutonic invaders were Pagans when they arrived in this country is shown by the many place-names derived from the names of their gods, some of which I have already quoted; that they did not establish themselves west of the Wye until after their religion was changed, might also be asserted from the nomenclature of the Marches, if we had no historical records to prove it. No Saxon idol names are to be found in Herefordshire or Salop.

The early history of Christianity in Old English times has not left so many traces in the nomenclature of the country, as there would have been, had the Norman conquest not followed. The expulsion of the relics of English saints, and the re-dedication of their altars to saints of Norman lineage, were among the heaviest blows dealt by the invaders at the national feeling of the English people. As the monks and priests were in most cases displaced along with their patron saint, the old name soon died out of memory.

Here and there churches dedicated to Alphage or Alkmund, to Botolph or Ethelbert, to Milburgha or Frideswide, may still be found, but they are very rare.

In a few places, the word timber, as in Timber-land (Linc.), indicates the old English custom of bequeathing a piece of land for the maintenance of the fabric of some church. As the churches were mostly built of wood—the verb to build, 'getymbren,' means literally to put timbers together—at first probably the land so bequeathed was woodland. The establishment of *ciric-scot*, now called church-rate, put a check to the practice of leaving 'tymbre-land,' or we should probably have found more than two places named from it.

That there were monasteries among the Britons, is shown by such names as Ysbytty, now Spitty, from the Latin *Hospitium*; Mynach-dy, the monk's house; Tir-mynach, the monk's estate; Llan-llienu, now Leominster, the nun's church, &c. In like manner, the old English religious houses are traceable in Abban-dun, now Abingdon; Abban-haela, now Abinghall, Abberley, and Monkland.

The worship of relics and images in the Old English period is shown by such names as Halifax, from a *fax*, or tress of hair, which was supposed to be holy; and Spon (as in Spondon), where a *spon* or splinter of the 'true cross' seems to have been preserved.

V.

NAMES WHICH HAVE OUTLIVED THE MEMORY OF THE PERSON OR EVENT WHICH THEY WERE MEANT TO COMMEMORATE.

Among the British place-names of this class we may instance Cwmgaedwin, named after some forgotten saint called Caedwin; Adfor-ton, from Cadfor; and many names of particular fields, hills, rocks and other natural objects. Upon a single estate in Monmouthshire, for example, the following place-names are found:

Gworlod-y-merthyr, the martyr's meadow.
Cae-croes-faen, stone cross field.
Pen-y-beddau, hill of graves.
Gworlod-y-tin, meadow of the fortifications.
Coed-crau-lyn, the wood of the pool of blood.
Gworlod Oswyth, St. Oswyth's meadow.

In like manner, every good guide-book to Wales * points out places in almost every neighbourhood which are known by such names as 'Stone of Weeping' or 'Place of Slaughter,' or 'Pool of Blood;' and the reader may be reminded of the practice of other nations. Near Rhuddlan (Flints.) a remarkable group of names indicates a series of sad events of which history says nothing:

Bryn-y-saethau, the hill of arrows.
Bryn-y-lloddfa, the hill of slaughter.
Pant-y-gwae, the vale of woe.

* Cliffe's Books of North and South Wales, for example.

Bryn-y-coaches, the hill of war chariots.
Pwll-y-crogwen, the pool of executions.
Braich-y-dadleu, the hillock of strife.
Pant-erwin, the vale of severity.
Cae-yr-orsedd, the field of the tribunal.

At Beaumaris (Angl.), a tract of land now covered by the sea is known as Traeth-wylofaen, 'the sands of weeping.'

Near Chirk in like manner we find:

Castell-crogwen, the castle of the executions.
Adw-yr-beddau, the fallow-field of graves.

And a part of the town of Oswestry commemorates in the name of Pentre-poedd, 'the burnt village,' some one of many times when it has been sacked and burnt in the border wars. Rhos-ddiarbed, 'the field of no quarter,' now Caersws (Montgomeryshire), commemorates the slaughter of the army of Locrinus by that of his injured wife Gwendoline, as the tale is told by Geoffrey of Monmouth, and is retold by Spenser in his 'Faëry Queen,' and Milton in his 'Comus.'

Washington Irving's description of the hill near Granada from which the last Moorish monarch of that kingdom took his last sad look of his lost realm, which was called from that fact, 'The last sigh of the Moor,' indicates a similar habit among the Spaniards, like ourselves, half-Celtic, half-Gothic in race.

In the case of Pwll-meuric (Mon.) we see commemorated one of the heroes of a legend known only to readers of the Liber Landavensis. But for the old monk's labour, corroborated as it is by the name, we should have known nothing either of the battle of Mathern or of the heroism of the chief Meurig. So, too, that better known but still shadowy personage, the British king Aurelius Ambrosius, is commemorated in the names of Croft Ambry, Amesbury, (anciently Ambrose-burh), and Amber-ley; while his great descendant Uther Pendragon (dragon-crested) still survives in Hudders-field, the local pronunciation 'Huthers-field' being in this as in many other cases a safe guide to the derivation; and Arthur, the hero of a beaten nationality, is commemorated in the name of many a hill, wood, or cairn. The story of Brychan Brycheiniwg, with his twenty-five sons and twenty-five daughters, all saints and most of them martyrs, has been handed down along with the name which the royal martyr has left to Brycheiniwg and its county, although English eyes can scarcely discern it through the modern disguise of 'Brecon.'

The Old English place-names are remarkable for the number of forgotten personages whose names they preserve. Some of these are probably the originals of many of our common surnames. Thus Ealdred, 'aged counsellor,' has become successively Aldred and Aldridge; Ulfwin, 'victorious wolf,' has been softened into Allen; Æthelred, 'noble in council,' has passed into Audry, and Æthelred's-ley (land) is now Audley; Billings-gate is a memorial of a once-noted chief named Belin; Briht, 'illustrious,' survives as Bright, Brett, and Birt; Cuccwin, 'the cock of victory,' has passed into Cocking; Cwicchelm is preserved in Cuckams-ley; Ilcat or Elchat, the founder of Ilkeston, has given rise to the name of Halkett, Hridel to Riddell, Gippa to Gipps, Londa to Lund, Sigbert to Cibber, Flacca to Flack and Affleck, Wihtred to Wither, Webherd to Webber, Cenred to Kennard, Cynric to Kenrick and Kendrick, Lilla to Lilly, Godmund to Goodman, and Godwin to Goodwin. So in more recent times the same race have evolved such names as Littler, Golightly, and

Longfellow out of Laidlaw, Longueville, and Gellatly. To this day, English readers, when perusing Scott's 'Waverley,' generally pronounce the name of the huntsman as Davie Gellátly; placing the accent on the second syllable instead of its proper place, the first.

In Hingham (Norf.), Hubbers-ton (Pemb.), and Engle-field (Berks.), we have memoranda of the great Norse invasion of 866, which ended in the subversion of the East Anglian monarchy, then wielded by the good king Edmund whose canonised name is preserved in St. Edmund's bury. Hingham seems to be named from Hingua, and Hubberston from Hubba, two brothers who led the Norsemen in that invasion; both perished in battle, but the invasion succeeded, Alfred's victories barely saving Wessex from the grasp of the invaders, which fell permanently upon the eastern half of England. One of the battles fought in 870 was fought at the place thence called Engle-field, 'The field of the English,' who were there victorious. The men of Wessex under their leader Æthelwulf, who (says Bromton) 'raged like a lion in battle,' defeated the Norsemen with great slaughter, giving them a foretaste of the still heavier punishment which was in store for them. A few weeks later, at Assan-dun (now Ashdown), Æthelred and his more famous brother and successor, Alfred the Great, inflicted upon the savage invaders the heaviest defeat which they ever sustained.

The words Holm and Hulm indicate clearly the footsteps of two distinct branches of the Norse race. When we refer to the map of the Scandinavian countries, we find the form 'holm' occurring only in Denmark and Sweden, and the islands of the Baltic, while the form 'hulm' is found only in Norway. In like manner, we find the latter word occurring only on the western side of Britain, while 'holm' is frequent in the eastern, southern, and south-western sides of the island, although both words are used in the same manner, as designating a grassy hill near water, or an island. Starting from Hulmitey and Hulmey, in the Hebrides, we find the next occurrence of the word in Lancashire and Cheshire, where there are eight Hulmes. The chain of 'Holmes' may be traced from Stockholm, the Swedish capital—which is situated on two grassy hills near the water, and was probably defended with a palisade fortification as its name implies—down through Bornholm, 'the bear's island,' and other holms, all of which are situated on the north side of the Baltic, until we reach South Norway, in which country we find two examples; Holmstrand and Holmsdal. In Denmark, the corresponding word for island is *öe.* Stretching across on the Norseman's old track from the Norwegian Holmes-dal, we pass by Helleneholm, the cavern-island, and Holmr, one of the Orkneys, until we reach another Holmesdale, in that part of the Scottish mainland called by the Norse settlers Sutherland, from its position due south of Norway. The Norsemen do not seem to have made much impression upon the eastern or Pictish part of Scotland, stretching from the Cromarty Firth (*fiord*, Norse) down to the Firths of Tay and Forth. Passing down the coast we find a trace of them at Ber-wick, the seaside village on the Britons' *ber*, or boundary; but the first *holm* after leaving Sutherland is in Durham. Then they increase in number as we pass to the south, North Yorkshire containing four, the East Riding seven, the West two, Lincolnshire one. East Yorkshire has, too, another trace of the Norsemen in its many 'dales.' The Norse element made its way up the Trent into Nottinghamshire, Derbyshire, and Staffordshire, and up the

Ouse into Huntingdonshire, each of those counties containing a place named Holm, with some English word appended. Norfolk contains three *holms*. There are few traces of Norse settlement on the south coast, the only Holms in that part of the island being found in Sussex, Dorset, and Devonshire, one in each county. Along the Bristol Channel, the Norseman has left his mark in many places, but conspicuously on the Steep and Flat Holmes and King's-holm. That he ascended the Severn, the Avon, and the Wye, we find not only from the *wicks* (villages) which remain by the shores of the former streams, but also from Holm Lacy, the grassy hill near the latter. Priestholm, on the Anglesey coast, shows where the Norseman rested on his path of ravage, and two Holmes in Westmoreland and one in Cumberland point out his permanent stations among the British population of the north-west; in all there are thirty-one places in England which bear the Norse word *holm* as their name, alone or in combination.

Some names are finger-posts to nooks of history; thus Goodrich (Herefords.) was given by Edward the Confessor to his sister Goda, under whose *ric* (sway) it thus passed. In other cases, the finger-post remains, while the nook is filled up, and its place obliterated. So with Wigmore. This ancient castle, at the Conquest the possession of Edric the Forester, was in after ages the cradle of the gallant Mortimers, but its name points to a forgotten fact of a time long anterior to either. Camden tells us—on what authority he does not say, and Domesday Book does not corroborate his statement—that it was originally called Wigcyngamere, 'the lake of the war-king or of the victory.' Probably the allusion is to some conflict, in which the intrusive Saxon thegn defeated an attempt of the

Britons to expel him from his conquest; but the mere has long been dried up, and all memory of battle or of combatants has exhaled like its waters.

So with Kemps-ford (Glouc.), called in the Anglo-Saxon Chronicle 'Cynemæres-ford,' which I take to mean the ford of some forgotten chief named Cynemær. Bede records a battle fought there in 800, between the Wiccii, or men of Worcestershire, and the West-Saxons. Bosworth, overlooking the s which marks one form of the possessive case, treats the whole name as descriptive; on which hypothesis it means 'the famous royal ford.' If so the name may have been as significant to the Gloucestershire man of 869 as Alma or Inkermann is to his descendants a thousand years later; but we know neither why the ford should have been called royal (cyne), nor from what event it became famous (maere).

In like manner, Ellesmere (Salop) hands down to us the name of some chief named Ella; but whether the fierce ruler of the as fierce Northmen of Northumbria left his name to the mere as a grim memorial of some slaughter which stained its waters with blood, or whether the name is that of some obscure thegn or jarl, we can but conjecture. The former is the more probable solution, but I am not aware that there is any historical record of Ella's conquests being extended so far beyond the recorded boundaries of his kingdom.

In Pensnett (Staff.), we have a less doubtful record of the terrible Penda, king of Mercia, whose *snaed* or portion it may have been, while his wars against the West-Saxons render it not improbable that Pendo-mere (Som.) may be a memorial of his having conquered the land around that mere. His relative Peada (A.D. 652) seems in like manner to have left his name to Ped-mere (Bucks), Pedwardin (Heref.), Peada's water-camp, Peatling (Leic.), 'Peada's possession,' &c. The death of the turbulent Algar Earl of Mercia is commemorated in Algar-kirk (Sus.), which was erected on the site of his last fight.

Aegelmod, or Aylmer, the eolderman of Mercia, and (if I mistake not) the husband of Alfred's mannish daughter Ethelfleda, survives in Alme-ley and Aymestre in his county of Hereford, but we know little of him beside the name and the fact of his having lived and ruled. Besides those which have already been mentioned, I give below a few of the names of men and women of old English times whom we know only as having 'called their places after their own names,' and who are themselves utterly forgotten. Many of these names are beautiful both in sound and in sense, and might wisely be restored to use. Their revival would at least relieve our ears from the wearisome iteration of a few names, most of which are merely the corrupt forms in which the translators of the Bible have disguised Eastern appellations. Suitable as they no doubt seemed to the people who originated them, these over-worked Scripture names harmonise ill in sound with our northern surnames, and in meaning often seem grotesque. In many cases the name given in the English Bible is neither Hebrew, Greek, nor English, but a barbarous coinage. What ancient Israelite could recognise Chavah in Eve, or Showl in Saul, or what erudite Greek of the first century would suspect the identity of Ἰακώβ with James?

The use of these barbarous names is not even endeared by old associations, having originated in the seventeenth century, previous to which time the names of the apostles were the only Scripture names in use in this country. The practice of using such names exclusively, or at least commonly, was in fact one of the badges of a political party, the leaders of which, although great men intellectually, morally, and religiously, were not free from small affectations, of which the adoption of Scripture names is almost the only one which has survived to our time. It is true that they had a precedent. The astronomer Kepler had, in a like spirit, supplanted the twelve signs of the zodiac with the twelve apostles, and had substituted Scripture names for the ancient names of other constellations; but neither the effect thus produced upon the study of the heavens, nor the amount of public favour which the experiment received, was such as to recommend the practice for imitation.

The Old English names which are preserved in the names of places in England are the following:

Adda
Aegelburh
Aegmond
Ael
Æthel
Æthelburghu
Æthelredu
Æthelred
Æthelstan
Aisbur
Aldhelm
Alfage
Alkmund
Andred
Aylburh
Babba
Badda
Barthold
Bebba
Beda
Bega
Belin
Beorlaf
Beorna
Bera
Beramund
Billung
Binna
Blanda
Blunda
Bonna
Brechla
Bridla
Briht
Brihthelm
Cadda
Catta
Caver
Cendred
Cenric
Cenwulf
Ceolred
Chetel
Chivel
Clappa
Cran
Craw
Creoda or Crida
Cuccwin
Cwicchelm
Cynmaer
Cynwold
Dagga
Dodda
Donna
Dorma
Eadburh
Eadgithu or Edith
Eadmund
Eadred

Eadwin
Ealdred
Eappa
Eata
Ebbe
Ecca
Egelburh
Egelwin
Egon
Elchat
Ella
Elmund
Elva
Elwy
Fava or Fyva
Finc
Flacc or Flecc
Frideswide
Fridu
Gelinga
Gilmor
Godmund
Godred
Godu or Godgifu (corrupted into Godiva)
Godwin
Granda
Grena
Hadda
Hand
Hara
Hawk
Hern
Hicc
Higg
Hildu (corruptly Hilda)
Hinc
Hold or Hould
Hucc
Hunna
Lamba
Lassa
Lecha
Leddan
Lilla
Lodda
Loppa
Lufa
Lulla
Lutta
Maegla
Maeldulf
Massa
Meopa
Milburghu
Naffa
Nigel
Oddo
Orchil
Osbald
Osbeorn
Osmund
Oswyth
Pacca
Pebba
Pega
Penga
Peowa
Pippa or Pappa
Pudda
Putta
Rodmer
Sebba
Sedberghu
Sedla
Sibbald or Sigbald
Sida
Sidmund
Sigbert
Snell
Tetta
Theoca
Theoda
Thorca
Throcca
Throg
Tod
Ulfor
Ulfwin
Walbeof
Wanda
Wibba or Wiba
Wigmund
Wimbot
Winbald
Withyel
Wivel
Wolstan
Wracca
Wrenna
Wulfhere

Many of these names as noticed *ante* survive as surnames, either simply or in combination with the descriptive words with which they are united to form place-names. In addition to those already noticed, we may detect the name Adda in Addis, Æthelstan in

Ethelstan and Huddleston, Babba in Babb, Bebba in Bebb, Beorna in Barnes, Bera in Berry, Billung in Billing, Binna in Binns, Blanda in Bland and Blandy, Bonna in Bonner, Briht in Bright, Cenric in Kenrick, Clappa in Clapperton, Cran in Cranston, Craw in Crawley, Dogga in Doggs, Dodda in Dodd, Dorma in Dormer, Ȩappa in Yapp, Finc in Finch, Gelinga in Jelinger and Challinger, Godu in Goode, Godmund in Goodman, Gomond, and Gammon, Godred in Goddard, Granda in Grandison, Grunda in Grundy, Hara in Hare, Hawk alone and in Hawksworth, Hern in Heron, Hicc as Hicks and in Hickson, Higg as Higgs and in Higginson (Higg's kin's son), Hucc in Huckson, Lamba in Lambe, Lecha in Letcher and Lechmere, Pacca in Pack, Packington, Pakenham, Peck, &c., Pega in Pegge, Pippa in Pepper and Piper, Tod in Todd, Throg in Throgmorton, Wimbald in Wimbold and Wimble, Wivel in Wyvil, Wracca in Wragg, Wrenna in Wren, &c.

The Norse names are not in all cases distinguishable from those of the Old English, a fact which is due partly to our receiving them through the latter tongue, partly to the use of the same name by both races—a proof of their kindred origin—and partly to the mingling of men of various nations in the piratical hordes.

This illustrates one fact of history, and is corroborated by another. We know that the host led by William at Hastings was in like manner made up of adventurers from many lands, and we know, too, that they, like the Norsemen, were soon absorbed into the mass of the English people.

The frequency of the termination *a* in Old English male names seems odd to eyes accustomed to Latin, in which that termination is in most cases feminine. In some names it seems to be a substitute for the Norse termination *ur* or *r*, the English in old times as now being apt to drop the *r* when it followed a vowel; in other cases the *a* seems to have been added to the name to make it accord with English usage. But the great majority of the names ending in *a* are certainly Old English.

Among the Norse names given below, we recognise some as historical. Thus in Bebban-burh (now Bamborough) we see a record of Bebba 'the flame-bearer;' in Hacconby a trace of the bold Haco, perhaps the monarch who fell at the battle of Largs, in Scotland, so fatal to his race: while the once-dreaded name of Hasting, whose wife and children our great Alfred sent back to him without ransom—a truly noble deed in days when ransom was one of the main objects of war—is perpetuated at Hastings-leigh. The town of Hastings must have been named from some earlier bearer of the name, since it was founded and named long before the ninth century. The name Gunner, or Gunnr, which appears in some half-dozen places, has mythological associations. In the old Icelandic or Norse poem of 'The Völuspâ,' the most ancient song in the 'Edda,' to which I have elsewhere alluded, Gunnr is commemorated among the Valkyries or 'war-dæmons,'—

> 'Skuld hêth skildi, ën Skögol önnur
> Gunnr, Hildr, Göudul ek Geirskögul.'
>
> Skuld held the shield, Skögul followed her,
> Gunnr, Hildr, Goudul and Geirskögul.

Ormr, the serpent, is mentioned also in the same poem, as 'raising the waves'—

> 'Ormer, knyr, unnir.'

As the 'Völuspâ' is attributed by Mr. Beckman to an

unknown poet of the latter half of the ninth century, there is at all events a respectable antiquity, whatever may be said as to the amount of credit, due to the legend of the Sea-serpent.

The place-names which are undoubtedly Norse preserve the memory of many otherwise unknown rovers, e.g.:

Bab, now Babe.
Brand, still a surname.
Brice, now Bryce.
Bulla, now Buller or Bulwer.
Cata, whence Catesby.
Feoda, whence Feather and Featherston.
Frene, now preserved in Freen.
Gamel, whence Gamble, Gemmel, Campbell.
Garbold, now Garrold.
Garmond.
Grim, now Grime and Grimes.
Grimald.
Gumba.
Gunnr, now Gunn.
Haela, now Hales and Hale.
Harding, whence Hardinge.
Harla, now Harlow.
Hasting.
Heming.
Hreopa.
Hretla, and Hridel, now Riddell, Ridley, and Rat(cliff).
Hrodmer.
Hrolf, now Ralph and Rolf.
Hrotan, now Rotton.
Hubba, whence Hubbard and Hubbersty.
Hungar.
Hunma.
Ingold.
Ingra, or Ingur.
Ketel, now Kettle.
Lapp, perhaps equivalent to Laplander.
Lond, still a name and also as Lundy.

Lothbrock, may be the original of the name Lethbridge.

Lutgar.

Olaf, now preserved in Olive and Oliver, and with the prefix St., forming the word Tooley, still given to a street in London, near St. Olaf's church.

Ord, still a name in Northumberland.

Ormr, the serpent, preserved in Orm, Oram, Ormsby, and Ormathwaite.

Osgar.

Ran, or Hran, preserved in Rann, Randal, Randerson.

Scrivel.

Scrop, whence Scrope and Scroop.

Sebba, Sibr, or Sigbert, whence Sibthorp.

Sifa or Sufa.

Sigweard, or Siward, whence Seward and Sheward.

Skendla.

Snorro, or Snorr.

Spald.

Swark.

Themel.

Thorgar, the hammer-god of war, one of the most poetical of the Norse names.

Thorold, now surviving as a surname.

Torkil, sometimes Gallicised to Torquil.

Tostig, perhaps the unworthy brother of Harold II., who when at Hereford murdered his attendants, and had their limbs put in the casks of wine and beer provided for the household.

Trant, a name still surviving.

Ubba, perhaps the same as Hubba.

Uggar, apparently from the same root as the words ugly and ogre.

Ulf, i.e. 'the wolf.'

Umba, the same as Humba.

Wigbold, 'bold in war.'

Wigmond, 'protection in war.'

Wilbur, still preserved in Wilbraham (pronounced 'Wilburum,') and in Wilberforce.

Worla.

VI.

NAMES WHICH SHOW THE TRIBAL DIVISIONS OF THE OLD ENGLISH PEOPLE.

Side by side with the strong individualism of the Gothic races, there seems to have existed also a strong feeling of clanship. This is shown by the large class of place-names which end in *ington*, *ingham*, *ingworth*, *ingwalls*, *ingland*, *ingsett*, or *ingthorp*, the *ing* in which words (as Bosworth remarks) represents the word *incga*, meaning children or descendants. This tribal organization is most strongly marked in the Anglian part of England, appears less frequently in Saxon districts, and is still rarer in the Jutish counties. In Norfolk and Suffolk, the number of these tribal settlements is remarkable, suggesting the reflection that the Anglian immigration must have been conducted chiefly by tribes; that of the Saxons by individual adventurers. The coast district, too, is richest in these tribal names; a fact which shows that the Angles did not penetrate very far inland, at least for the first two or three generations after their arrival. It might take even a longer time before the tribes could muster a sufficient number of young men to form a band. This consideration goes to explain the lateness of the foundation of the Mercian kingdom, which was in truth an independent extension westward of the East Angle kingdom. Crida, an Anglian chief, founded the kingdom of Mercia in 586: i.e. he penetrated into the country west of the Severn, destroyed the Romano-British city of Magna, and reduced the British chiefs into tributaries. The Mercian power seems to have grown very slowly, and never to have become very compact. It is curious, too, that Offa, the greatest of the Mercian kings, distinguished himself by nothing so much as by his conquest of the kingdom of East Anglia, the cradle of his race.

To return to the tribal settlements: we notice in Norfolk twenty-four *inghams*:

Antingham	Deesingham	Massingham
Barmingham	Ellingham	Sanderingham
Basingham	Felmingham	Saxlingham
Beckingham	Gillingham	Sherringham
Bedingham	Gimingham	Walsingham
Briningham	Honingham	Wessingham
Burlingham	Itteringham	Whittingham
Cressingham	Lessingham	Witchingham

Norfolk affords one *ington* in Alpington; one *ingthorp*, Redlingthorp; one *ingtoft*, marking a Danish settlement, viz. Berningtoft, 'the grove of the children of Bjorna,' the bear; and two of an unusual form—Irmingland, the land of the children of *Er*, the war-god, and Haveringland, which seems to mean the land of the children of a chief named Haver.

Suffolk contains nine *inghams*:

Aldringham	Finingham	Iclingham
Barningham	Gislingham	Mettingham
Cretingham	Helmingham	Worlingham

Upon these names we may note in passing that we find from history that there was a Mercian tribe called Iclingas, of whom Iclingham was probably the paternal seat, but we know nothing of their history.

There are three *ingtons* in Suffolk: Tannington, Lavington, and Dennington. Of these three, Lavington does not fall within the tribal class, since it occurs also in the British district at the south side of Salisbury plain. It is probably named from the British saint Lefan.

The form *ingworth* occurs at Worlingworth; and Dallinghoo is the only example of the termination *inghoo* (*hoo*, Danish, a hill).

Ingfield, a not very frequent form, occurs in five instances in Suffolk:

Bedingfield	Redlingfield	Woldingfield
Fressingfield	Shadingfield	

The word Bedingfield is remarkable because Bedfield is also to be found in the district. Both names come from the same root; and as Bedfield points out the field of Beda, Bedingfield indicates the possession of the tribe named from him.

Cambridgeshire contains seven *ingtons* and two *inghams*, but in Huntingdonshire there are only two of the former and none of the latter class.

The recurrence of like names in the Saxon and Jutish parts of England, although infrequent, is sufficient to show that all the three sets of immigrants spoke the same language; and the persistence of these names may help to teach another equally important truth. The Danes and the Normans successively conquered these tribal settlements as well as other parts of the country, but the names remain; and the inference is that neither of those bodies of invaders were very numerous. Except in Lincolnshire, which is a second Denmark in the multitude of *bys* which it contains, Danish names are thinly strewn, examine what English county we may. The Norman names are also few—the scattered abodes of new lords of the soil, too jealous of each other to desire close neighbourhood, and too self-reliant to fear the subjugated people around them.

That this reading of the names which I have called tribal is correct, two historical facts go far to prove. The Saxon Chronicle tells us that the kings of East Anglia were styled Uffingas, i.e. the children of Uffa, who founded that monarchy about A.D. 575, and from whom the tribes who gave name to Uffington, in Berkshire, Lincolnshire, and Salop, claimed descent, either metaphorical or real. A renown which extended from Norfolk south to Berkshire and west to Salop, was for those days considerable. The Chronicle tells us also that the men of Kent were called 'Centingas,' or children of Kent. It is recorded, too, that the kings of Kent called themselves 'Oiscingas,' that is, the children of Oisc, the son of Hengist. In some cases, our Teutonic forefathers, like our countrymen at the present day, when settling in a colony, named their new abode from the place which they had quitted in the motherland; probably the word England itself is but a form of 'Anglen,' the name of a part of continental Denmark; but more frequently they gave to their new possession a tribal name. Selecting the name either of their leader or of some famous ancestor, they called their settlement the home, the farm, the town, or the estate of his children. It would seem that the settlements made by bands of adventurers were thus distinguished from those which were made by single adventurers.

Some tribal names represent the handicraft carried on by the ancestor and continued by his descendants in their new home. Such place-names as Walker-ingham, from *wealcere*, a fuller of cloth (already noticed); Whipp-ingham, from *wiba*, a weaver; Arl-ingham, from *yrthling*, a farmer; and Millington, from *milnere*, a miller, with *inga* added in each case, show some of the principal trades carried on in Old English times. The smith, as the maker of weapons, was accounted the first of craftsmen, but, as he was needed everywhere, no places seem to have been especially set apart for him or his trade. The only exception to this remark is Smethwick, the smith's village, unless indeed we are to accept Mr. Toulmin Smith's ingenious etymology of Birmingham, from *Brimi* and *incgaham*, i.e. the home of the children of flame. Certainly it is reasonable enough to fancy that Birmingham was, twelve hundred years ago, as now, the seat of the smith's trade; but it remains to be shown that Birmingham, and not Bromwycham—the common word, and the common word in such cases is generally the correct form of the name—is the ancient appellation of the place.

The arrogance of the Saxons and Angles towards the Britons whom they dispossessed is amusingly shown in the term by which they designated these children of the soil. Not satisfied with having deprived them of their lands, the intruders called them Wealas, i.e. strangers. The word survives in the term 'Welsh,' which expresses a historical truth: the Briton did become a stranger in his native land; but the term came with a bad grace from the *strangers* who had disinherited him. Here again nomenclature corroborates history: Wallingford (Berks.), anciently called Wealas-incgaford, 'the ford of the children of the strangers,' seems to mark one of the spots where a remnant of the aboriginal people remained in the midst of their supplanters; and the village of Wales, on the confines of Yorkshire and Derbyshire, is apparently another of these British settlements.

Another of this class of names is remarkable as establishing what will be a startling proposition to many readers: that there was a tribe of old English troglodytes, of whom we have no other trace save in a single passage of a forgotten chronicler. The word Snot-ingaham, now disguised as Nottingham, means 'the home of the children of the excavations,' or of the cave-dwellers. The correctness of this rendering is proved by the authority of Asser, the friend of Alfred the Great, who says:

'Subterraneis speluncis et meatibus quæ in receptacula et in habitationem,' etc.

Of the greater number of the tribes who marked their settlements with the word *incga*, we have no information beyond the name. Thus Kens-ington (Midd.) is 'the town of the children of the Cynes,' or royal tribe, but of what royal tribe we know not.

Att-ingham (Salop) is an example of the use of the word *ingaham* in a figurative sense. Local history and tradition concur in explaining the word as meaning 'the home of the children of Eata,' abbot of Lindisfarne in the seventh century. Probably Attingham was a mission station occupied by monks from Lindisfarne, who carried into the Welsh border land the doctrine and the rule of their spiritual father. Kedd-ingham (Suff.) and Eck-ington (Derb. and Worc.) are probably examples of stations named in like manner after Ceadda or Chad, the famous bishop of Mercia, and Ecca bishop of Hereford in the eighth century.

In Swann-ington, Ell-ingham, Bab-ington, and Padd-ington, we recognise the settlements of the children of Sweyn, Ella, Bebba, and Peada, and we know that kings of those names ruled in the districts where those places are situated; but whether the connection was a literal or a figurative ancestry we know not. The names may have been, as in the case of the Uffingas (noticed *ante*), commemorative of remote ancestors of either the inhabitants or the monarchs. In many instances, however, the direct testimony of historians connects the place with a famous bearer of the name—as Algarkirk (Sussex) is recorded to have been named from Earl Algar who was slain there—and mentions the incident out of which it sprang. In such cases, there is no more room for reasonable doubt than there is on the proposition that Battle in Sussex was named from the great conflict fought there in 1066.

Six names of this class are noticeable as evidence that the founders believed in the Northern Paganism. In Berkshire we find Sunningwell, i.e. 'the well of the children of the sun;' in Yorkshire we have Lockington, 'the town of the children of Loki;' and in Suffolk, Thorington, 'the town of the children of Thor,' the thunder-god. A parallel is suggested by the word Thormanby (Linc.), which I read as 'the abode of Thor's servant;' or, taking the syllable *man* as a corruption of *mund*, the meaning would be 'the Thor-protected abode.' On either reading it designates a place at which Thor was specially worshipped.

Setterington (Yorks.), 'the town of Seater's children,' points out a probable seat of the worship of the god from whom Saturday is named; while Baldringham in like manner indicates the abode of a tribe who called themselves 'the children of Baldur,' the sun-god, and who probably had there a temple dedicated to his worship.

Ermington (Devon) seems to have been the seat of the children of Erm. Erm is a cognate word with the Greek Ἄρης, and like it designates the war-god, whose image, the 'Ermingsul,' was set up at the side of the military road called Erming Street, as we learn from the Saxon Chronicle. Woden, although a favourite deity of the

Saxon warriors, was really only a deified hero. His name occurs in a single instance as connected with a tribal appellation. Waddingham (Linc.) is 'the home of the children of Waddy;' and we find in one of the royal pedigrees given in the Saxon Chronicle the name of Waddy as a son of Woden. Most of the Old English kings, we may note, traced their lineage to Woden through one or other of his many sons.

The names of the other Dii majores of the Northern faith—Tiw or Tuisco, Freya, and Weland—do not occur in connection with *inga*.

The word Scrayingham (Yorks.) is curious as bearing on the theory that Hengist and Horsa were the names, not of the chiefs, as historians aver, but of the vessels in which the invaders arrived. Here we have a name which seems to have been founded on that of a ship. Scra-ingaham, literally rendered, is 'the home of the children of the sea-swallow.' This may, of course, be merely one of the many indications of the use of armorial bearings among the Northern rovers, but it may also be read as a commemoration of the name of the *chiule* which brought to the Northumbrian shore the founders of Scrayingham. Both Angle and Norseman were then in the imaginative youth of their national existence, and 'the sea swallow' would be at once a poetical and an appropriate name for one of those 'skimmers of the seas,' in which adventurers from the North sought empire and renown.

Some light is thrown, too, upon the costumes of both races of Northmen by the occurrence of the words Blanda and Seolc, in connection with words signifying possession or habitation. Bland-ford (Dorset) and Seolces-tun, now Silkston (Derb.) are examples. Blanda, being cognate with the verb to *blend*, seems to point to the habit of wearing parti-coloured dresses, which was common among the Northern nations. Seolc is our word *silk*, and may be taken as designating the man who wore a robe of that material, then very costly, and therefore a mark of distinction which would readily pass into a personal name. Parallel cases among the Greeks and the Romans will readily suggest themselves to the reader, in the names of Porphyrios, the wearer of purple; Caligula, and Caracalla, the latter derived from a cloak, and the former from a shoe.

Walsingham (Norf.) is a trace of the old Anglian poetry. Living around an ancient holy well, which continued to be frequented by devotees long after it had been adopted into Christian superstition as St. Mary's well, the people seem to have regarded themselves as in some sense its progeny. Hence they styled their village Wals-ingaham, 'the home of the children of the well.'

Fremington, 'the town of the children of the Frem,' or the stranger, Framling-ton and Framling-ham, 'the town and the home of the stranger's possession,' may be taken as marking the settlements of a band of adventurers, neither Norse, Angle, Saxon, nor Jute in race, although (as the word *frem* suggests) from some Teutonic country. Some learned etymologists have found a Wendish or Vandal element in our language; and possibly the 'Frem' may have been the rover to whom we are indebted for it.

Domesday Book (Herefordshire) gives a place called 'Wiboldingtun,' not now to be identified, but which appears to have been one of these tribal settlements. I read the word as meaning 'the town of the children of Wibold,' a manifest softening down of the name

Wigbold, 'bold in war,' a not uncommon Saxon appellation.

Whippingham, already noticed as a seat of the weaving trade, is literally 'the home of the children of Wiba,' the weaver. The trade seems to have been hereditary, like most other trades in rude times.

A few names which include the word *seat*, *sett*, or *set* —from *setu*, the station or seat of a tribe—point out still more distinctly the clannishness of the old English. The *setu* class of names, like the *inghams*, are most frequent in Anglian districts. Norfolk and Suffolk furnish eight of the whole twelve, viz.:

Wetheringsett	Wissett	Hethersett
Elmsett	Whissonsett	Forncett
Bricett	Letheringsett	

Woodsett, Dorset, and Somerset are supposed to indicate the seats of the Wood, Dor, and Sumor tribes; and Wetheringsett (Suffolk) may be added, as being the seat of a tribe called the Wether, i.e. *the* band, by way of excellence. Swettenham (Ches.), from *sweot*, a band, is a parallel case. Mr. E. A. Freeman, the distinguished antiquary and historian, has remarked that the syllable Wilt, in the word Wiltshire, is a contraction of Wilset, and designates the *setu* of a tribe called the Wil. Perhaps this is the tribe of which we read in Bede, under the name 'Wiltes.' A tribe so called appeared in North Germany in the sixth century, and it is probable that some of them joined in the migration of their neighbours to this country, which was then going on. It is noticeable that Sir Thomas More, in his 'History of England,' and his continuator Halle, spell the name of the county 'Wylshire.' The Wil, Wyl, or Wilte tribe probably came to England from the banks of the Lower Rhine: there at least a part of the tribe were seated in the time of Pepin, the father of Chárlemagne. Bede, writing of Wilbrod, a missionary sent from England, says:

'Pepin gave to him a place for his episcopal see in his famous castle, which in the language of those people is called Wiltaburg, i.e. the town of the Wiltes.'

The same historian gives us a word of the *setu* class which is now quite forgotten in the district of which it was the appellation. When referring to a part of the country of the Wiccii, which included Gloucestershire and Worcestershire, he says that it was called Magesetania. This evidently means 'the country of the station of the Mage tribe.' Domesday Book gives Mage as the name of a place in Herefordshire, thus showing that the tribe had at least one settlement beyond the confines of the Wiccii. Mage has disappeared from the rural nomenclature, but a conspicuous hill in the centre of what was the Mage country is still known as May hill.

The place-names of which Wis and Whis form part seem to countenance the theory that there is an admixture of Sclavonic blood in the English people. In Wis-sett and Whisson-sett, we have the *setu* of the same race as that which gave name to Whis-by (Linc.), and Whissen-dine (Rutl.). In each case I read the first part of the name as identical with the Saxon name (Wisle) for the *Vis*-tula river. Part of Poland is designated by one of the Saxon writers by the kindred word Wisle-land.

Whiston (Worc.) belongs to a different category, being a local contraction of *white nuns' town*.

VII.

NAMES WHICH PRESERVE TRACES OF THE BRITONS AMONG THE TEUTONIC INVADERS.

The remark already made, that the invaders did not exterminate, but settled down among the Indigenes, will have prepared the reader to expect more important traces of the latter than the few names already cited. There are, indeed, many large groups of names of British origin, even in the most completely Saxonised or Anglicised districts, which are intelligible only as indications of the persistence of the British race. Overflowed as they were by successive waves of the great invasion which began with the coming of Hengist and Horsa; broken up into patches, here a town, there a group of uplands—in one place a solitary village, in another a city, with a circle of surrounding settlements, the race has left its presence as unmistakeably in the names of places as in the speech of the inhabitants. The habit of putting an *h* before every word which begins with a vowel, which is a rule of Welsh orthoepy, is an anomaly and a vulgarism in Saxon speech, although universal among the peasantry of the Saxon districts. When we find this peculiarity disappear, as we advance northward, that is, as we leave the Saxon settlements, and pass into the Anglian, Norse, and Danish districts, until, in the vale of the Clyde, we are reminded of the Strathclyde Britons by hearing the peasant say 'huz' for us, it is as difficult to resist the evidence of British descent in the speakers, as it is to doubt that the *try* of Mercia or the *combes* of Wessex point out British settlements. History comes in to corroborate our deductions by incidental notices. The Saxon Chronicle records battles between the invaders and the Britons, at Sears-byrig (Old Sarum), Berin-byrig (Banbury), Gloucester, Cirencester, Bath, and other places which we now find surrounded more or less densely with place-names wholly or partly British. The term Welsh seems to have come into use about 597, and is applied in the Chronicle to distinguish the Britons of Wales and the marches from those who remained amid the Saxons and Angles. The only exception is a remarkable one, which tells strongly in favour of my interpretation. Under the year 614, we read that 'Cynegils and Cwichelm fought at Beándune,' which Dr. Giles thinks to be Bampton in Oxfordshire, 'and slew two thousand and sixty-five Welshmen.' Bampton lies in the midst of a circle of British-named places, amid which the Thames (Taf) flows past Wallingford—Wealas-incga-ford, 'the ford of the children of the Welsh,' or 'strangers.'

In the Saxon districts, which may be rudely included in a sort of parallelogram, the north side of which is a line drawn from Gloucester to the estuary of the Thames; the west is formed by the Bristol Channel, and a line passing from near Bideford down through the middle of Devon; the British Channel forms the east; and the south is the coast of Sussex, Hants, Dorset, and a part of Devon, the British settlements may be distinguished by the word *combe*, which is always by natives of the district pronounced *coom*, and is the exact word in meaning and in pronunciation which appears in Wales as *cwm*. This word is not found anywhere in the Anglian or Norse districts, which have other British words marking the places retained by the Indigenes.

Beginning from the eastward, we find in Kent a British settlement indicated by the river Darenth (*dwrwent*, shining water), the town of Darentford, now Dartford, and Swanscombe, i.e. the hollow or dingle seized by some Norseman named Sweyn.

Surrey has no *combes*, and reveals no traces of Britons except in its river Wey (*wy*, water), and in Kew, the ancient shrine of St. Cewydd.

Sussex has its river Arun (*eiren*, fruit-bearing), and five *combes*, to show that the Britons once held its fertile valleys and its pleasant dingles.

Hants has no *combes*, but has a curious group in three places called Meon (*min*, a brow), all of which are situated upon and near conspicuous hills. The only other place in Great Britain of like name is Meon camp, a conspicuous hill in Gloucestershire.

Dorset has not only its Froom (*ffraw*, gentle) on the banks of which the Briton lingered, but it has also two *combes*, Kingcombe and Batcombe. The north-east part of the county, too, properly forms with South Wilts what seems to have been a very populous and important British district, dependent on Old Sarum or Amesbury, as its capital. In this place we find Britford (the ford of the Britons); Lavington (the town of St. Lefan, a British saint); the river Avon (*afon*, a river); and four *combes*: Boscomb, the dingle of Bosa; Motcomb, the dingle of the mote or meeting-place; Uggscomb, the dingle of Ugga; and Burcomb, the dingle near the burying place, or barrow—a kind of tumulus which is more frequently met with on the Wiltshire downs than in any other part of the kingdom. Perhaps the Britons fought more desperately to retain the district in which were situated the town named after their great king Aurelius Ambrosius, and the solemn temples of Avebury; and if so, we can understand why the ill-omened banquet of British and Saxon chiefs, so familiar to schoolboys, should be described as taking place on Salisbury plain, near the centre of this British district. The whole story of this feast of blood—the wholesale murder of Britons by Saxons at the signal, *nemet eure seaxas*—may be a myth enshrining the national antipathy of the beaten race; but its localisation in this district corroborates the view of its British character which is suggested by the place-names.

The *combes* are more plentiful in Somerset than in any other county, there being eighteen places so named, arranged in five groups. The most important of the five in number as in position is that of which Bath, the British royal city of Caer-badon, forms the centre. In this group we find Charlscomb, the ceorl's, or husbandman's dingle; Widcomb, the wide dingle; Moncton Comb, the dingle near the monks' *tun*, or farm; Comb-hay, the inclosed dingle; and English Comb, a name which shows by suggested antithesis the British character of the neighbourhood.

This British character is more strongly shown in the little group of Croscomb, the dingle of the Cross—probably a preaching station of the early missionaries—and Winscomb, the dingle of Win, a Saxonised form of the British Gwyn, fair, which is still a common Welsh surname.

A larger group, in the south-west part of the county, includes five *combes*, two of which, by the position of the specific name after the generic term—Comb St. Nicholas and Comb Henry—seem to have become inhabited or appropriated first in Norman times. Near to them is a trace of the Briton in the word Creach, in which (as in Crich, in the British part of Derbyshire) we recognise the British word *crûg* [pronounced *creeg*] a heap or small hill. Timberscomb, in like manner, seems to be *twmpath-cwm*, the dingle of the artificial hillock or tumulus, still called in Herefordshire a *tump*.

Devon (Brit. *dyfneint*, the land of hollows or valleys) never was fully conquered by the Saxons, and its abundance of British place-names corroborates history in that respect. Besides its six *combes*, it has the great table land of Dartmoor (named from the Darent or Dwrwent, now the Dart), with its peaks called *tors*, and its eight streams, all bearing British names, with the single exception of the Erm, which is probably cognate with the Worm rivers of Herefordshire and Derbyshire, so called from their sinuous course. Avon is the common British word for a river. Wrey is a kindred word with the English *awry*, and the Brit. *gwragen*, a bow; Teign is equivalent to Tayn and Tean, from *tân*, the sacred fire or altar; Carey is from *carreg*, a rock; Lid is from *lyd*, country; Tamar is from the same root as Tame, Teme, Thames, Taff; Taw seems to be but another form of Tywy, now called Towy, in South Wales, from Dû-wy, dark water.

Gloucestershire, only part of which was conquered by the Saxons, contains several groups of British place-names, the most important of which consists of Glevum, the Romano-British city now known as Gloucester (Glouw-cestre of the Saxons, Caer-gloyw of the Britons), and the dingles of Harescomb, the hare's dingle; Finchcomb, the finch's dingle; Shepscomb, the sheep's dingle; and Whitcomb, the white dingle, so called probably from the colour of the soil. In other parts of the county, we find traces of the Briton in Comb, Brimscomb, Stinchcombe, the Froom river, and Frampton, or the town on that river. Winchelcomb, now Winchcomb (*wincel*, S., a nook), stands alone among the hills, although not far from the other *combes* which have been mentioned above.

In the great district of Middle or Anglian England, we find very few traces of the Briton; here and there a town whose name ends in *try*, as Coventry and Daventry (British, *tref*, a town); and the fact is explained by the statement in the Saxon Chronicle that that district remained for several centuries a waste between the West Saxon kingdom in the south and the Anglian kingdoms north of the Humber and the Ouse. Near the end of the sixth century, we find Crioda or Crida crossing this waste, and founding beyond its extreme western border the kingdom of Mercia; but the district intervening between him and East Anglia does not seem to have been fully conquered and settled until a much later period. Nearly all its place-names are Saxon and Anglian, and it is not until we reach the hill country of Derbyshire that we again meet with traces of the Briton.

Derbyshire seems to have remained British down to the time of the Danish conquest. Its capital was a Danish *by* or abode, but the Britons kept the hills even against the Danes. Its peaks are still called tors (*twr*, British); its chief streams, the Wye, the Derwent, and the Rother (*yr odor*, the boundary), still retain their British names; one of its most ancient towns is still the Chapel (*capel*, British) in the *frith* or wood of the Britons; and its many broad hills are called lows, from *llo*, a hill.

Yorkshire is almost destitute of British place-names, yet in the East Riding we find the Esk river (*ysc*, water), the Derwent, and Glaisdale (*glâs*, bluish-green, or verdant), and Humber (*hymyr*, the gathering of waters).

VIII.

NAMES WHICH INDICATE THE SEVERAL IMMIGRATIONS TO THIS COUNTRY, AND THE ORDER IN WHICH THEY OCCURRED.

THAT the Britons were the earliest of existing races in their arrival in this country, which they styled Ynys Prydain, is shown by the frequent recurrence of short names belonging to their language, either pure or as the nuclei around which other names have been formed. Even in a district so early wrested from them as was Kent, the word Dover (*dwfwr*) attests that Britons once dwelt there by the water. In the word Thames, too, as already remarked, we recognise the British *Tam* or *Taf*, a river—cognate with the root of the Greek πο-ταμός—which is preserved more purely in Tame and Taff, the names of streams over whose banks the Briton ruled until times much later than those which saw him driven from the valley of the Thames.*

As the rule, it may be laid down that the principal rivers and hills in any country retain the names given to them by the Aborigines, while less conspicuous elevations and smaller streams either lose their original names or are not named until, by subsequent immigrations, the country has become more densely settled. In England and Wales, all the rivers of first and second magnitude are still known by British names; and the same remark applies to all the mountains and most

* See my essay on 'Etymology of Names in Herefordshire,' published 1849.

conspicuous hills, Snowdon alone excepted. In this case, the Saxon 'Snaw-don,' the snowy hill, has supplanted the more poetical but less easily pronounceable British name, 'Creigiau yr Eryri,' the eagle's rocks. The British names are retained, more or less modified, by Skiddaw, Helvelyn, Mam Tor, Carnedd Dafydd, the Wrekin, and Malvern; while the list of rivers in England includes only two of any magnitude, Ouse and Trent, which bear appellations conferred by Teutons or Norsemen. One of these excepted words is in itself doubtful. The word Trent is derived by Bosworth from 'Drouent,' *a flexu sive ambitu sui cursus*; but he does not state, nor can I guess, to what language 'Drouent' belongs. About the word Ouse there is no difficulty: it represents the fact that the rivers so named wind their sluggish way through alluvial soil. We still speak of water which percolates as *oozing*, and of the mud of rivers as *ooze*, which are different forms of the word applied by the Old English to the river.

The confluence of the Yorkshire Ouse with the Trent and the Don forms a gathering of waters which still bears the British name of Humber, a slight corruption of *Hymyr*, 'the place which is worthy to be called seas.' So, too, the impetuous stream which descends from Plinlimmon, and rushes wildly through the rocky passes of Radnorshire and Breconshire until, having reached the rich vale of Herefordshire, it becomes a majestic stream, justifies by its magnitude its British title, Wye, 'the water.' In the earlier part of its course, the resemblance to the scenery of Derbyshire—the most British part of England—is sufficient to account for the application of the same word Wye to the chief river of the Peak. The Severn is little changed in name since the Britons called it Hafren; while a dozen rivers retain as their proper name the word Avon (*afon*), the common British word for a river.

In the marches of Wales, all the rivers—with the doubtful exception of the Leddon, which may be only the British *lyd*, country, with the Saxon *don*, a hill, added—retain their British names. The turbid river which flows past Chester, for instance, is still called Dee (from *dû-wy*, dark water), and the meadow between its bank and the city wall is still the Roodee (*rhos-dû-wy*), the moist plain by the dark water. So again the Tam is visible in the modern Tame; the turbulent Arrow is still *garw*, rough and headstrong; the Lugg is still *llug*, bright; and the rapid stream which parts Herefordshire and Monmouthshire is still known as the Munnow, a contraction of *mynydd-wy*, the mountain water. I need not say that in Wales all the rivers retain their immemorial British names.

The word *wy*, water, seems to be a primitive word belonging to the Celtic family of languages, and its presence in Holland—where it is the name of a river sometimes grotesquely represented on maps by the letter Y—is one of the traces of the Celtic race. Intensely Teutonic as the whole of the west coast of Europe is now, it was once Celtic.

In Wales, the word *wy* forms the basis of the names of all the principal rivers, viz.:—Wye, Tywy, Teifwy (now Teifi), Cynwy (now Conway), Menwy (now Menai), Dûwy and Dywy (now Dee).

The Roman conquest of Britain is shown by the Romanisation of many of the names. That the dominion of Rome was introduced in British and not in Old English times, is shown by the inclusion of the British term within the Latin, while the English includes or modifies both. Thus the British *din* is included in the Roman *dunum*, which the English modifies into *don*; and the Romano-British Caer Legionum becomes Caerleon. *Castra*, a fortified town, is thus modified by the English tongue into *caster*, *cestre*, *cester*, *ceter*, or *chester*. Gloucester is another example of the inclusion of both British and Roman terms in an English name. Caer-gloyw, the fair city, became in Latin Glevi Castra, and out of both the Saxon has formed Glou-cester.

So, too, with a group of Salopian names. Wrekin, Wrexham, Wrickton, Wrockwardin, Wroxeter, and its Roman name Uriconium, all include the same British word *wr*, which was probably the name of the tribe of dwellers round the Wrekin two thousand years ago. The word seems to be from *gwr*, a man, i.e. a warrior, war being the only pursuit then accounted manly. Thus the Greek idea of virtue was ἀρετή, resemblance to Ἄρης, the war-god; the Roman type of excellence was *vir-tus*, manliness; and the ancient Germans may have meant that the males of their race were all warriors, when they described themselves as *Alemanni*, or all men.

That the Romans made roads in this as in other lands which they conquered, is attested by the British word *sarn*, and the English words, *street*, *stret*, *strat*, and *portway*, all meaning a Roman road. An example of the former is found in Sarn Helen, so named from the mother of Constantine; and the word reappears with a Saxon suffix in Sarnsfield, 'the field of the causeway.' An attempt has been made to deduce *street* and its cognate words from *ystrad* (British), a meadow or level place; but two considerations show the fallacy of this notion. Of the fifty-six names beginning with *street*, *stret*, or *strat*, nearly all are the names of places situated upon hills, in which *ystrad* would be a contradiction in terms; while all are situated on the line of some Roman road, some 'foss-way,' or 'stony-street,' or 'watling-street'—a fact which is inexplicable on the *ystrad* etymology.

The Roman habit of choosing for permanent camps sites near water is shown in many names of places, e.g. the group of names ending in *wardin*, all to be found in that Silurian country which it took the Romans so much time and trouble to subdue. Not to speak of their summer camps, only for actual warfare, which are very numerous on the hills west of the Severn, there are groups of camps along the rivers and conveniently near the waters, which are marked by the word *wardin*, from *dwrdin* (B., water camp). On the Severn, lie Wrockwardin, the water camp of the *wr* tribe; Cheswardin, St. Chad's water camp, so named of course ages after the destruction of Uriconium had obliterated Roman civilisation from the district; and Bedwardin (bais-dwr-din, the water camp of the ford). On the Teme, we find Leintwardin (llain-dwrdin, 'the water camp of the strip of land'); on the Lugg, Pedwardin (Peada's water camp); Lugwardin* (Lugg water camp), and Mar-wardin (Mae'r-dwr-din) the field of the water camp; and on the Wye, Bre-dwr-din, now Bredwardin, the water camp of the promontory.

The word *wall*, which seems to be a Saxon form of the British word *gwawl*, marks the site of Roman works. The word was probably received by the Britons from the Romans along with the works to which British writers apply it. The etymon is evidently *vallus*, a

* Spelt Lugg-dwr-din by Lady Brilliana Harley, in her Letters (temp. 1640–50).

stake, from whence came *vallum*, a fortification, i.e. a mound with the ditch (*fossa*) excavated in order to throw up the heap or ridge, and the row of stakes, or, in later times, the stone fence erected upon the ridge. It may or may not be correct to say that the *v* in Latin was sometimes pronounced as *w*, but it is certain that the Romans on landing in Britain first came in contact with the Belgic population of the south-east coast, whose posterity—the uneducated Londoners to wit—still use the *v* and the *w* interchangeably. The hard *g* was prefixed by the Celtic Britons according to the rule of their language; and thus *vallum* became *gwawl*. That the word was used by them to designate Roman works, is shown by a passage quoted by Richards (Welsh Dictionary, edition 1815) from an old British bard. Speaking of the wall of Severus, erected to keep out the Picts, he says:—

'Rhag gwerin gythrawl, gwawl faen.'

Which I render—

'Conspicuous against the people, a stone wall.'

The British for the wall of Severus was 'Gwawl Severus.' This view of the etymology of *wall* is strengthened by the consideration that the Romans, when adopting British words commencing with *gw*, represented the *w* with a *v*, and dropped the *g*. In this manner Gwrtheyrn and Gwrthefyr appear in Latin as Vortigernus and Vortimerus.

The Saxon word for a wall is *dic*, which in Yorkshire and South Scotland still (pronounced *dike*) designates a stone wall.

If the word *wall* were Saxon, we should find it most frequently in the Saxon kingdoms of Essex, Sussex, and Wessex; but in fact there are only two examples in those parts of the country, viz. Blackwall, near London, and Bower Walls, near Bristol, at the extremity of Wessex. Against these two, we have to place eleven instances, one of which—Walls End, the eastern termination of the wall of Severus—is in the Anglian kingdom of Bernicia, and the other ten are in the Anglian kingdom of Mercia. All these are to be found in districts full of evidences that they contained a large British population under Anglian sway.

In Worcestershire, we meet with four, viz. Wall-hills, near Suckley, Cradley, and Eastham; and Wall-batch, near Grimley.

In Herefordshire, there are six, viz. Wall-hills, near Ledbury, Thornbury, and Orleton; Cox-wall Knoll, on the Teme, where it divides the county from Salop; Walls-field, near Cradley; and Wal-ford, on the Wye, near the site of the Roman town of Ariconium.

All these places are either the names of camps of Roman or Romano-British construction, or are situated on the roads which those camps were meant to command.

The usual word for a Roman road, as already shown, is *street*; but in the Eastern counties, the word Fossway is sometimes found applied in that sense: Fossway dike (Linc.) for example. This word seems to be meant to distinguish such roads as were protected by a *fossa* or ditch on each side. It is customary to derive *fossa* from *fodio*, but I think it is the elder word of the two, and is cognate with the British *ffos*, a ditch.

The Romano-British class of names is most common west of the Severn; the English to the east of that river, and the Norse further eastward still. This is a corroboration of history, it being certain that the

Angle was long in the country before he established himself west of the Severn, and that the Norse or Danish kings never crossed that river at all. The few traces of the Norseman which are to be found beyond the Severn all lie along the sea-coast or the banks of the rivers, and are due to the fact that he reached that part of the country from the south or the west, whereas the Angle made his way thither from the east.

In a few cases, the Englishman not only retained the British or Romano-British word, but appended to it certain words of his own language. In other cases, he seems to have contented himself with merely shortening the name which he found in use. Thus the Latin Regulbium was curtailed into the English Reculver, a more compact but meaningless word. The only excuse for the Teuton is that he was as careless of the names he found, as the Roman had been before him. Regulbium was a mere pompous and unmeaning tomb, in which the original appellation *Rhagolwg beu*, 'the conspicuous abode,' was buried out of sight and out of hearing. The lofty commanding site, however, still vindicates the British name as an accurate description.

In the great majority of cases, the English obliterated the British names; and the mode and the principle of the change are equally curious as illustrations of national character. The personal element in war—the individualism out of which the feudal system was to spring—made itself felt among the Northern races at a very early period. Their wars were the result of the ambition and cupidity, not of the sovereign, but of the warriors individually. Bands of adventurers united in a common design for the distinct advantage of each. In the words of a proverb long current among their descendants in Eastern Scotland, 'like Harry o' the

Wynd, each fought for his ain hand.' The humblest of the Norse rovers was—to quote their own cherished title—one of the *vikingr*, or sea-kings, who obeyed the elected leader of his party just so long as he chose, and fought with or against his countrymen just as it suited his perception of his own interest. The sea-kings had long been the terror of Europe before any of their monarchs appeared at their head; and when they settled down in any country, they divided their conquests among themselves, and established themselves as independent rulers, without any idea of fealty to the monarch whom they had left at home. Almost every man among them seems to have given proof of his independence by calling his conquest after his own name. Unlike the Saxon, the Norseman had no tribal settlements, and among the Saxons such settlements were but few in comparison with those made by individuals.

With the Briton and the Roman, the nation was everything; the individual nothing. No Roman, with the exceptions of Ostorius, commemorated at Oyster hill, and a Caius whose name remains at Conwyl Gaio (Carmar.), has left his name to any spot in Britain; while the British place-names are in most cases descriptive and not personal. Occasionally the hero King Arthur, or Ambrosius, or Uther, or Brân 'the blessed,' or the wizard Myrddyn, or some other personification of the race in whom clouds of legendary glory had at an early period half effaced the lineaments of man, is remembered in connection with a hill-top, a wood, or a camp; but these cases are rare, and none of them can be traced with any certainty into Pagan times. The persons whom the Briton loved to commemorate are in almost all cases heroes of religion—saints kingly, episcopal, or monastic, teachers or martyrs. No ordinary chief, still less any private man, seems to have given his name to his possession; and where religion was not the occasion of a place being named, its appellation may be traced to either poetry or patriotism, or to both combined.

The Teutonic invader, on the contrary, however poetical at first, soon came to care little about poetry and much about property; little about his nation, but much about his own personal possessions. The Briton had carried self-government very far, as the wretched disunion of the people, and their readiness to betray each other, from the times of the Romans down to that of Edward I., abundantly prove; but the Old English carried out the principle still further. The Saxon Chronicle is full of evidence of the miserable disunion which made the country an easy prey to the Danes; and the same disunion made all their valour fruitless when the Norman William invaded the land. Had they been united, and disposed to obey their chosen leader Harold, they could have won the battle of Hastings; and the history of England would have been changed. Up to the afternoon of that disastrous 14th of September, 1066, the English were victors: it was their sallying forth from their camp, in defiance of Harold's orders, which saved the Normans and ruined their own country. Yet what good thing is there which man has not abused? The Englishman's self-reliance has produced many good as well as many evil results; and it has been an infinite advantage both to his race and to the world that he was conquered by the Danes and by the Normans.

Here we have not to do with the results: we merely adduce evidence which shows how early this self-reliance showed itself. That evidence is abundant in the place-names of England. Many of the most remarkable of these names have been already given; and it is now necessary to show how they enter into combination with descriptive prefixes and suffixes. Thus Aylbur's town has become Aylburton; the wood, the land, and the town of King Wulfor (A.D. 656) are now Wolferwood, Wolverley, Wolferton, and Wolverton; Alfred's town is known as Alfreston, or Alfreton; and the fierce Cerdic, founder of the monarchy of Wessex, is all but forgotten in his town of Chard.

The disappearance and reappearance of some names tells the story of successive immigrations in a still more forcible manner than any cases hitherto cited. The ancient city of Hereford has changed its name not less than four times. First it was called by the Britons *Hên-ffordd,** from the *old road* which there crossed the river Wye; a road which was so called in allusion to the new Roman road, now called Stony-street, which connected the towns of Gobannium (now Abergavenny) and Magna Castra, destroyed by the Angles. In Roman times the city was styled Caer-ffawydd, the city of beech-trees. The Angles called the place Fern-lege, or the ferny place, but this name did not long supplant that which had been left by the Romans. Caer-ffawydd was restored, but was gradually softened, *H* taking place of the hard *c*, and *ffawydd* being changed by Anglian tongues into *fort* or *ford.* Thus the name appears successively in mediæval and later writings as Harifort, Hariford, and Hereford.

Leicester is another example of a similar substitution of one name for others. The British Caer-Lloegr was Romanised to Ligera, which the Angles changed to

* Welsh people still know Hereford best by its original name, Hên-ffordd.

Legera-cestre, and this name became softened into Leycestre, and finally to the present form Leicester. It still survives as a personal name in the form Leycester.

Peterborough is a name which points to an interesting episode of Anglian history, which lies buried in the pages of Bede and the Saxon Chronicle. Its first name was 'Medèshamstede,' the station in the meadows; and the change of the appellation to Peterborough was a memorable incident. The abbey was founded in A.D. 655 by Peada, king of Mercia, but he was murdered by his wife in the same year, when the foundations had barely been laid. His successor Wulfhere carried on the work, and under his patronage it was completed in a very few years; and the Chronicle gives a full and glowing description of the solemn dedication, in A.D. 664, by Deus-dedit, Archbishop of Canterbury, and the bishops of Rochester, London, and Mercia, in the presence of the king and his brother and sisters. The king's deed of gift to the abbot is stated to have been subscribed by himself and by the thegns who witnessed it 'with their fingers on the cross of Christ,' a practice which still survives in the sign of the cross which is made by witnesses who cannot write their names. Pope Vitalian granted a receipt, confirming the king's grants and exempting the abbot of Medeshamstede from all jurisdiction except that of the Holy See and the Archbishop of Canterbury. The abbey flourished and 'waxed rich' for two centuries, and then the storm of destruction burst upon it. In A.D. 870, the Danes under Hingwar and Hubba 'came to Medeshamstede, and burned and beat it down, slew abbot and monks and all they found there; and that place which before was full rich, they reduced to nothing.' The abbey remained desolate until 963, in the reign of Edgar, when Ethelwold, Bishop of Winchester, undertook the task of restoring the minsters which had been destroyed by the Danes. First he went to Ely, and 'caused the minster to be made;' and then he made his way to Medeshamstede, but he 'found nothing there but old walls and wild woods.' Hidden in these old walls, however, he found writings left by one of the dead abbots, telling how royally the abbey had been built and consecrated and endowed. Guided by these writings, Ethelwold 'caused the minster to be built,' and set therein an abbot and monks. He then went to King Edgar, showed him the writings which he had found, and induced the king to give much land and a number of towns and villages, along with the singular addition of 'one moneyer in Stamford.' The famous Dunstan, then Archbishop of Canterbury, with the Archbishop of York and a number of bishops, ealdormen, and thegns, witnessed the king's grants; and the abbot Aldulf not only 'bought lands and enriched the minster,' but also made the wall about it, thus converting it into a *burh* or fortified place; and then he 'gave that to name Peterborough, which before was called Medeshamstede.' Thus the abbot's gift has permanently supplanted the ancient name, although the facts which it represents have long been forgotten.

Malmesbury is another place which has for ages borne a name totally different from that which it once bore. It was a British town, the centre of a district where many British names remain, and was then called (says Leland) Caer Bladon, *i.e.* the Roman camp converted into a city by a British prince named Bladon. It seems to have retained its name until A.D. 642, when Maildulf, one of the band of missionaries from Ireland who preached among the Saxons, received permission from Ina king of Wessex to build on the spot a church and a monastery. In this work his coadjutor was Aldhelm, the king's nephew; and the popular memory combined their names in the word Mealdelmes-byrig, which has been by time reduced into the more managable word Malmesbury.

Queenborough (Kent) is an example of a rare kind—the conversion of a masculine into a feminine appellation. Known to the Jutes and Saxons as Cyninga-burh, the king's fortification, it retained that name, merely modified into Kingborough, down to the time of Edward III. In his wars with France, the little town at the mouth of the Swale was a convenient port, and he rebuilt the ancient castle which commanded the entrance. On visiting the town shortly afterwards, he was much pleased with it, and left a twofold testimony of his satisfaction, first in altering its name to Queenborough, in honour of his wife Philippa, and next in granting to the inhabitants the privileges of a free borough, and 'the staple of wool,' *i.e.* the right to hold a market for that product. The new name was given in 1366; the wool market was granted in 1369.

Horne Tooke has shown that the word tawdry has come from overdressing the image of St. Etheldreda, whose name was colloquially shortened into Awdrey; and it would seem from a remark by Coles (quoted by Mr. Halliwell in his 'Dictionary of Provincialisms') that the festival of the saintly lady was held as a fair for the sale of articles of women's finery. His words are:

> 'Tawdry lace—fimbriæ nundinis sanctæ Etheldredæ emptæ.'

It is probable, too, that the word *Tab*, in Tabley

(Glouc.), like our children's word tabby, for a cat, is a similar corruption of the name of St. Ebbe or Abb, a nun of high saintly renown, and (like many other saints of her nation) the daughter of a king, the otherwise undistinguished Ethelfrid, who reigned about 660.

The words Yap, as in Yapton, and Yat, as in Yatton, may be taken as reminiscences in like manner of Eappa and Eata, two priests of great renown among their countrymen, as shown in the 'Ecclesiastical History' of Bede. Eappa was a zealous and devoted missionary to the South Saxons, circa 681; and we are not surprised, therefore, to find his name preserved in a place included in his labours. Yapton, in Sussex, is however the only place which bears his name. Eata was bishop of a see which included Mercia, and it is within the limits of that kingdom that we meet with the name of Yatton. There are two places of that name, both in Herefordshire.

Amwell (Herts) may be taken, not only as a trace of early history, but as an example of the method pursued in this inquiry. The known part of the name, the syllable *well*, being an English word, we seek first in the same tongue for the other syllable. The probability, judging from analogy, is that *Am* is the name of the person to whom the well belonged, or upon whose estate it was situated. With that clue we soon reach the name Emma, of which Am is an obvious contraction. The next step is to inquire whether history records the connection of any person with the place, and by so doing we learn that the ancient name was 'Emma's well.' Perhaps Queen Ælfgivu Emma, mother of Hardicanute, Harold Harefoot, and Edward the Confessor, was the Emma alluded to; but whether that conjecture stand or fall, the case establishes the correctness of the inductive system of interpretation.

The manner in which the study of the names of places illustrates history may be shown in fuller detail by the consideration of a group of names in Herefordshire. Four miles south-east of the town of Leominster lies the camp of Risbury, in the midst of a number of places which bear names mostly of Anglian origin. The formation of the camp appears to have been an incident of the final war for the sovereignty of the country lying between the Severn and the Wye, which was waged in the early part of the tenth century. Risbury, the Riseberie of Domesday Book, and the Risebiria of a charter given in Dugdale's 'Monasticon,' is a word of obvious derivation: *Rise*, a hill, as in Highgate Rise, Clapham Rise, &c.; and *bury*, from *burh*, a fortified place. The names of the neighbouring parishes—Marston, Humber, Hennor, Eyton, Ford, Docklow, and Stoke*—are all proofs that the Angles settled in those places. Pencomb (from *pen*, a hill, and *cum*, a dingle); and Blackcaer-dun, an Anglicised British word, meaning 'the black hill-camp,' are the only traces of the Briton to be found within some miles. The names indicate that Herefordshire was then a land of woods and pools, with here and there a few huts in a 'thwaite' (clearing), or on a dock-covered 'low' (*hlaew*, a hill), while devious paths concealed rather than led to the chief's palace at the head of the dingle (Pen-cwm), or on some quasi-island in the marshes, known to the Britons by the term *ynys*, to the Angles as an *ey-tun* or a *mares-tun*

* It should be remembered that the Roman word *vallus*, the etymon of the word 'wall,' meant originally a stake driven into the ground, e.g. 'Induere se acutissimis vallis aut stimulis.'—*Cæsar*. This was precisely the Saxon *stoc* or *stoke*.

(Eyton and Marston). Such words as Wood-field and Woot-ton (wood town) show the cleared spots in which the settler dug a ditch and threw up a mound around his dwelling. A house so defended was called in Saxon a *tun*, and the word still survives in the Scottish lowlands, where a farm-house with its outbuildings is still called a 'farm-toon.'

It was only the lower hills, however, which were thus settled by the invaders: the loftier hills—as their names show—still remained in British hands long after the vales and the lesser eminences had been wrested from them. Although the kingdom of Mercia is said to have been founded by Crida, in 586, it would appear to have really existed only in the champaign country up to the time of Æthelstan, three centuries and a half after Crida's conquest. It was a league of British princes of the district which that king (as already noticed) overcame at the battle of Malvern, in A.D. 924, and which he 'held hard and drave across the Wye, so that they possessed not Wye afterwards.' * The princes were expelled, but the people remained. The Briton not only kept his hills, but disputed with the invaders the possession of the valleys. When opportunity served, or beef grew scarce on the hills, a British band would make a foray upon the herds of an Anglian thegn in the vales, and then hurry back with their booty to their fastnesses.

The nursery rhyme of 'Taffy' is a mere condensation of the history of these marches for many centuries:

Taffy was a Welshman,
Taffy was a thief.

* Chronicle of Brut, edited by Sir F. Madden.

Here is Anglian prejudice, abusing by wholesale the people whom Anglian invasion had dispossessed.

Taffy came to my house,
And stole a leg of beef.

Here is the raid upon the Angle's homestead, and the capture of his cattle. By and bye the visit would be repaid:

I went to Taffy's house,
Taffy wasn't at home.

He was too prudent to await his visitors when they came in inconveniently large numbers; but whilst they were seeking for him he sometimes made a wide detour, came down like a thunderbolt upon the homesteads which had been left unguarded, and carried off all that remained of the herds which he had previously thinned:

Taffy came to my house,
And stole a marrow bone—

that is, all that was left worth taking. It is unnecessary to pursue the story, as told in the ballad with the characteristic coarseness of mediæval times. The substantial meaning is enough for our purpose. It teaches us how Taffy's retaliation hurried on the catastrophe. Probably, in such cases, there would be a grand gathering of the Anglian settlers, to which every man who was not a 'niddering,' or utterly worthless, would be summoned on pain of being harried out of house and home by his compatriots; and then the hills would be surrounded and stormed, and the troublesome hill-men captured for slaves or slaughtered.

IX.

NAMES WHICH ILLUSTRATE OLD ENGLISH AND NORSE SOCIAL LIFE.

The frequent recurrence of the words Folley and Foxley in the vicinage of our most ancient cities and towns seems to be a trace of an important fact of Old English social life, viz. the reservation of tracts of land as the property of the people at large. It is admitted that there was a large public domain in times preceding the Norman Conquest; and as we find no mention of it in Domesday Book, we reasonably conclude that the Conqueror had seized not only the domains of the Old English kings, to which he had the sort of title conferred by the slaughter of the previous possessor, but also much land of which they were merely the custodians, and which was really folc-land. This view is strengthened by the significant distinction made in Domesday Book between the lands held by Harold—over whose name *comes* is always written, as though to avoid even the appearance of a recognition of his kingship—and the lands held by his predecessor Edward, which are always described by the initials 'T. R. E.,' for *terræ regis Edwardi*. These latter I take to have been the folc-land, while the lands designated as Harold's property I understand to have been partly his own ancestral estate, and partly the Royal domain. The cities and towns seem to have retained such portions of the folc-land as had been assigned to them; and these tracts of land in some cases still belong to the townsmen, having escaped the rage for enclosure down to our own times. In the words Folley and Foxley, we have apparent traces of the *folces-lege* or people's land. The only explanation of these words hitherto offered, that the places so named were often the scenes of sport and festivity in the middle ages, so that the word Folley came to be associated with fooling, tends to strengthen this view. The public land would naturally be the site for the public sports. It is worth note, too, that in old deeds and grants of land, wherever the Folley is mentioned, the word is not translated but transferred, appearing as 'Folleia,' which would scarcely have happened if the word had merely meant a place of fooling. The name would be a reflex of the public opinion, which did not consider sports to be folly, although it might fairly enough look upon the folc-land, being the citizens' property, as the proper place for their amusements.

Another illustration of Old English social life is afforded by place-names drawn from the tenure of land. The only real tenures in pre-Norman times were allodial and feudal, the latter being granted by the lord for military service; the former absolutely. All land which was not held by or from a lord was folc-land, and where any of this was granted to an individual, it was called boc-land. We shall find traces of all these tenures among the Old English place-names. There being no British place-names indicating that it was customary among the Britons to let land to tenants, it would seem that the Old English introduced the practice. In the names of King's Lynn (Norf.), and King's Len—now corrupted into Kingsland (Midd. and Heref.), we see a record of the historical fact that the land belonged to some one of the Old English kings, who let it out on what lawyers call fee-farm tenure, and that the town or village which arose on the spot was thence named King's *len* or laen—a word of cognate origin with the verb to lend and the substantive loan. Len-ton (Notts) and Len-ham (Kent) indicate that the site was let, but do not preserve any trace of the name or rank of the owner. Len-aelh (Heref.), which afterwards became Linhales, and has within the last two centuries been strangely transformed into Lyonshall—apparently from the reason that it had *no* connection with the king of beasts or any of his namesakes—is the sole example of a *len* which included the *aelh* or residence of the owner. Usually the thegn or hlaford seems to have retained the hall and its precincts in his own possession; but as the jarls and thegns accumulated property non-resident landlordism became inevitable, and the hall was made a *len*. In Norman times, the *aelh* was replaced by the castle of the baron, who brought in a new tenure, which for a time superseded that of the *len*. Having received his lands from the king on the condition of military service, the baron sub-granted to his friends parts of his fee on condition of their rendering military service to him. The idea was not quite new: there had been under the latest kings before the Conquest 'Radcheni' or 'Radmen,' whose lands were held on the tenure of serving the State in war. Domesday Book mentions them in a great number of instances, and this kind of tenure gradually became general. When the baron thus sub-feued his estates, he generally retained in his own hands the part surrounding the castle, which became the *demesne*, while land sub-let was called *mesne*. As the Norman kings claimed to be the absolute owners of all lands in the kingdom—the crown is still so in law—the baron was accounted the mesne lord or middleman, and all his land, whether sub-let or not, was strictly mesne land, but in practice the term was restricted to that which he sub-let or granted. Both words are still in use in law; in nomenclature only one is preserved. Land surrounding a mansion is called a demesne, but the word does not occur as a place-name. *Mesne* is retained in one instance—Clifford's Mesne (Glouc.)—indicating land originally part of Dean Forest, but granted to a Clifford. This scarcity of names indicating the Norman land-tenure is itself a corroboration of history; an echo of the truth that that tenure has died out of use, while the older English mode of letting land has survived, and has become universal.

Soc-bourn (Dur.) and Soc-lege, now Suckley (Worc.), preserve in the root-word the memory of another Old English tenure. The soc-men were freemen and tenants, but were privileged, i.e. they were exempt from the jurisdiction of all courts but that of the district included in the *soc.* Littleton defines tenure in socage to be when the tenant holds his tenement of the lord by any *certain* service, so that it be not knight's service.

The existence of intermediate classes between freemen and theows is also shown in place-names. The *bordars*, who held small portions of land on the tenure of rendering services, in tending the cattle of their lord, are visible in such place-names as Bordesley (Warw.). Domesday Book, it may be noted, records the fact that there were 'five villani and four bordarii' in Birmingham, of which Bordesley is part. Borden (Kent) seems to be the *dene*, or hollow, occupied by Bordars. The next class, the Cottarii, or cottars, are commemorated at Cotter-stock (North.), the stoke or palisaded station of the cottars. Probably the reason why we have no more places named from these tenures is that the Norman crushed *len*-men, bordars, and cottars alike into serfs, and recognised no freemen save those who held land by military tenure.

The Saxon practice of dividing lands at the owner's death among all his children equally, which in Kent was styled 'gavelkind,' supplies the only probable explanation of a number of names of which the root is *snaed*, a piece of land separated from a manor. This word appears modified by the various Old English dialects as Snad, Snaith, Snea, Snead, Sneyd, Snen, and Snod; and is the root of many names of places in Yorkshire, and of one in each of the following counties:—Stafford (in which county Sneyd is also the name of an ancient family), Montgomery, Hereford, Nottingham, Kent, and Sussex.

The tendency of invaders, and indeed of settlers in a strange land generally, to keep as near as possible to each other for mutual protection, is evident in the grouping of names from one language in the midst of those which belong to another. Thus in the Forest of Dean, which is divided by the Wye from the British districts of Irging and Gwent (now parts of Herefordshire and Monmouthshire), thirty out of thirty-six place-names are Old English, while the rest are British names Anglicised. In Lydan-ey (now Lydney) and Lydbrook, the root is the British *lyd*, country; in Ruardean, we see the *rhiw-ar*, or sloping-path field held by Britons, adjoining the *dene* or hollow in the possession of the English; and in Longhope we see the two races united, the *hwpp* or sloping plain between hills so fully Anglicised as to be distinguished from all others by the English adjective *Long* prefixed, instead of the British word *hir* added to the root-word.

A parallel fact is the group of bilingual names around the junction of the Munnow and the Wye. The modern name of the district on the north side of the junction, Archenfield, means the field of Irging, the British name of part of it; and the same mingling of races is shown in the words Monmouth, the mouth of the Munnow, Mitchel-tref-wy (now Mitcheltroy), the greater village by the Wye or water, Wyesham, the home on the Wye, and Osbaston, the *tun* or farm of Osbald. Such names show the English settling down in a group among the Britons, seizing their lands, and Anglicising their names at will.

Another group of names of which worth (*wyrth*, Saxon; *werth*, German) forms part, is confined to the North Midland counties and South-West Yorkshire, where the word is very frequent. Originally, *wyrth* meant a well-watered estate, although in course of time its meaning was extended so as to mean any estate; and the *worths* of England, like the *werths* of Germany, are still the well-watered spots which the word implies. In Hants, Somerset, and Devon, the word *ey* (water) is appended, as in Worthey, Clatworthy, &c.; and this tautology seems to mean that the settlements so named were not formed until the later times of pre-Norman rule, when the meaning of the word *wyrth* had been lost. This conjecture is strengthened by the historical truth that the English had not fully conquered Devonshire at the time of their own subjugation by the Normans. So late as 1064, the northern coast of both Devon and Somerset was treated by Harold as an enemy's country.

The next group covers a larger space, but is not less sharply defined. The word *thorp* (German *dorf*), meaning a farm-house, is scarcely to be found outside of the Norse or Danish district of England. It occurs in twenty-eight names as a prefix, and in 281 as a suffix; and seems to be the equivalent of *hám* in the Saxon and Anglian districts. On the other hand, it is very rare in the Danish county of Lincoln. The word does not occur in Norway or Iceland, while it is found only in those parts of Denmark which adjoin Germany. If originally Danish, it must have belonged to the southern section of the people. The analogous word in Norway, in North-East Scotland, and in Lincolnshire, is *by*, just as in those Norse countries *vic* or *wick* (village) takes the place occupied by *tun* (town) in Old English place-names.

This debateable word naturally leads to a consideration of other and more certain traces of the Norseman. Although, as remarked above, it is in some cases difficult to distinguish them from the Old English, there are certain broad distinctions between the two sets of names which can be easily grasped. If we look closely at the map of England, we shall be able to trace the footsteps of the Norseman with tolerable accuracy. On the East coast, the word *by* as a termination of place-names is very frequent in the district extending from the Tees to the Welland, now divided into the shires of York, Derby, Nottingham, and Lincoln, but disappears when we turn inland and reach the hilly district which bounds Yorkshire and Derbyshire on the west. There are two *bys* in the low country of South Derbyshire, but none among the hills. In the district indicated, *by* occurs in 150 names; in Durham and Northumberland there are no *bys*, but a small group of ten is strewed along the banks of the Eden, in Cumberland. To the south of the Welland there are only two *bys*, one in Norfolk and the other in Suffolk: in South and West England there are none.

In all these cases, *by* is a suffix or appendix to the proper name of the place. As a prefix it occurs in two places, both in Saxon and Anglian districts, and seems to be in each a form of *big*, from *biggin*, a building, indicating the spot where the lord built a house.* Such are By-worth (Suss.) and By-ton (Hants). West of the Severn a single example is found; Byford (Heref.) appears in Domesday Book as 'Bviford,' in which spelling we see the British origin of the name, viz. Buwch-fford, the cow's way. This name is in keeping with Bu-allt, the steep place of the cow, Hên-ffordd, the old way, and other place-names in the same district. The only instance west of the Wye in which *by* occurs as a suffix is Tenby, in South Wales, which is well known to be a corrupt Anglicising of the original name, Dinbychan, the little fortification.

The *bys* in Cumberland and Westmoreland mark those parts only which were accessible to the Norse rovers by water; and this fact is analogous to the occurrence of names containing *holm* and *ness* on the banks of rivers in other parts of England. Even the remote Wye and Severn thus bear traces still extant of the Norseman's *chiule* upon their banks. They are evidence that, while the great body of Norse invaders seized the large district of Eastern England, which was consequently known as the Danelagh, or Danish land, there were many small bands which wasted the island, forced their way wherever there was water to float their

* The verb *to big* is still used in Scotland in the sense of *to build*:

'The rising moon had climbed the hill,
Whaur eagles *big* aboon the Dee.'

barks, and appropriated to themselves any fertile river-island or meadow which took their fancy.

That they did not exterminate the English, but settled down among them, is curiously shown in the modifications of the same word which occur almost side by side. The same word in English lips seems to have always tended to become softer in sound; in Norse lips, to harden. The *c*, originally hard in all the Old English words in which it occurred, becomes softened into *ch* or *sh*, while it is preserved as *k* in the pronunciation of the Norseman and his posterity. The learned Dane Worsaae remarks, I think, that Sweyn the king was called by his Norse subjects 'Sven tvae-skaeg,' and by the Saxons 'Sweyn twa-shag,' both titles being the same words, and meaning Sweyn the forked bearded. Here are some parallel instances from place-names,* some of them among the commonest in England:

Old English	Norse	Meaning	Example
Ælh	Skeal	a drinking hall	Lin-ælh, Skelton
Æsc	Ask	an ash-tree	Ash-ton, Ask-ham
Cealc, Chalk	Cawk	chalk	Chalk hill, Cawk-well
Ceorl, Charl	Carl	a husbandman	Charl-ton, Carlton
Chetel	Kettle	a possession	Chittleham, Kettle
Ciric, Church	Kirk	a church	Churcham, Kirkham
Cissa	Kessa	a king's name	Chichester, Keston
Scear	Scar,	a precipice	Shares-hill, Scarcliffe
Sceaf	Skeff	a sheaf	Shefford, Skeffington
Sceol	Skel	a shoal	Shelford, Skelton
Scua, Shaw	Scaw	a wood	Shaw-hill, Scaw-fell
Scyp	Skip	a sheep	Shipton, Skipton
Scyr	Skir	a division	Shire-brook, Skir-brook
Nash	Naze	a headland	Rodd-nash, The Naze

* For a part of this list I am indebted to Ferguson's 'Northmen.'

X.

NAMES PRODUCED BY THE NORMAN CONQUEST.

NOT long after the Norsemen came their French-born cousins, the Normans, the nature and extent of whose conquest is not less clearly indicated in our local nomenclature. The list of place-names traceable to the Normans is a scanty one, from which we conclude that the number of the invaders was small in proportion to that of the people among whom they settled. Most frequently the Norman name is an appendage to the Old English, thus suggesting that the Norman was the conqueror of the landowners rather than of the people. The ordinary form is exemplified in Stretton Grandison, Moreton Say, Stoke Bliss, and Redmarley d'Abitot, where the name of the Norman lord follows that of the place, which is Old English. In such names as Alan's mere (now corrupted to Allensmore) we have exceptions to the usual sequence, the lord's name coming first; but the explanation is easy: Alan was originally a Saxon name. Alan de Ewyas was one of the Barons of Herefordshire in 4 Edward III., but the name is a coinage of the dim ages when the Saxon or Angle was a poet. Common as it became among the Normans, Alan was a corruption of the Saxon Ulwin or Ulfwin, the wolf of victory.

In the group of Flyfords (Worces.), we have a trace of the historical truth that the king was a feudal baron. Flyford Grafton, Flyford Flavell, and Flyford Kings, are the names of contiguous parishes, which belonged respectively to the baronial families of Grafton, and Flavell (or De Freville), and the king.

Another group in the same county illustrates the old law phrase, 'a knight's fee,' viz. Knight-wick, Knight's-ford, and Knight-town, now Knighton, all which were probably held on the tenure of knightly service.

In rare cases, the Norman name is adopted into the English tongue, as in Rowlstone and Walterstone (Heref.), in which Rowland's Town and Walter's Town are evident. The English habit of shortening words in common use is further exemplified in Wistanstow and Wistaston, which are remarkable as instances of the havoc which the vulgar tongue sometimes makes. In the latter case, the original name was Stephen's town, which was first curtailed to Stenston, then to Steston, then somehow assumed the prefix *wi*—which may be the British word for water, the place being subject to inundation from the river Lugg, so as to be inaccessible sometimes for weeks together in the winter—and has in these later centuries blossomed into Wistaston! Had I not seen the word in its several stages in Camden, and in the report of the trial of an action at law, about a century ago, to decide the ownership of the estate, I should not have ventured upon an etymology so incredible-looking. In Wistaston we have a clue to Wistanstow (Salop), i.e. Stephen's station. Whether those places were named from the first of Christian martyrs, or from the Conqueror's nephew, who resembled his namesake in neither Christianity nor martyrdom, it is impossible now to ascertain, if it were worth while to inquire; but the saintly nomenclature is the more probable, as the affixes *stow* and *ton* indicate the pre-Norman period as the time when the names were given.

Pure Norman names are sometimes found side by

side with Old English or British. In Herefordshire, St. Devereux—so named from the famous abbey of Evreux in Normandy—is overlooked by the British village of Cil-Pedawc, St. Pedawc's retreat, now Kilpeck. From the former doubtless originated the patronymic of the Norman baronial family, which is now represented by Devereux, Viscount Hereford. In many other cases, the estate in like manner gave name to the lord, as De Hereford, De Bermingham, &c.; but in some the process was reversed, the lord giving his name to the place. Rich-mond (Yorks.) was thus named from Rich, who built a castle on the *mount* which he had seized. Gros-mont (Mon.) is an instance of the settlement of a Norman lord and the erection of a castle near the broad massive hill which the Britons called *y Graig* (the rock). History justifies this conclusion from the name, since we know that the castle was built by Hubert de Burgh, in the reign of Henry III. Probably in all places of this class the castle preceded the town.

In a kindred class of names, we perceive the British name of the town supplanted by that of the Norman castle. Thus in Breconshire, the old *Tref-celli* (town among the hazles) has been superseded by the Norman La Hay (the enclosure), which is now used in the half-translated form of The Hay. In like manner, the feudally-named Knighton (Radnor.) represents the British Tref-y-clawdd, 'the town on the dike' (of Offa). Montgomery seems to be a Norman corruption of Mynydd Gymry, 'the mountain of the Britons,' a name which the Britons probably applied to the border hills generally, but which was in its corrupted form first given to the Norman castle, and was afterwards assumed by its lord, who certainly showed good taste in his choice of so euphonious a cognomen. When the district was formed into a shire (temp. Henry VIII.) there was a certain historical justice in calling it Montgomeryshire, although Powis-shire would have been more accurate, as the district was styled by its inhabitants Powis. The correctness of this etymology is proved by the common pronunciation of the word. Our spelling and our pronunciation alike are corruptions of Montgumry. In the West of Scotland, the family name of the House of Eglintoun, a branch of the same great Norman family, is pronounced as in Wales. Hence Burns writes:

> Ye banks and braes and streams around
>   The castle o' Montgomerie,
> Green be your woods and fair your flowers,
>   Your waters never drumlie.

Norman place-names record the sway of many families once mighty and wealthy, but now either wholly extinct or at least dissevered from their ancient possessions. Say of Moreton Say—Bliss of Stoke Bliss—De Gamages of Mansell Gamage—Bowdler of Ashford Bowdler—Brian of Brampton Brian—Carbonell of Ashford Carbonell—Gifford of Fonthill Gifford—Bagot of Hope Bagot — D'Abernon of Stoke d'Abernon — Bigod of Weston Bigod (now Beggard) are no longer owners of the places which bear their names. In the expressive language of the Bible, 'the place which once knew them knoweth them no more.' But that the family which produced the worst of English judges once owned Moreton Jefferys, its name would suggest nothing, powerful as the family may once have been; while Stretton Grandison only reminds us of the hero of the longest of Richardson's long novels, now known but by name even to inveterate devourers of fiction.

It has been remarked above that the Norsemen did

not exterminate, but settled down among the English, and the persistence of some British place-names in the midst of the settlements of both those invading races shows that the English had previously followed the same policy. The existence of a large class of names of which *tre* or *try* forms part, justifies this conclusion. With (I think) only three exceptions, however, these names are found only in Wales or Derbyshire, the most British parts of the island. The etymon I take to be *treu* (as given in Domesday Book), which is apparently a modification of the British *trêf*, a town, or more strictly, the abode of the person whose name (in British place-names) follows the word. Thus tre-Faldwin is Baldwin's abode; tre-Madoc (Brecon.) the abode of Madawc, one of the heroes of British legend. Sometimes the word appended is descriptive, as Tre-gwyn (Mon.), the white house, or Tref-eglwys, church house. When the word occurs eastward of the Severn, it is usually in conjunction with English or Norse words, and is thus—in accordance with the idiom of those tongues—always a suffix. Thus we have Coven-tre, the protected town, Alles-tre (Derb.), the abode of Ella, &c. Daven-try is one of the rare cases in which a British name has survived all but unchanged amid a wholly Anglianised district. Dwy-afon-tre, 'the town of two streams,' it still is, although the streams have dwindled into brooks. Baw-try (Notts) in like manner retains almost unaltered its Anglianised British name Bawn-tref, 'the town of the cattle-fold.'

XI.

NAMES WHICH RECORD THE CONNECTION OF THE CHURCH WITH THE SOIL, AND THE RANKS AND ORDERS OF THE HIERARCHY.

In Section III. I have to some extent forestalled the inquiry under this head; and it may suffice to indicate here the large class of names which show the position of the Church as one of the great landowners, and the gradations of rank among its ministers. Bishop's town (now Bishopston), Bishop's Frome, Eaton, and Hampton Bishop, and Bishop Thorp may suffice as traces of the episcopal landowner; while Canon-bury, Norton Canon, Canon Pyon, &c., prove that there were capitular bodies which held estates; and the names of which Priest or Prest forms part help us to trace the subordinate clergy. In England there are forty-six place-names of this last-mentioned class, of which thirty-six are Preston, i.e. the priest's town; two are Prestbury, the priest's fortified town; two Prest-wolds show that the towns were built on the wild or forest land; in two, Pres-cot indicates the pastoral character of the district; in one the position is shown by the suffix *cliff*; and one is named Prest-wick, or 'the priest's village,' in a Norse district. Pres-hute, 'the priest's hut,' is the only example of that combination of terms. Presteign, 'the priest's town before the eye,' i.e. outside the border, being just to the westward of the Welsh Marches, is the solitary instance of Prest occurring in Wales; and it is in the more than half English shire of Radnor.

Some few names of this class show the use of Latin among mediæval churchmen; and as one comes upon a gray old fane, standing among the solemn elms, amid which its tall ivied tower and battlements stained with yellow lichen seem to rise so appropriately, there is an apparent fitness of things, when we find that it bears a Latin name. A word from a tongue no longer living, which was ancient when the first stone of the time-stained structure was laid, seems to be in keeping with its venerable aspect. A Latin name jars somewhat when brought into close connection with a thriving seaport of to-day, such as Barnstaple, which its inhabitants call by its ancient name of Barum; and it sounds strange to hear Shropshire people styling their beautiful county proud Salopia; but usually the Latin word is not a substitute but an appended word, distinguishing adjoining parishes of the same Saxon or British name. The position of the Latin word after the principal name is a parallel fact to the usual position of the Norman lord's name, and indicates the prevalence of French habits of speech at the time when the name originated. Thus Monksilver has no connection with the metal, but merely points out the *sylva* or woodland belonging to a monastery. Buckland Monachorum distinguishes the place of the monks from the other Bucklands; and Kingsbury Episcopi marks one of the three fortified towns once belonging to Saxon royalty which afterwards became the property of a bishop. In another class of these bilingual names, the Latin word is an adjective indicating the respective sizes of the parishes: Birch Magna and Birch Parva (Heref.) are examples.

In one remarkable instance, the Latin name is the only appellation, and is composed of a noun and a participle in the ablative case, as though it were the commencement of a passage in some Latin chronicle. The name Pontefracto, afterwards corrupted to Pomfret—in which form it appears in Shakspeare's 'Richard III.'—and now more correctly written Pontefract, does indeed suggest a story, tragical enough, however briefly told. Seven hundred years ago, an Archbishop of York was passing with his train along the bridge at this spot when the structure gave way. Life was lost, and maimed survivors as well as bereaved relatives had ample reason to remember the 'broken bridge.'

In Monmouthshire, Latin is used in a manner which is peculiar if not unique. Instead of nouns or adjectives the appended words are prepositions or conjunctions. Llanwenarth parish having been divided, the two portions are distinguished as Llanwenarth *ultra* and Llanwenarth *citra*, as they lie near to or far from the Priory of Abergavenny, to which probably the patronage belonged. In the same district, one of the many parishes named Llangattoc is distinguished from the rest by the words '*juxta*-Usk,' pointing out its position on the bank of that river. In the Saxon, Anglian, and Norse districts, the construction is the same, but the words are English, as in Kingston-on-Thames, Ashton-under-Lyne, Newcastle-upon-Tyne, &c. The only other instances of the use of Latin in this connection are Attercliffe-*cum*-Darnall (Yorks.), Sutton-*cum*-Duckmanton (Derb.), Duddeston-*cum*-Nechells (Warwicks.), and a few others which need not to be cited.

The monastic orders have left equally legible traces of their presence among the owners of the soil. The Old English word Abban (corrupted to Abing) shows that the place was 'the abbot's.' *Mynstre* (from *monasterium*) survives as minster, now restricted to mean a cathedral;* and it seems from the half-British word Leominster (*llian*-mynstre) that there were minsters for nuns as well as for monks. The pure Old English words Nun-Upton and White-ladies' Aston (both in Worces.), and the half-Norse Nun-thorp, show also that there were nunneries in pre-Norman times, and that they held estates.

The monastic houses were in many cases hospitals, as the frequency of the words *spital* in England, and *ysbitty* in Wales, sufficiently proves. Both seem to have come from the Latin *hospitium*. Such names remind us of one of the best uses to which monastic institutions were applied, but there are others which record a fact less creditable to the cowled fraternity. In such words as Llan-y-mynach, the monk's church, we have a trace of the long and angry contention for patronage and possessions between the regular and the secular clergy, of which the double churches of Leominster, Abergavenny, and other parishes, give more tangible evidence. Judging from nomenclature, monkery throve equally well on both sides of the Severn, taking into account the greater fatness of the land on the English side. Monk-house, Monk-land, Monk-ley, Monk-moor, have their equivalents in Mynach-dy, Tir-mynach, Waun-mynach. About twenty-four places in England are named from abbey or abbot, nearly the same number from monk, and about a dozen contain the word nun. In some the possessive case is disguised: Nonnan, belonging to a nun, having been corrupted into Nunning, as in Nunnington. Generally monastic words are prefixed to the original names of the places, thus indicating that the town or village was first founded. Thus in

* All cathedrals were mynstres, but there were many mynstres which were not cathedrals.

Devon we find Abbot's Teignton, Abbot's Kerswell, &c. Where the town grew up around the abbey, we find the monastic word constituting the name, as in Westminster, and in Abingdon, 'the abbot's hill.' The word *grange* indicates the farmhouse of the monastic lands.

We know from history that there were but few priories in England; and this testimony is corroborated by the names. Originally the priory was an offshoot or colony from an abbey, and the prior ranked beneath the abbot, whose deputy at first he was. In course of time the priors became independent, but were always accounted inferior; just as the vice-comes was at first the count's deputy, but now, when there is no official subordination, the viscounty is a lower grade of the peerage. According to Sir Edward Coke, at the time when the monastic orders were in their heyday of power, only two priors sat in Parliament, which contained twenty-six abbots; a number greater than that of the bishops at that time. The names which commemorate the priors are in England only eight; in Wales none. In four of the eight cases, the word *prior* is a prefix to the original name, which is always English; an indication that the priory was post-Saxon in its introduction to this country. Prior's Halton is the prior's hall-town; Prior's Lee, the Lee belonging to a priory; Prior's Ditton, the prior's ditch-protected town; and Prior's Marston, one of seventeen marsh towns. Out of sixty-six Stokes, there is one Stoke Prior; and Leamington Priors and Hardwick Priors in like manner distinguished the prior's property from six other Hardwickes and one other Hastings. Prior's Dean is one out of nine 'hollows,' which became the sites of villages.

A curious couplet of names in Dorset suggests a comical juxtaposition of ideas. Remembering the Saxon habit of feeding immense herds of swine, we see that Toller Fratrum is plainly the Toller which belonged to a body of monks, but we do not see why it should be accompanied by Toller Porcorum, 'of the pigs,' as though they were the owners of the estate. We often hear of the pig being called in Ireland 'the gintleman that pays the rint,' but this is the only instance that I know of in which the unclean animal is ranked as a landowner.

XII.

NAMES WHICH BELONG TO THE PERIOD OF THE BREAKING-UP OF FEUDALISM.

Of this mighty change, the Wars of the Roses were the immediate although not the only cause. Before those wars broke out, the system had begun to totter, and it must ere long have fallen, even if Henry VI. had never left the business of governing to his tyrannical wife and her paramour De la Pole. Richard of York might have died peacefully in his bed as a subject, and yet the feudal system must have gone down before the rising tide of civilisation. The war simply accelerated the process by sweeping away the old baronial families, which formed the breakwater: thenceforward the tide was unobstructed, and the great middle class caught the truncheon of power as it fell from the unnerved hands of the last of the barons. This great revolution has left very few traces in the names of places; a fact which shows that it occurred when the land was fully occupied, and that its immediate effects on the great body of the people were but slight. There is no place named from any of the actors or events in that struggle. St. Albans, Barnet, Wakefield-green, Mortimer's Cross, Towton, Hexham, and Bosworth Field, were all known by those names long before they were drenched with the blood of Yorkist or Lancastrian. Mortimer's Cross, for example, could not have been named from the 'bloody Candlemas day' of 1461, on which the young Edward won the crown, for the sufficient reason that Edward was not a Mortimer, but the son of the last heiress of that great house, by her marriage with Richard Plantagenet; nor, if we may judge from the silence of history and the absence of any architectural remains, was any cross ever erected on the spot, which was merely the crossing of two main roads.

The connection of the House of Lancaster with Herefordshire has left a single vestige in the term 'King's-acre,' which designates a part of the lands of the earldom. By marriage with Mary, coheiress of the last of the Bohuns, Henry of Bolingbroke became possessor of a moiety of the Bohun estates, which passed with the title. When 'Harry of Hereford, Lancaster, and Derby' became King Henry IV., the earldom of Hereford vested in the Crown, and has never been regranted. The lands have been given away piecemeal, to one favourite and another; and the term King's-acre (in modern English, the king's land) is actually the only trace of the vast power and immense possessions of the long line of earls of Hereford, who for three centuries ranked among the greater barons of England.

XIII.

NAMES OF RECENT ORIGIN.

This class of names belongs to the colloquial English which is still in use. It comprises a great number of names of natural objects, such as hills remarkable in form, promontories, waterfalls, caves, and woods. Some of these names are picturesque and suggestive, others grimly comic. Thus, following the Old English and Norse habit of likening a jutting point of land to the prominent feature of the human face (in Saxon *naesse*, in Norse *naze*), the people of South Devon have named a rocky headland near Torquay 'Bob's Nose.' Whether 'Bob' is in this case a corruption of Hob or Robin Goodfellow, the fairy jester, we have no means of deciding. On one point alone we are sure; if the Nose near Torquay be a faithful portrait of that of Bob, he must have been one of that class of humble heroes who do the fighting and bear the wounds while more fortunate men got the rewards. Bob's Nose is so battered and broken, having in fact nothing of a 'bridge' left, that it requires an intensely believing eye to see the nasal shape at all.

Along the south coast especially, almost every point of land which is not called a nose is called a head. There are but three exceptions, all of an ornithological kind: Portland and Selsea have 'bills,' while the chief headland of Devon is called 'the Start,' a name taken from the opposite extremity of the bird. Thus one of our winter birds, which has a red tail, is still known as the Redstart.

The same habit of metaphor describes the junction of a river with the sea, not by the Latin term æstuary, which pictures the boiling mass of waters, where tide and current meet, but by the homely appellation of 'the mouth.' Yarmouth and Wearmouth are examples.

Hand and Arm seem to have been adopted as personal names, since we meet with Handsworth and Armley, both in Yorkshire, which evidently point out the abodes of chiefs bearing those names. Hand is still a surname; but I have met with no instance of Arm being so used in the present day except in the singular phrase Strongitharm, which seems to have been originally a war name, assumed by some vainglorious chief or conferred by his admiring followers. The contraction of 'in the' into 'ith' is a peculiarity of the dialect of Lancashire, and seems to point to that county as the abode of the original Strong-in-the-Arm.

The hair has also furnished us with a place-name. A wooded hill in Northumberland seems to have reminded the beholders of a rough shock head of hair, and so they called it Roseberry Topping. The latter word is still in use in Yorkshire with the same meaning.

The same love of metaphor has shown itself in terms borrowed from the dairy. The curiously twisted rocks at Cheddar have been likened to cheeses, and a well-known granite mountain in Cornwall is universally recognised as 'the Cheesewring.'

In Derbyshire a friable cliff, portions of which are constantly falling, is known locally as the Shivering Mountain.

The lofty conical hill near Abergavenny is as well known by its modern English name of the Sugarloaf as by its true name, Pen-y-fal, the head of the bare hill.

With an equally homely and less appropriate metaphor, the shapeless masses of rock at the western end of the Isle of Wight have been named the Needles, since there are few objects which bear less resemblance to the slender-pointed tool of the seamstress. Perhaps the use of the word is an indication of French rather than of English habits of thought, the French word *aiguille* being applied to any mountain peak, however broad or shapeless.

With more fitness of metaphor, the Herefordshire peasant applies the name of Saddle-bow to a little hill separated by a shallow valley from a large hill in the same line; and in Worcestershire the most rugged-looking of the Malvern range is known as 'Ragged Stone Hill.' This range, it may be noted, has suggested poetical ideas to the peasantry who dwelt upon it. Its chief passes are severally named the Wych (i.e. the sudden turning), the Winds' Point, and the pass of the White-leaved Oak; while one of the most beautiful of the summits bears the picturesque title of Midsummer or Midsomer hill. This last is a case of distinction *with* a difference, and tends to make out the name to be not quite so poetical as it seems at first hearing. Possibly, it means merely the middle of the Somers' estate, of which it is at least the most conspicuous feature.

On the other hand, in some of the most picturesque parts of Devon, the local names are remarkable for want of poetry. For the picturesque caves near Torquay, no better term than 'hole' has been found; and nothing can be more stiffly prosaic than 'The Waters' Meet,' applied to that grand wild scene, the junction of the East and West Lynn, near Lynton, except it be the tame designation 'Valley of Rocks,' given to the strangely picturesque dale strewn as it were with the tombstones of giants.

On the same North Devon coast, a succession of names in a very curious manner indicates the habits of the people throughout a long period, which has ended within the lifetime of many persons now living. Passing eastward from Ilfracombe, 'the dingle of Aelfric,' some Saxon pirate, the tourist first reaches Helsborough, 'the fortification of Ælla,'* who (if the king of that name, founder of the South Saxon monarchy) was a marauder of a somewhat higher stamp. From Ælla's hill camp, the tourist looks down upon a little nook known as 'the Rapparee's Cove,' thus recalling the banditti who in Ireland plundered and murdered their neighbours out of loyalty to the worthless Stuarts, and who were at all times ready to transfer their operations to the wealthier side of St. George's Channel, when shipowners were willing to run the risk of combining a little treason with their habit of smuggling. Passing onward, the visitor comes successively to Pillage Point, a reminiscence of the times of the wreckers, and Smuggler's Cove, a bit of history still nearer to our own times; while, as he raises his eyes, the huge stern-looking hill called Hangman's Head—long the place of execution for pirates—with grim appropriateness closes the series. Thus we have ancient and modern piracy, partisan warfare, the cruel robbery and frequent murder which made up the practice of wrecking, the daring frauds of the smuggler, and the usual ending of all those 'gentlemanly practices': the history of the coast for a thousand years told in a series of names.

* Ælla landed in Sussex in 477, and in 493 had made his conquering way west to Somerset; when to Devon is uncertain.

In Radnorshire, which is emphatically English Wales, although almost all its parishes retain their ancient British names, the genius of each race exemplifies itself in the name which it gives to a waterfall. The picturesque falls of the Wye have originated for the little Welsh town built around them the poetic and sonorous name of Rhaiadr-a'r-Gwi, 'the waterfall on the Wye;' while the loftier if less important fall of the Ithon has received from English tongues the homelier title of Water-break-its-neck. There is, however, about this name a certain wildness of portraiture which shows that a little of the Old English poetry still survived when this name was given. The Old English race was once imaginative, fond of song, and full of metaphor, as witness such names as The Strid, the terrible chasm in Craven, which has been in our own age endowed with undying interest by the English poets Rogers and Wordsworth; witness also the laconic and grandly suggestive names of two hills in Derbyshire, near which was fought the great battle between the heathen and the Christian Angles. Win Hill marks the station of the victor, and Lose Hill that of the vanquished.

There is a still loftier class of ideas suggested by the term applied to many boundary trees; and we perceive a grand fitness in the name of Gospel Oak, when conferred upon a venerable tree towering high above its neighbours, covering a large area with its shade, and nourishing a myriad birds with its fruit. Some of these trees are merely the descendants of the oaks to which the name was first given: for example, we cannot hope to identify the Gospel Oak described by Bede as the scene of the conference between Augustine the missionary from Rome and the British bishops, in the year 603. The narrative shows that the scene was somewhere in the southern part of Gloucestershire, the only part which fulfils the description of Bede, since it is the only district in which the territories of the Wiccii (the people of Worcestershire) and those of the West Saxons met;* and we further learn from the narrative that the place was still known in the historian's time, a century and a quarter after the event, as 'Augustine's Ac,' a designation which he himself translates as Augustine's Oak; but, as no place or tree so named is now known, we are unable to ascertain the locality more clearly. It is certain that no oak situated between Worcester and Hereford can be the right one, and therefore the local tradition and some modern writers (D'Aubigné, for example) are both wrong. Bede says:

'In the meantime, Augustine, with the assistance of King Ethelbert, drew together to a conference the bishops or doctors of the next province of the Britons, at a place which is to this day called Augustine's Ac, that is, Augustine's Oak, on the borders of the Wiccii and the West Saxons.'—*Ecclesiastical History*, l. ii. cap. 2.

There is a curious parallel between these 'Gospel Oaks' and such names as Christ's Oak and Christ's Well, which survive in the corrupted forms of Cressage and Cresswell. That similar corruptions of the holy Name were common, is shown by the appellation given to a game popular among idle schoolboys. When the master's back was turned, nothing used to be so frequent in schools forty years ago as a game at 'Cris-cros-row,' none of us having the least idea that the words meant Christ's cross row, in allusion to the crosses which each player makes alternately with circles.

The moral of the whole is that place-names change

* Dr. Giles thinks it was at Aust.

in form, but rarely perish. Amid all Time's mutations these shadowy landmarks remain. Man's industry has drained the marsh, turned the moor into corn-fields, cut down the primæval forest, exterminated its ferocious beasts, cultivated the wolds, and dwarfed the rivers into brooks; but the ancient name of each in almost all cases still lives upon the people's tongues, ages after it has ceased to be applicable. *Voces et prœterea nihil* are these names; but they outlast races, tribes, families, orders, and thrones. Yet each place-name is but the result of a fortuitous concurrence of causes. To establish an appellation as the name of a place required at first the concurrence of many independent wills, about a mere matter of taste; and its persistence has depended in like manner upon the agreement of succeeding generations, over whom the wills of the namer and his contemporaries have no power. In all its history, the name is beyond the reach of law, while all the probabilities are against the vitality of a thing so unsubstantial and evanescent. Yet place-names survive. *Stat nominis umbra*; and the shadow stretches down the long vista of ages, even when the substance which cast it—the event or the person—eludes the search of historian and antiquary. Astronomy yields us a parallel fact. The seer tells us that the star which we see at night is but the image created by light which left the real Sirius or Aldebaran long ages ago, and that the star may have ceased to exist long since that light streamed off. Thus, to compare small things with great, the names of places carry down to future ages a picture or a reminiscence of a forgotten fact or person. For the future student the name preserves the physical aspect of the site, the deed which distinguished it, or the name of its possessor, of which perhaps there are no other traces. Thus we can recreate to the mind the Ynys Prydain of pre-Roman times, the Britain of later ages, and the Engle-land of the Saxons, Angles, and Jutes; can realise much of the religion, the manners and customs, the institutions, the trades and occupations, of the different races who have blended to form the Briton of to-day. It is all extant in the names: the student needs but to read them.

NOTE TO THE READER.

In the vocabulary which follows, he will find the alphabet of the study, all the root-words out of which the place-names now existing in England and Wales have been formed, with examples of all the modes in which they are combined. Wherever it was practicable, I have given the most ancient form of the name from the best authority, which in many cases is Domesday Book. Although written by French-speaking men for a French-speaking king, and therefore expressing sounds according to rules of pronunciation very different from those of our modern English, there can be no doubt that the compilers faithfully wrote down the names as spoken to them. The substantial agreement between many of those names and the pronunciation of the peasantry at the present day is a proof of the accuracy of the Conqueror's scribes eight centuries ago.

It will be seen that the *roots* of place-names only are given; and in order to make the Vocabulary available, the student has merely to look for each part of the word separately. The first syllable, or the first two syllables, of a place-name, usually contain one root, and the remainder contains the other. If the word be British, the first syllable will be the generic term, as *llan* or *ty*; and the rest of the word will be the specific term distinguishing the particular *llan* or *ty* from all others. If the word be Saxon or Norse, the rule will be the reverse, and the generic term will be found last. Under each root examples are given of all the modes in which it enters into combination, the earliest known spelling being always given.

VOCABULARY.

A

B. British. *C.* Celtic. *E.* The Old English, commonly known as Anglo-Saxon.
D. Old Danish. *G.* Greek. *L.* Latin. *N. F.* Norman French. *N.* Norse. *qu. v.* which see.

Ab, Abbas, Abbey, Abber, Abbots *E.* pointing out the site of an abbey or land belonging to one. Ex.: Ab-Kettleby (Linc.); Abbey-dore (Heref.), the abbey on the bank of the river Dore; Cerne Abbas (Dorset), the abbot's dairy or cheese farm; Abbey-Huton (Staff.), the hut-town belonging to an abbey, in distinction from other Hutons; Abber-ley (Worc.), the abbey land or place; Abber-ton (Essex and Worc.), the abbey town; Abbot's-bury (Dorset), the abbot's fortified town.

Abb *E.* from Ebbe, name of a saint. Ex.: St. Abb's Head (Northumb.), contracted into Tabb's Head; Abs-ton, Ebbe's town; Ab-don (Salop), Ebbe's Hill.

Aber *B.* the place where a small river flows into a larger, or any river falls into the sea. Ex.: Aber-ayron (Card.), the place where the Ayron falls into the sea.

Abing *E.* from *abban*, belonging to an abbot. Ex.: Abban-dun, now Abingdon (Berks); abbot's hill; Abban-hæla, now Abinghall (Glouc.), the abbot's hall; Abban-gyrwe, now Abinger (Surr.), the abbot's moor.

Aby *E. D.* from *abba*, an abbey, and *by*, the Danish word for an abode or a town. Ex.: Aby (Linc.), the abbey town or village.

Ac *E.* from *æc*, an oak. Ex.: Ac-ton, 8 places, oak town; Acaster (Yorks.), the oak *cestre*, or fortified town on the site of a Roman camp.

Accr *E.* from *acer*, a piece of cultivated land; whence God's-acre, a churchyard. Ex.: Accrington (Lancas.), the acran-tun, or town in the cultivated land.

B. British. *C*. Celtic. *E*. The Old English, commonly known as Anglo-Saxon.

Ack, Acomb *E*. from *æc*. Ex.: Ack-worth (Yorks.), oak estate; Acomb (Northumb.), oak dingle. *See* Comb.

Ackl *E*. from *æc*, and *hil*. Ex.: Acklam (Yorks.), oak-hill village.

Acorn *E*. from *æc*, and *corn*, a seed. Ex.: Acorn-bury (Heref.), acorn camp.

Acrise, Cryse *E*. from *æc*, and *rise*, an ascent. Ex.: Acrise (Kent), oak ascent, or hill; Green Cryse (Heref.), the green ascent of the oaks.

Ad *E*. a heap, probably monumental; equivalent to *carn*, British. Ex.: Ad-wick (Yorks.), the village of the heap.

Adfor *B*. from Cadfor or Cadfawr, great warrior, the name of a British chief. Ex.: Adfor-ton (Salop), Cadfawr's town.

Adder *E*. from *ættor*, an adder, probably first the cognizance and afterwards the name of a chief. Ex.: Adder-ley (Salop), adder meadow or land.

Adding *E*. from Adda, the owner's name, and *incga*, descendants. Ex.: Addington, 5 places, the town of Adda's descendants. There was an Adda missionary to the Mercians, *a.d.* 653.—*Bede*.

Adl, Addles, Adling *E*. from Æthel, name of a man, and *incga*, descendants. Ex.: Adling-tun, now Adlington (Lanc.), the town of the descendants of a noble, probably such as bore no title, being younger sons and their posterity; Addles-trop (Glouc.), the farm-house of Æthel. *See* Trop.

Admis *E*. from Edmund, the owner's name. Ex.: Admis-ton (Dorset), Edmund's town.

Ædan *B*. a saint's name. Ex.: Llan-ædan (Angl.), St. Ædan's church.

Afal *B*. an apple. Ex.: Llangattoc-fibon-afal (Monm.), St. Cattog's church by the apple-stump.

Afan *B*. raspberry trees: also a saint's name. Ex.: Llan-afan (Brecons.), St. Afan's church.

Aig, Aigh *E*. from *haga*, land hedged in. Ex.: Aig-burth (Lanc.), the hedged burh or fortification; Aigh-ton (Lanc.), the hedged town.

Ais *N*. from *As*, belonging to the gods; whence the supposed paradise of As-gard, the gods' garden. Ex.: Ais-thorp (Linc.), the gods' farm-house.

Aismunder *E*. from *as*, and *mund*, a protection. Ex.: Aismunder-by (Yorks.), the god-protected place.

D. Old Danish. *G.* Greek. *L.* Latin. *N.F.* Norman French. *N.* Norse. *qu. v.* which see.

AIT *N.* from *aith*, a tongue of land.* Ex.: many islands in the river Thames.

AKE, AKEN *E.* from *æc*, an oak. Ex.: Ake-ly (Bucks), oak-land; Aken-ham (Suff.), the home among the oaks.

AL *E.* from *eald*, old. Ex.: Al-tofts (Yorks.), the old groves; Al-thorp (Linc.), the old farm-house.

ALBER, ALBRIGH, AYLBUR *E.* from Aylburh, or Egelburh, the eagle's fortification, a man's name. Ex.: Alber-bury (Salop), Alburh's camp; Albur-ton, now Aylburton (Glouces.), Alburh's town; Alburh-ton, now Albrighton (Salop), the same.

ALBURGH, ALBURY *E.* from *ægl*, an eagle, and *burh*, a fortification Ex.: Alburgh (Norf.), eagle fortress; Albury (Surr.), the same.

ALBY *E. D.* eagle's abode. Ex.: Alby (Norf.).

ALCESTER *E.* from *eald*, old, and *cestre*, a fortification on the site of a Roman castrum. Ex.: Alcester (Warw.), old fortress town.

ALD from *eald*, old. Ex.: Ald-wark (Northum.), the old castle; Ald-ham (Suff.), old home or village.

ALDEN, ALDING *E.* from Eald or Ald, adopted as a name, and still preserved in Scotland as Auld. Ex.: Ald-incgaham, now Aldenham (Herts), and Ald-ingham (Lanc.), the home of Ald's *incga*, or descendants.

ALDER *E.* from Aldred, old in counsel, a man's name. Ex.: Alder-ley (Ches.), Aldred's land.

ALDERMAS *E.* from eolderman. Ex.: Aldermas-ton (Berks.), the eolderman's or lord-lieutenant's town.

ALDRIDGE *E.* Aldred's. Ex.: Aldridge (Staff.)

ALDRING *E.* from Aldred and *incga*. Ex.: Aldr-incgatun, now Aldrington (Suss.), the town of Aldred's descendants.

ALE *E.* from *eala*, a hall. Ex.: Willing-ale (Ess.), the hall among the willows.

ALF, ALFRE, ALFRIS *E.* from Alfred. Ex.: Alf-rick (Worc.), Alfred's rule or territory; Alfre-ton (Derb.), Alfred's town; Alfris-ton (Suss.)

ALGAR *E.* from Algar, Earl of Mercia, eleventh century. Ex.: Algar-kirk (Suss.), the church built on the spot where he was killed.

* Professor Munch (Mémoires de la S. R. de Copenhagen).

B. British. *C.* Celtic. *E.* The Old English, commonly known as Anglo-Saxon.

ALK, ALKMON *E.* from St. Alkmond. Ex.: Alkmon-ton, the town of Alkmond; Alk-ham (Norf.), Alkmond's village.

ALL *E.* from *æla*, a hall. Ex.: All-stretton (Salop), distinguished from the neighbouring Stretton, which is church property, by being the site of the hall, or abode of the feudal lord; All-cannings (Wilts), the hall Cannings, in distinction from some other Cannings.

ALLEN *E.*, *N.F.* from Alan or Ulfwin 'wolf of victory,' the chief's name. Ex.: Allen-dale (Northumb.), Alan's dale; Allens-more (Heref.), Alan's mere or pool.

ALLER *E.* from Aldred. Ex.: Aller-ton (Yorks.), anciently Alred-istun, Aldred's town.

ALLES, ALLI, ELLES, HELLES *E.* probably from Ella, a famous Northumbrian king. Ex.: Alles-tree (Derb.), the British town (*tref*), seized by Ella; Elles-mere (Salop), Ella's pool; Helles-don (Norf.), Ella's hill; Alli-thwaite (Lanc.), Ella's clearing.

ALLING, ELLING *E.* from Ella and *incga*. Ex.: Alling-ton (Northum.), the town of Ella's descendants; Elling-ham, 4 places, the home of the same.

ALLT *B.* from *gallt*, a steep place. Ex.: Allt-mawr, a common term for a high hill in Wales, the great steep place; Bu-allt, now Builth (Brecons.), the steep place of the cows.

ALME, ALMER, AYLMER, AYMES, AYME *E.* from Ælmer, or Ægel-mod, a man's name. One Ægelmod was eolderman of Mercia in the ninth century. Ex.: Ægelmodes-ley,* now Alme-ley (Heref.), Ægelmod's land; Almer (Dorset); Aylmer-ton (Norf.); Aymes-tre (Heref.) Ægelmod's town.

ALMOND, HAUGHMOND, HAYMOND, HECKMOND, AGMOND *E.* from Ægmond, the protecting eye, a man's name. Ex.: Almond's, anciently Haymond's Froome (Heref.), so distinguished from other Froomes in the vicinity; Haughmond Abbey (Salop); Heckmondwick (Yorks.), Ægmond's village; Agmondesham, now Amersham (Bucks), Ægmond's home.

ALN, OLN *E.* from *olan* or *holegn*, the holly. Ex.: Aln-wick (Northumb.), holly village; Oln-ey (Bucks), holly water.

ALPH, ALPHE *E.* from Ulfa, a man's name, a form of Wulfhere. Ex.: Alphe-ton (Suff.), the same; Ulfan-tun, now Alphams-ton (Ess.), the same.

* Domesday Book.

D. Old Danish. *G.* Greek. *L.* Latin. *N. F.* Norman French. *N.* Norse. *qu. v.* which see.

ALPHING *E.* from Ulfa, and *incga.* Ex.: Alphing-ton (Devon), the town of Ulfa's descendants.

ALRES *E.* from *alar,* the alder. Ex.: Alres-ford (Hants), the ford of the alder-tree; Alre-was (Staff.), the moist place of the alder-tree.

ALS, ELS, *E.* from Ella, the owner's name. Ex.: Alston (Camb.), meaning Ella's town; Elsdon (North.), Ella's hill.

ALTCAR *B.* from *allt* and *car.* Ex.: Alt-car (Lanc.), the steep place of the pool.

ALTON *E.* anciently *Ethelinga-dean,* the valley of the nobles.*

ALV, ALVE, ALVER, ALVES, ALVING *E.* from St. Elva. *See* Elva.

AM *E.* probably from Emma, queen, mother of Edw. Conf. Ex.: Am-well, Emma's well.†

AMBER, AMES, AMBREY, AMBROS, EMBREY *B.* probably from Ambrosius, the famous British king. Ex.: Amber-ley (Suss. and Worc.), Ambrose's place; Ambrose-burh, now Amesbury (Wilts), Ambrose's fortified town; Croft-ambrey (Heref.), Ambrose's field; Ambros-den (Oxf.), Ambrose's hollow; Ember-ton (Bucks), Ambrose's town.

AMERS. *See* Almond.

AMES. *See* Amber.

AMLWCH *B.* from *am* high, and *llwch,* a lake. Ex.: Am-lwch (Angl.), the high place by the pool.

AMP. *E.* *See* Hamp.

AN, AND, ANDR, ENDER *N.* from Andred, or Andrew, the owner's name. Ex.: Andreds-cestre,‡ now An-caster (Yorks.), Andred's fortified town; Ans-ton (Yorks.), Andred's town; And-efer, now Andover (Hants), Andred's place on the brink of a stream; Ander-by (Linc.), the abode of Andred; Anders-ton (Dorset), Andred's town; Ender-by (Leices.), Andred's abode.

ANGER *E.* a steep hill. *See* Hanger.

ANNES, ANS *E.* from Anna, a male name among the Saxons.§ Ex.: Annes-ley (Notts), Anna's place; Ans-ley (Warw.), the same; Anstey, 5 places, Anna's stow or station.

* Bosworth's Anglo-Saxon Dict. † Bosworth's Anglo-Saxon Dict.

‡ Anglo-Saxon Chronicle. § Bede mentions a king of East Angles so named.

B. British. *C.* Celtic. *E.* The Old English, commonly known as Anglo-Saxon.

ANNO *B.* a saint's name. Ex.: Llan-anno (Radn.), St. Anno's church.

APPER, AP. *See* Abber and Ab.

APPLE, APPUL *E.* from *æpl,* the apple-tree. Ex.: Apple-thorp (Notts), apple farm-house; Appulder-comb (Devon), apple-tree dingle.

AR, ARE *B.* ploughed land. Ex.: Ar-ley (Warw.), the place on the ploughed land; Are-ley (Wors.), the same.

ARD *C.* a promontory; Saxon, *gara.* Ex.: Ard-leigh (Ess.), the meadow by the promontory.

AREN *B.* from Ereinwg, the ancient name of the district. Ex.: Aren-dale (Heref.)

ARFON *B.* opposite to Fōn or Mōn, the Brit. name of Anglesea. Ex.: Caer-yn-a'r-fon, near Carnarvon, the Roman city opposite to Anglesea.

ARLING, HARLING, IRLING, IRTHLING, ARTHING *E.* from *yrthling,* a son of the earth, that is, a farmer. Ex.: Arling-ham (Glouc.), the farmer's village; Harling-ton (Bedf.), the farmer's town; Irling-borough or Irthling-borough (Northamp.), the farmer's fortified town; Arthing-worth (do.), the farmer's estate.

ARM *E.* the arm, also a personal name. Ex.: Arm-ley (Yorks.), Arm's land or place.

ARMITAGE *E.* a hermitage. Ex.: Armitage (Staff.)

ARNE *E.* from *ærn,* a place. Ex.: Arne (Yorks.).

ARROW *B.* from *garw,* rough or impetuous. Ex.: the river Arrow (Heref.)

ARTHING. *See* Arling.

ARTHUR *B.* King Arthur. Ex.: Arthuret (Cumb.), perhaps the Saxon *yth,* water, added to the king's name; Coed Arthur, Arthur's wood.

ARTH *B.* from St. Arthan. Ex.: Llan-arth (Monm.) St. Arthan's church.

ARVAN *B.* from St. Garfan. Ex.: Arvans (Monm.), St. Garfan's church.

AS, ASGAR *N.* probably from As-gard, the fabled garden of the gods. Ex.: As-by (Westm.), Asgar-by (Linc.), the abode of the gods, or the place supposed to be comparable to Asgard.

ASH *E.* from *æsc,* an ash-tree; the root of 83 names of places, of which there are 17 named Ashby, ash abode; 9 Ashton, ash town; 7 Ash-ford, etc.

D. Old Danish. *G.* Greek. *L.* Latin. *N. F.* Norman French. *N.* Norse. *qu. v.* which see.

Ashbur, Ashper, Aisber *E. B.* from *as*, belonging to the gods, and *ber*, a boundary; combined into a man's name. Ex.: Aisbur- or Ashbur-ton (Devon); Ashper-ton (Heref.), Aisber's town.

Ask, a form of *æsc*, an ash-tree, probably indicating a Danish settlement, as *scyp* becomes *skip* in like circumstances. Ex.: Ask-ham, 4 places (Yorks, Notts, and Westm.), ash home or village; Ask-rigg (Yorks.), ash ridge.

Asp, Aspe *D.* from *asp*, the aspen-tree. Ex.: Asp-ley Guise (Bedf.), Guise's aspen-meadow; Aspe-den (Herts), aspen hollow.

Ast *E.* a kiln, cognate with *ustus*, Lat., burnt. Ex.: Ast-tun, now Aston, 21 places, kiln town; Ast-wick (Bedf.), kiln village.

Atch *E.* from *haeca*, a bar or bolt, hence a dwelling. Ex.: Atch-ham (Salop), the barred home. *See* Hatch.

Athan *B.* from St. Aedan. Ex.: St. Athan (Glam.)

Atheling *E.* from *æthel* a nobleman, and *incga* descendants. Ex.: Ethelinga-tun, now Atheling-ton (Suff.), the nobleman's son's town; Ethelinga-ig or ey, now Athelney (Som.), the nobleman's isle or water.

Athering, Athers. *E.* *See* Adder.

At *E.* from *ettin*, a giant. Ex.: Atwick (Yorks.), the giant's abode; At-worth (Wilts), the giant's estate.

Attingham *E.* from *Eata* and *incgaham*, the house of the children of Eata, abbot of Lindisfarne, seventh century. Ex.: Atting-ham (Salop.)

Au, Aw, Ow *E.* from Offa, King of Mercia. Ex.: Au-bourn (Linc.), Offa's brook; Aure (Glouc.); Ow-field (Heref.), and Ow-borough (do.), Offa's field and camp.*

Auck *E.* from *hafoc*, a hawk, the cognizance, and thence the name, of the landowner. Ex.: Auck-land (Durham), Hawk's land; Auck-borough (Linc.), Hawk's fortified town.

Aud, Audl *E.* a contraction or colloquial form of Æthelred, noble in council, as tawdry comes from St. Æthelredu.† Ex.: Aud-ley (Staff.), Ethelred's land; Audl-em (Ches.), Ethelred's ham, or home.

Ave, Aven, Aving, Awene, Aw, corruptions of *awen*, *B.* divine inspiration. The common pronunciation of the name of the

* Camden. † Horne Tooke.

Druidic temple in Wilts is Awbury. The word means the fortification of the inspired ones, which the Druids claimed to be. The word *awen* is now used to describe poetic inspiration. Ex.: Awenburi,* now Aven-bury (Heref.), the same as Avebury; Ave-ton (Devon); Aving-ton (Hants), all probably indicating Druidic sites.

Avon *B.* from *afon*, a river. Ex.: rivers in Somerset, Warw., Wilts, etc.; and the Welsh still call the Wye and other rivers by the same word used as a prefix, *e.g.* Afon Gwy, etc.

Axe *E.* from *aesc*, an ash tree. Ex.: the river Axe (Som. and Devon); Acsan-mynstre, now Axminster, the monastery near the Axe.

Ay, Ey, Ea *E.* water, or a piece of land wholly or partly surrounded by water. Ex.: Ay-thorp (Yorks.), water farm-house; Eye (Suff.); Ey-ham, now Eyam (Derb.), water village; Ea-ton, 10 places, water town; frequent also as a suffix.

Ayles, Ayl, Ayls, *E.* a contraction from *ægle's*, belonging to a chief who called himself the Eagle; in Heref. a contraction from Athel. Ex.: Aylesford (Kent), anciently Ægles-threp, Eagle's meeting place of cross-roads; Ayles-bury, anciently Ægles-burh (Bucks), Eagle's town; Ayls-ham (Norf.), Eagle's village; Ayl-mer-ton (Norf.), Eagle's pool town; Aylston-hill and Aylston wood (Heref.), Athelstan's hill and wood.

Ayn *E.* from *ey*, water. Ex.: Ayn-hoe (North.), the hill of the waters.

Ayott *E., D.* from *ey*, water, and *hut*, a hut. Ex.: Ayott (Herts), the hut near the water.

* Domesday Book.

D. Old Danish. *G.* Greek. *L.* Latin. *N. F.* Norman French. *N.* Norse. *qu. v.* which see.

B

BAB, BABBA, BABRA *E.* from Babba, or Bebba, the chief's name. Ex.: Bab-worth (Notts), Babba's estate; Babba-comb (Devon), Babba's dingle; Babra-ham (Camb.), the home or village of Babba.

BABING *E.* from Babba and *incga.* Babing-ton (Som.), the town of Babba's descendants.'

BAC, BACK *E.* from *bac*, a ridge, so called from its resemblance to the back of an animal. Ex.: Bac-ton, 3 places, ridge town; Back-well (Som.), ridge well; the Hog's Back, a ridge near Guildford (Surrey).

BACH, BAGE *E.* a path. Ex.: Mere-bage or Mere-bach (Heref.), the path by the pool; Sand-bach (Ches.), the path on the sand; Efes-bach, now Evesbach (Heref.), the path on the brink.

BACH, FYCHAN, BYCHAN, FECHAN *B.* little. Ex.: Mynydd-bach, little mountain; Pont-nedd-fychan (Glam.), the bridge over the lesser Nedd river: Castell-bychan, little castle; Ecclefechan, little church.

BAD, BADDES, BADDI, BADS, BADN *E.* from Badda, Bieda, or Baeda, a man's name.* Ex.: Bad-ley (Suff.), Badda's place; Baddes-ley, 3 places, the same; Bads-worth (Yorks.), Badda's estate; Bad-hoe, now Baddow (Ess.), Badda's hill; Baddiley (Ches.), Badda's place; Badn-age (Heref.), Badda's edge or ridge.

BADARN *B.* St. Padarn or Patarnus, who is recorded to have come with St. Cadfan from Britanny at the head of 847 missionaries to South Wales, A.D. 524, and to have afterwards founded a college at Llanbadarn.† Ex.: Llanbadarn (Card.)

BADING *E.* from Badda and *incga.* Ex.: Bading-ham (Suff.), the home of Badda's descendants.

BADOC, *B.* from St. Madawg. Ex.: Llan-badoc (Monm.), St. Madawg's church.

BADRIG *B.* St. Patrick, who arrived in Wales from Ireland in 430. Ex.: Llan-badrig (Angl.), St. Patrick's church.

* Bosworth. † Myfyrian Archæology, vol. ii. p. 50.

B. British. *C.* Celtic. *E.* The Old English, commonly known as Anglo-Saxon.

BAES *B.* from *bais*, shallows, or a ford. Ex.: Baes-aleg (Monm.), the ford of Aleg, *i.e.* Alexander.

BAGLAN *B.* a saint's name. Ex.: Baglan (Glam.), St. Baglan's place; or from *bag* and *llan*, *i.e.*, peak church.

BAG *B.* the point or top of a thing, a form of *pig* or *pic*, a peak.

BAG *E.* from Bega, the owner's name. Ex.: Bag-burh, now Bagborough (Som.), Bega's fortified town; Bag-thorp (Norf.), Bega's farm-house.

BAIN *N.F.* contracted from Pagan or Payn, a common name among the Norman knights. Ex.: Bain-ton (Yorks. and North.), Payn's town. *See* Pains.

BAKE *E.* contracted from *bedican*, protected with a dike. Ex.: Bedican-well,* now Bakewell (Derb.), the bediked well, there being a mineral spring at that place.

BAL, BALE *B.*, *E.* a knob or prominence. Ex. Bal-thorp (Notts), the farm-house by the knob or round hill; Bale (Norf.).

BALA *B.* the place where a stream issues from a lake, answering to Balloch in Scotland. Ex.: Bala (Merion).

BALD, BALDON, BALDER *D.* from Baldur, the sun, a Norse deity. Ex.: Bold-ock (Herts), Balda's oak; Balder-ton (Notts), Baldur's town; Baldon-toot (Oxf.), the teotha or tything of Baldur.

BALDRINGHAM *E.* from Baldur and *incgaham*. Ex.: Baldringham (North.), the home of Baldur's children, probably a place where the worship of Baldur, the sun-god, was carried on.

BALLING *E.* from Belin, a chief, whence comes Belin's-gate, now Billingsgate. Ex.: Ballingham (Heref.), Belin's home or village.

BAM, BAMP *E.* from *beám*, a tree. Ex.: Bam-ford (Devon), tree ford: Bamp-ton, anciently Bean-dune (Oxf.), tree hill.

BAMBOROUGH *E.* from Bebban-burh,† Bebba's fortification. Ex.: Bamborough (Yorks.)

BAN, BANNAU, VANS *B.* high. Ex.: Ban-gor, the high choir, or cathedral; Bannau Brycheiniwg, the high hills of Breconshire; The Vans (Carm.), the high hills.

BANBURY *E.* contr. from Beran-burh,‡ Bera's fortified town. Ex.: Ban-bury (Oxf.); Ban-stead (Surr.), Bera's station.

BANT, PANT *B.* a valley or bottom. Ex.: Pant-y-goitre (Monm.), the valley of the town in the wood.

* Camden. † Saxon Chronicle. ‡ Anglo-Saxon Chronicle, anno 556.

BARING, BARRING *E.* from Beran and *incga*, children. Ex.: Baring, Bera's children's place; Barring-ton (Camb.), the town of the same.

BAR *B.* a bush. Ex.: Bar-comb (Suss.), bush valley; Bar-low (Derb.), bush place or hill.

BAR, BARR *B.* a bar, fence, or gate. Ex.: Great Barr (Staff.); Bar-ford (Oxf.), the fenced ford; Barham, 3 places, the fenced or gated home.

BARGOD *B.* a border. Ex.: Ynys Bargod (Flints.), border island.

BARK *E.* from *birc*, the birch-tree, still called birk in Scotland. Ex.: Barking (Suff. and Ess.), the bircen or birches; Barks-ton (Leic. and Linc.), birch town.

BARL, BARLAVING *E.* from Beorla or Beorlaf, the chief's name, and *incga*, children. Ex.: Barl-borough (Derb.), Beorla's fortified place; Barling (Ess.), the place of Beorla's children; Barlaving-ton (Suss.), the town of Beorlaf's children.

BARM *E.* from *bere-ern*, a barn. Ex.: Barm-by (Yorks.), barn abode.

BARMOUTH *B.* corrupted from Aber-mawddach, the estuary of the Mawddach. Ex.: Barmouth (Merion).

BARN *E.* from *bere-ern*, corn-place, or barn. Ex.: Barn-et, i.e. barn hut (Mid.), the hut near the barn; frequent also as a suffix.

BARNES, BARNS *E.* from Beorna (the bear), afterwards latinised into Berinus, and Normanised to Berners, the name of the lord. Ex.: Barnes-wood (Leices.), Berners' wood; Barns-ley (Yorks.), Berners' place.

BARNING, BERNING *E.* from Beorna and *incga*. Ex.: Barning-ham and Berning-ham (Yorks.), the home of Beorna's descendants.

BARROW *E.* from *bærw*, a wood or grove, being probably derived from the Brit. *bar*, *q. v. supra*. Ex.: Barrow, 8 places; Barrow-den (Rutl.), grove hollow.

BARS *E.* the perch fish, probably assumed as the owner's cognizance, and thence his name. Ex.: Bars-ham, 4 places, Perch's village; Bars-ton (Warw.), Perch's town.

BARTESTREE *E.* anciently * Bartholdestreu, Barthold's trees. Ex.: Bartestree (Heref.)

BARTHOM, BART *E.* St. Bartholomew. Ex.: Barthomley (Staff.), St. Bartholomew's place; Bart-low (Camb.), St. Bart.'s hill.

* Domesday Book.

B. British. *C.* Celtic. *E.* The Old English, commonly known as Anglo-Saxon.

BARTON *E.* from *beretun*, corn farm. Ex.: Barton, 21 places.

BARWICK *E.* from *bar* and *wic*, the barred or fenced village. Ex.: Barwick, 3 places.

BAS *B.* from *bais*, a ford or a low place. Ex.: Bas-church (Salop), Basing (Hants).

BASILDEN *E.* St. Basil's hollow. Ex.: Basilden (Berks.)

BATTERS, perhaps corr. from Peter's. Ex.: Batters-ea (Midd.), Peter's water; Batters-by (Linc.), Peter's abode. Or perhaps from Badda or Beda. *See* Badder.

BAYN. *See* Bain.

BAW *B.* from *bawn*, an enclosure for cattle. Ex.: Baw-tre, now Bawtry (Notts), the town of the cattle-yard.

BEACONS *E.* from *becn*, a beacon, or from *bæcen*, beech-trees. Ex.: Beacons-field (Hants).

BEAU, BEL *N. F.* beautiful. Ex.: Beau-manoir, the beautiful manor; Beau-desert (Warw.), the beautiful place in the desert; Bel-voir (Rutl.), the beautiful view.

BEAUMARIS *B.* probably from *buw*, a cow, *mor*, the sea, and *ys*, low. Ex.: Beaumaris (Angl.), the low place of cows by the sea.

BEBLIG *B.* St. Peblig, said to have been a son of the Emperor Maxentius. Ex.: Llan-beblig (Carnarv.), St. Peblig's church.

BECK *D.* from *bec*, a brook, chiefly found in the Dan. district of England. Ex.: Skir-beck (Yorks.), the dividing brook; Sand-beck (Notts), the sandy brook; Beck-ford (Wilts.), the ford of the brook.

BECKEN, BECKING *B.* from *bæcen*, the beeches. Ex.: Becken-ham * (Kent), beech home: Becking-ham (Notts), the same.

BED *B.* contr. from *bedican*, bediked or protected. Ex.: Bedican-well, now Bakewell (Derb.), the protected well.

BEDD *B.* a grave. Ex.: Bedd-Gelert (Flints.), Gelert's grave; Bedd-lywelyn (Brecons.), Llywelyn's grave.

BEDFORD *B.* anciently Beadanford, from *beado*, slaughter, and *ford*, a ford. Ex.: Bedford, slaughter-ford.

BEDSTON *E.*, *B.*, from *Bedr* and *ton*. Ex.: Beds-ton, St. Peter's town (Salop).

BEDW, FEDW *B.* the birch-tree. Ex.: Pen-bedw, birch hill; Bedw, now Beddoe (Salop), the birches; Bedw-gwâl-ty, now

* Anciently Baccancelde, *A. S. Chronicle*, 694.

D. Old Danish. *G.* Greek. *L.* Latin. *N. F.* Norman French. *N.* Norse. *qu. v.* which see.

Bedwelty (Mon.), the house of the wild beast's couch among the birches.

BEDWARDIN *B.* from *bais-dwr-din,* the ford of the water-camp. Ex.: Bedwardin (Worc.)

BEDWAS *B.* a saint's name. Ex.: Bedwas (Glam.)

BEDWIN *B.* the name of one of the knights of King Arthur.*

BEE *E.* from *beoh,* a bee.† Ex.: Bee-by (Leics.), bee abode; Bee-don (Berks), bee-hill.

BEECH *E.* from *bæce,* the beech tree. Ex.: Beech-ham-well (Norf.), the well of the beech village; Burnham-beeches (Bucks).

BEER *B.* from *ber,* a hedge. Ex.: 4 places in Dorset, Som., and Devon. Or from *bere, S.,* corn.

BEES *E.* from Bee, the name of a saint. Ex.: St. Bees (Cumb.); Bees-ton, 6 places, St. Bees' town.

BEG, BEIGH *E.* from Bega, or Beya, the owner's name. Ex.: Beg-brook (Oxf.), Bega's brook; Beigh-ton (Derb.), Bega's town or enclosure.

BEL *N. F.* fine or beautiful. Ex.: Bel-champ (Ess.), beautiful field; Bel-voir (Rutland), beautiful prospect.

BEL *E.* perhaps from *bæl,* a sacrificial fire. Ex.: Bel-ton, 5 places, the town of the sacrificial fire. [In Scotland the 20th of May is still called Beltane, the sacrificial fire.]

BEMP *E.* from *beám,* a tree. Ex.: Bemp-ton (Yorks.), tree town.

BEMFLEET *E.* from *beám* and *fleot,* the harbour by the tree.‡ Ex.: Bem-fleet (Essex).

BEN *E.* from Binna, the owner's name. Ex.: Ben-field (Northamp.), the field of Binna; Bengeo (Herts), Binna's hill; Benworth (Linc.), Binna's well-watered estate.

BENT *E.* contracted from Bennet or Benedict. Ex.: Bent-ley, 6 places; Bent-ham (Yorks.), the place and the home of Bennet, probably indicating the property of Benedictine monks.

BEOWULF *E.* a man's name, from *beado,* slaughter, and *wulf,* a wolf, the wolf of slaughter.

BERE *B.* from *ber,* a hedge, or from the Saxon *bere,* barley or corn generally. Ex.: Bere-church (Ess.), Bere (Dorset).

BERG *E.* from *burh,* a fortification. Ex.: Berg-holt (Suff.), the fortification in the wood.

* Lives of British Saints.

† The beoh-ceorl or bee-keeper was an important person on a Saxon farm.

‡ Bosworth.

B. British. *C.* Celtic. *E.* The Old English, commonly known as Anglo-Saxon.

Berke *E.* from *berc*, a birch-tree. Ex.: Berke-ley (Glouc.), birch place or meadow.

Berkshire *E.* from *barruc*, a bare or polled oak, and *scyre*, a shire; so called from the shire-motes being anciently held under the shade of a polled oak in that shire.

Bermonds *E.* from Beramund, the protecting bear, the owner's name. Ex.: Bermonds-ey (Surr.), Beramund's water.

Berning *D.* and *E.* from *beorn*, Danish, a bear, and also a man's name, and *incga*. Ex.: Berningham (Norf.), the home of Beorn's descendants.

Berrick. *See* Barwick.

Berring *E.* from Bera, the owner's name, and *incga*, descendants. Ex.: Berring-ton (Salop and Heref.), the town of Bera's descendants.

Berriw *B.* from *ber*, a hedge, and *rhiw*, a sloping path. Ex.: Berriw (Montg.).

Berrow, Berry *E.* from *bærw*, a grove. Ex.: Berrow (Worc.); Berry Pomeroy (Devon), Pomeroy's grove.

Berryn *E.* perhaps from Birinus, missionary to the West Saxons A.D. 635. Ex.: Berryn-Arbour (Devon), Birinas's retreat.

Berwick. *See* Barwick.

Bet, Beth, Bethers, Beltes, Bettis *E.* from Bieda or Beda, the name of the owner. Ex.: Bet-ley (Staff.), Beda's land; Bednal, now Bethnal (Midd.), Bedan-hall, *i. e.* Beda's hall; Bether's-den (Kent), Beda's hollow; Bettes-hanger (Kent), Beda's hill; Bettis-comb (Dorset), Beda's dingle.

Bettws *B.* a piece of land lying between a river and a hill. Ex.: 13 places.

Bever *E.* from *beofor*, a beaver. Ex.: Bever-ley (Yorks.), the beaver's place; Bevers-ton (Glouc.), the beaver's town.

Bew, Bewd *B.* from *buw*, a cow. Ex.: Bew-castle (Cumb.); Bewd-ley (Worc.). Perhaps the former may rather be from *beau*, the N. F. for beautiful.

Bicester *E.* perhaps from *biliges-cestre*, the camp of the bean-field. Ex.: Bicester (Oxf.). *See* Bis.

Bick *E.* from *bæce*, the beech-tree. Ex.: Bick-leigh (Devon), beech meadow; Bæcen-or, now Bicknor (Monm.), beech boundary; Bicker (Linc.), the beech; Bickers-taffe (Lancas.), the beech toft or grove; Bic-ton (Devon), beech town.

Bid, Bidden, Bide, Biddles *E.* from Bieda, the owner's name. *See* Bet and Bad.

D. Old Danish. *G.* Greek. *L.* Latin. *N. F.* Norman French. *N.* Norse. *qu. v.* which see.

BIG, BIGGIN, BIGH *E.* from *biggin*, a building. Ex.: Big-bury (Devon), the building on the anciently fortified place; New-biggin (Westm.), the new building; Bigh-ton (Hants), the town of the building, *i. e.* the town formed around a previous building. Or from *bige*, a bending or bay.

BIL, BILLING, BILN, BILS *E.* from Belin or Billung, the owner's name. Ex.: Bil-borough (Notts and Yorks.), Belin's fortification; Billings-gate (Midd.), Billung's gate; Bils-ton (Staff.), Belin's town; Biln-ey (Norf.), Belin's water.*

BILLOCK *E.* from *bilige*, a bean-field. Ex.: Billock-by (Norf.), bean-field abode.

BIN, BING *E.* perhaps from *byan*, to abide. Ex.: Bin-ley (Warw.), the abiding place; Bing-ley (Yorks.), the same.

BINNING *E.* from Binn and *incga*. Ex.: Binningtun, now Bennington, 3 places, the town of Binna's descendants.

BIR *E.* from *burh*, a fortified place. Ex.: Bir-ley (Heref.), the fortified place in the meadow.

BIRCH, BIRCHING, BIRK *E.* from *birce*, the birch-tree. Ex. Birch-holt (Kent), birch wood; Bircen-tun, now Birchington (Kent), the town of the birches; Birkland (Notts), a part of Sherwood Forest.

BIRD *E.* from *beord*, a bird, adopted as a man's name. Ex.: Birds-all (Yorks.), Bird's hall; Beordan-burh, now Birdinbury (Warw.), Bird's fortification.

BIRK. *See* Birch.

BIRLING. *See* Barl.

BIRMING, BRIMING *N.* perhaps from *brimi*, flame, the name of a magical sword mentioned in Norse poetry,† and *incga*, children. Ex.: Birming-ham (Warw.), Briming-ton (Derb.), the home and the town of the children of flame.

BIRT *E.* from *briht*, illustrious, or a form of *beord*, a bird, and the owner's name. Ex.: Birt's Morton (Worc.), Birt's mere or pool town; Weston-birt (Glouc.), Birt's Weston, in distinction from other Westons.

BIS *E.* from *bylges*, beans. Ex.: Bylges-ley,‡ now Bisley (Glouc.), the bean meadow.

* Brandenburg was officially reckoned Saxon; part of the big duchy of Saxony; where certain famed Billungs, lineage of an old Count Billung (connected or not with Billings-gate in our country, I do not know), had long borne sway.—Carlyle's *Life of Friedrich II. of Prussia.*

† Toulmin Smith. ‡ Bosworth.

B. British. *C.* Celtic. *E.* The Old English, commonly known as Anglo-Saxon.

BISHOP, BISP, *E.* from *biscop*, a bishop, indicating episcopal property. Ex.: Bishops-ton, 6 places; Bishop-thorp (Yorks.), the bishop's farm-house; Bisp-ham (Lanc.), the bishop's village.

BITTA, BITTER, BITTES *E.* from Bieda or Beda, a man's name. *See* Bet and Bad.

BLACK, BLAKE *E.* from *blæc*, black, assumed as a personal name, and still common as such. Ex.: Black, 12 places; Blake and Blaken, 5 places. Blaecen, pronounced Blaken, is the possessive case of Blake.

BLAEN, BLAENAU *B.* the beginning or summit, or the source of a stream. Ex.: Blaen-afon (Monm.), the source of the river; Blaenau (Monm.), the sources of several streams.

BLAND *E.* from Blanda, a man's name, still preserved as Bland and Blandy; probably a kindred word to *blend*, and may have arisen from the parti-coloured dress worn in Saxon times, like the Scotch tartan. Ex.: Bland-ford (Dorset), Blanda's ford.

BLATCH, BLECH, BLETCH *E.* from Blecca, a heathen chief converted by Bishop Paulinus, A.D. 634. Ex. Blatch-ington (Suss.), the town of Blecca's descendants; Bletchington (Suff.), the same; Bleching-don (Oxford), Blecca's hill.

BLAZEY, BLAIS, BLEA, BLEAS *E.* from St. Blaize or Blasius. Ex.: Blazey (Cornw.); Blais-don (Glouc.), Blaize's hill; Blea-don (Som.), the same; Bleas-by (Notts), Blaize's abode.

BLAU *B.* blue. Ex.: Blau-reng (Monm.), the blue range of hills.

BLED, BLEDD, *B.* from *blith*, giving milk. Ex.: Bled-low (Bucks), dairy hill; Bledd-fa (Radnors.), dairy place.

BLEECH. *See* Blatch.

BLETCH, BLETS. *See* Blatch.

BLICK *E.* from *blæcan*, to bleach.

BLO, BLEW, BLOOMS *E.* from *bloma*, a flower, and also a piece of iron when reduced from the ore. The sites of the Roman iron manufacture, in Dean Forest and elsewhere, are still called bloomaries. Probably the words Blo, Blew, and Blooms are traces of the Saxon manufacture of iron. Ex.: Blo-norton (Norf.), Blew-bury (Berks), Blooms-bury (Midd.).

BLOCK, BLOX *E.* from *blæc*, black, also a man's name. *See* Black and Blake.

BLUN, BLUNDES, BLUNTIS, BLUNS *E.* from Blunda, a man's name. Ex.: Blun-ham (Bedf.), Blunda's home or village; Blundeston (Suff.), Blunda's town; Bluntis-ham (Hunts), Blunda's home; Bluns-don (Wilts), Blunda's hill. Hence, too, the Giant Blunderbore, *i.e.*, Blunda the bear, of our nursery tales.

BLY, BLYTH *B.* from *blith*, giving milk. Ex.: Bly-borough (Linc.), dairy fortification; Blyth, 4 places, the dairy.

BOAR, *E.* from *bar*, a boar. The Saxons kept large herds of swine. Ex.: Boar-stall (Bucks), the boar's station.

BOBBING *E.* from Bebban, the possessive case of Bebba, a man's name. Ex.: Bobbing-worth (Ess.), Bebba's estate.

BOCK *E.* from *boc*, one of the forms of *bece*, the beech-tree. Ex.: Bocking, *i.e.* Bocen (Ess.), the beeches; Bock-le-ton (Heref.), the town of the beech meadow.

BOD *B.* an abode. Ex.: Bod-edeyrn (Angl.), Edeyrn's abode; Bod-min (Cornw.), the abode on the brow of a hill.

BODDING *E.* from Bieda or Beda, a man's name, and *incga*, descendants. Ex.: Bodding-ton (Glouc.), the town of Beda's children.

BODEN (doubtful) seems to mean a low, moist site. Ex.: Boden-ham (Heref. and Wilts). Boden-heim, in Germany, seems to be the same name.

BOL, BOLD *E.* the bole or trunk of a tree. Ex.: Bole (Notts), Bolen-brook, now Bolingbroke (Linc.), the brook near some noted tree; New-bold (Derb.), the new town beside the tree; Bol-ton, 8 places, bole town.

BON, BONNING, BONS *E.* from Bonna, a man's name (still existing as Bonner), and *incga*, children. Ex.: Bon-by (Linc.), Bonna's abode; Boning-ale (Salop), the hall of Bonna's children; Bonning-ton (Kent), the town of the same; Bons-all (Derb.), Bonna's hall.

BONT *B.* a bridge. Ex.: Pen-y-bont (Radn.), bridge head.

BOOK. *See* BOCK.

BOOTH *B.* from *bwth*, a hut. Ex.: Booths (Lanc.)

BOOTH *B.* a port. *See* Porth, *infra.*

BOOTLE. *See* Bottle.

BORD *E.* perhaps from *bordar*, a kind of tenant. Ex.: Borden (Kent); Bordes-ley (Warw.).

BOROUGH, BURG, BURGH, BURY *E.* from *burh*, *birg*, *burg*, *birig*, or *byrig*, a fortified hill, thence a town; Norse, *bor* and *bjerg*, a height. Ex.: Borough-bridge (Yorks.), the fortified town at the bridge; Burg-hill (Heref.), the fortified hill; Burgh-ley (Linc.), the fortified town in the meadow; Bury (Lanc.).

BOS *E.* from Bosa, consecrated first bishop of East Anglia, A.D. 669.

Ex.: Bos-ton (Linc.), Bosa's town; Bosanham, now Bos-ham, (Suss.), Bosa's dwelling; Bosworth (Leic.), Bosa's estate; Bos-ley (Cheshire), Bosa's land.

BOTES, BOTTES, BOTTIS *E.* contracted from Botolph's. Ex.: Botes-dale (Suff.), Botolph's dale; Bottes-ford (Linc.), Botolph's ford; Bottis-ham (Camb.), Botolph's village.

BOTTLE *E.* from *botel*, a dwelling or mansion. Ex.: New-bottle (Durh.), Bootle (Lanc).

BOUGH *E.* from *bog* or *boh*, that which bends down, a bough. Ex.: Bough-ton, 8 places, indicating a site among trees.

BOUGHROOD *B.* corrupted from *bwch ffrwd*, the cow's brook. Ex.: Boughrood (Radn.)

BOULS. *See* Bol.

BOURN, BURN *E.* a brook. Ex.: Bourn (Linc.), Burn-ham (Bucks), brook home or village.

BOW, BOWES *E.* from *bog*, a bending or turn of a stream or of a road. Ex.: Bow (Devon), Bowes (Midd.), the bendings.

BOWER *E.* from *bur*, a bower, or a cottage. Ex.: Bower (Wilts).

BOX *E.* from *boc*, the beech. Ex.: Box-ford (Suff.), the ford at the beech-tree.

BRACE *N. F.* from Bracy, the lord's name. Ex.: Brace-by (Linc.), Bracy's abode.

BRACK, BROCK *E.* from *broc*, a badger. Ex.: Brackley (Northamp.), Brocken-hurst (Hants), the badgers' wood.

BRAD, BRADEN, BRADDEN, BREDE, BRED *E.* from *brad*, broad or spacious. Ex.: Brad-ford (Yorks.), the broad ford; Bradden-ham (Bucks), the village in the spacious hollow; Bradden (Northamp.); Brading (Hants), the broad hollow; Brede (Suss.), Breden-bury (Heref.), Bredy (Dorset), broad water.

BRAILES *E.* from *broyl*, a park. Ex.: Brailes (Warw.), the park; Brails-ford (Derb.), the park ford.

BRAIN, BREIN *B.* from *brên*, a prince; hence the Brennus of Livy, the Romans having mistaken the title for a proper name. Ex.: Brain-tree (Essex), the prince's town; Breinton (Heref.), the same.

BRAITH *E.* from *brád*, broad. Ex.: Braith-well (Yorks.), the broad or large well.

BRAM, BRAMP, BROOM, BROM, BROMP *E.* from *brum*, a name applied to the Genista and also to the Reseda, *vulgo* broom and dyer's rocket. Ex.: Bram-dean (Hants), broomy hollow; Brampton, 11 places, broom town; Brom-ley (Heref.), broom land.

D. Old Danish. *G.* Greek. *L.* Latin. *N.F.* Norman French. *N.* Norse. *qu.v.* which see.

BRAN, perhaps from Brân, the first British Christian. Ex.: Brandon (Suff.), Bran's hill; Cwm-bran (Glam.), Bran's dingle.

BRANCE, BRANDES, BRANDS, BRANS, BRANT *N.* from Brand, a man's name. Ex.: Brance-peth, *i.e.* Brand's path (Durh.); Brandeston (Norf.), Brand's town; Brands-burton (Yorks.) so distinguished from other Burtons; Brans-by (Yorks.), Brand's abode.

BRANTING *E.* from Brand and *incga.* Ex.: Branting-ham (Yorks.), the home of Brand's descendants.

BRAT *E.* from *brád,* broad. *See* Brad.

BRATTLE *E.* from *brád* and *ley,* broad meadow. Ex.: Brattle-by (Linc.), the abode in the broad meadow.

BRAUNCE, BRAUNS. *See* Brance.

BRAY, BREA *E.* from *brego,* a ruler; hence the Danish name Brahe. Ex.: Bray-toft (Linc.), the ruler's grove; Bray-field (Bucks), the ruler's field; Brea-more (Hants).

BRE *B.* a promontory. Ex.: Bre-dwr-din, now Bredwardin (Heref.), the water camp of the promontory; Bredon (Worc.), promontory hill.

BREADSALL *E.* Breda's hall. Ex.: Breads-all (Derb.), Brede (Suss.), Breden-bury (Heref.), Breda's fortification.

BREDA, BREDEN. *See* Breadsall.

BREIDDIN *B.* from *bri,* honour, or *bre,* a promontory, and *din,* a camp. Ex.: Breiddin hill (Montg.), anciently called Dygen Freiddin,* the contest of the camp of honour, or of the promontory.

BRIAVEL *B.* St. Briafel, seventh century. Ex.: St. Briavel's (Glouc.).

BRICE, BRIS, BRIZE *E.* St. Brice, on whose festival, Nov. 13, 1002, the Danes in England were massacred. Ex.: Bricehut, now Bricett (Suff.), St. Brice's hut; Bris-lene-tun, now Brislington (Som.), the town of Brice's *lene,* or fee-farm land; Brize-norton (Oxf.), Brice's Norton.

BRICK *E.* perhaps from St. Brice. *See* Brice.

BRIDE, BRID *E.* from St. Bridget. Ex.: Bride-well, St. Bridget's well; Bride-stow (Devon), St. Bridget's station; Brid-stow (Heref.), the same.†

* 'The frail conflict of Breiddin.' Elidir Sais, 1200, in Stephens' Literature of the Kymry.

† Bridget was called by the Britons San Ffread. In the Liber Landavensis, Brid-stow (Heref.) is called Llan-san-ffread.

B. British. *C.* Celtic. *E.* The Old English, commonly known as Anglo-Saxon.

Bridg, Brig *E.* from *bricg*, a bridge. Ex.: Bridgnorth (Salop), the north bridge; Brig-house (Yorks.), the bridge house.

Bridling *E.* from Bridla (possessive Bridlan), the owner's name. Ex.: Bridlington (Yorks.).

Brig. *See* Brid.

Bright, Brightling, Brighthelm *E.* from *Briht*, illustrious, also a warrior's name, and Brihthelm, bright helmet, also a name. Ex.: Bright-waltham (Berks), Bright's town on the wold; Brightlinges-ea (Ess.), the water of Bright's possession; Brighthelmes-tun, now Brighton (Suss.), Brighthelm's town.

Brilley *B.* from *bre* and *lle*, promontory place. Ex.: Brilley (Heref.).

Brim *N.* from *brimi*, flame,* and also a man's name. Ex.: Briming-ton (Derb.); Brimscombe (Som.).

Brink *S.* the edge or margin. Ex: Brink-low (Warw.), the edge of the hill.

Brins *B.* from *brên*, a prince. Ex.; Brinsop (Heref.), the prince's sloping plain between hills.

Bris. *See* Brice.

Brit, from Briton. Ex.: Brit-ford (Wilts), the Briton's ford; Briton-ferry (Glam.), the Briton's ferry.

Brix *E.* from St. Brice. Ex.: Brix-ton, 4 places, St. Brice's town.

Bro *B.* a district. Ex.: Bro-bury (Heref.), the fortification of the district.

Broad *E.* from *brad*. *See* Brad.

Brock *E.* a badger or polecat. Ex.: Brockley (Suff.), the badger's meadow; Brockenhurst (Hants), the badger's wood.

Brom, Bromp. *See* Bram.

Broms. See Bram.

Broom. *See* Bram.

Bron, Fron *B.* a hill in the shape of a woman's breast. Ex.: Bron-llys (Brec.), palace hill; Fron-fraidd (Montg.), St. Bridget's hill.

Brother, Frother *B.* from *brawd*, a brother, indicating monastic land. Ex.: Brother-ton (Yorks.), the monk's town; Llan-frother (Heref.), the monk's church.

Brough *E.* from *burh*, a fortification. Ex.: Brough-ton, 22 places, fortified town.

* Toulmin Smith.

BROXASH *N. F.* and *E.* anciently Brewes-esc, from Bros, the Norman owner, and *esc*, an ash-tree. Ex.: Broxash (Heref.).

BRUM. *See* Bram.

BRUTON *B.* from Britwn, a Briton. Ex.: Tal-pont-britwn, now Bruton (Glam.), the foot of the Britons' bridge; Bruton (Som.).

BRYAN *N. F.* the chief's name. Ex.: Brampton Bryan (Heref.); Bryan's-ton (Dorset).

BRYN *B.* a hill. Ex.: Bryn-gwyn (Rad.), the white hill.

BU *B.* a cow. Ex.: Bu-allt, now Builth (Brec.), the cows' steep place.

BUB *E.* from Bebba, a man's name. Ex.: Bub-with (Yorks.), Bebba's willows.

BUCK *E.* from *boc*, a book; boc-land was copyhold. Ex.: Buckden (Hunts), the hollow which was held by copyhold.

BUCKING *E.* from *becen*, the beech-tree. Ex.: Becen-ham,* now Buckingham, the village among the beeches.

BUD, BUDEAUX, BUDOCK, from Budda, or Budeau, a man's name, perhaps a corruption from Badoc, name of a British saint. Ex.: Bud-brook (Warw.); St. Budeaux (Cornw.), *i. e.* St. Badoc's; Budock (Cornw.).

BUILD, BUILTH *B.* from *bu-allt*, the steep place of the cows. Ex.: Bu-allt-was, now Build-was (Salop), the moist place near the cows' steep; Bu-allt, now Builth (Brec.), the cows' steep.

BUL *B.* from *bul*, a bull, probably assumed as his cognizance by the owner of the land. Ex.: Bul-ley (Glouc.), the bull's meadow or place.

BULLING *E.* from Bulla (possessive Bullan), the name of the owner. Ex.: Bullan-hope, now Bulling-ham (Heref.), Bulla's slope.

BUMP *B.* from *pwmp* or *bwmp*, a protuberance. Ex.: Bumpstead (Essex), the station on or near the protuberance or small hill.

BUN (doubtful), but perhaps from *bôn*, *B.*, the trunk of a tree. Ex.: Bun-gay (Suff.), the *ga* or place of some noted treestump.

BUR *E.* from *bur*, a cottage, or from *burh*, a hill. Ex.: Bur-ton, 24 places; Bur-ford, 3 places.

* Camden.

B. British. *C.* Celtic. *E.* The Old English, commonly known as Anglo-Saxon.

BURCOTT *E.* anciently Brocote,* from *burh*, a hill, and *cote*, a sheepfold. Ex.: Burcott (Heref.), sheepfold-hill.

BURGH, BURI, BURY *E.* from *burg* or *burh*, a fortification or a hill. Ex.: Burgh, 16 places as a prefix; Buri-ton (Hants); Bury (Suff. and Lanc.).

BURLES, BURLING *E.* from Brechla, the owner's name. Ex.: Burles-comb (Devon), Brechla's dingle; Burling-ham (Norf.), the home of Brechla's descendants.

BURLINJOBB *B.* and *E.* anciently Brechlinchope, *i. e.* Brechla's *hupp* or slope. Ex.: Burlinjobb (Rad.).

BURN *E.* from *bourn*, a brook. *See* Bourn.

BURRING *E.* from Burra, a man's name, and *incga*, children. Ex.: Burrington, 3 places, town of Burra's children.

BURTH *E.* from *burh*, a hill. Ex.: Aig-burth (Lanc.), hawthorn or hedged hill.

BURWAR *E.* from *bærw*, a grove. Ex.: Burwar-ton (Salop), grove town.

BURWASH *E.* from *bur* and *wæs*. Ex.: Burwash (Suss.), the cottage at the moist place.

BURY. *See* Burgh.

BUSH, BUS *D.* from *bosch*, a shrub or cluster of shrubs. Ex.: Bush-ey (Herts), the bush near the water; Bus-cot (Berks); the hut among the bushes.

BUT, BUTT, BUTTER, BUTTS *E.* from *butte*, a mark for archers. Ex.: But-ley (Suff.), the archers' field; Butten-tun, now Butting-ton (Mont.), archers' town; Butts-bury (Ess.), archers' fortification; Butte-leigh, now Butterleigh (Devon), archers' land or place.

BUTTERLEY *B.* from *bu*, a cow, *tref*, town, and *le*, place. Ex.: Butterley (Salop), in Domesday Book "Butrelie," the place of the cows' town.

BUTTOLPH *E.* from Botolph, a man's name.

BUX *E.* from *buck*. Ex.: Bux-ton (Derb.), the buck's town; Bux-ted (Suss.), the buck's sted or station.

BUZZARD *N. F.* locally said to be a corruption of Beaudesert, the name or title of the Norman lord, but more probably from the name of the family of Bosard, seated here in *temp.* Edw. III. Ex.: Leighton Buzzard (Bedf.), Bosard's Leighton.

* Domesday Book.

Bwla *B.* a bull. Ex.: Croft-y-bwla (Mon.), the bull's field.

By (suffix) *D.* from *bye*, an abode, hence a town, answering to the Brit. *beu.* Ex.: Deora-by, now Derby, the deer's abode; Scroo-by (Notts), Scroop's abode; and 151 places in Linc., Notts, and Yorks. N. and E. This termination does not—except in Cumberland—occur beyond the limits of the Dane-lagh or Anglian England.

By (prefix) *B.*; west of the Severn it is a corruption of *bu*, a cow. Ex.: Byford (Heref.), which appears in Domesday Book as "Bviford," *i. e.* the *ffordd*, or way, of the cows. In the Saxon districts, it is a corruption of Beg, *q. v.*

C

In British words, *c* is always sounded like *k*; and it has the same sound in Old English words, except where it precedes *two* vowels, as in *ceorl, ceap, ceaster*, &c. In these cases it seems to have had in the southern dialects the sound of *tch*. *Caster* in Yorkshire answers to *Chester* in Mercian counties, and *Cester* and *Ceter* in Wessex; *ceald* (cold) in like manner becomes *chil* and *chilt*; *cawc* (Linc.) appears as *chal, challock*, and *chalk* in Kent and other southern counties; and *cyrc* (now kirk) in the north becomes *church* in the south.

Ca, Cae, Cay *B.* a hollow, and also a field. Ex.: Ca-wood (Yorks.); Cae, frequent in Wales; Cay-ton (Yorks.), th town of the hollow.

Cad, Cade *E.* from Cedda,* a man's name, perhaps derived from *cadr* (Brit.) strong, the root of the names Cadfan and Cadifor. Ex.: Cad-bury, 3 places, Cedda's camp; Cade-by, 3 places, Cedda's Danish abode.

Cadding *E.* from Cedda, and *incga,* children. Ex.: Caddington (Bedf.), the town of Cedda's children.

Cadle *B.* a battle-place. Ex.: Llan-cadle (Glam.), the church of the battle-place.

Cae. *See* Ca.

Caen, Cain *B.* from *cain,* fair, also the name of a female saint. Ex.: Caen-by (Linc.), Cain-ham (Heref.).

Caer, Gaer *B.* a camp, from *ca,* to enclose, supposed to point out the sites of Roman camps. Ex.: Caer-leon (Monm.), the camp of the legion; the Gaer (Monm.), the camp; Caersw (Mont.), probably from *caer-yswydd,* the camp of the privet-bush.

Cain. *See* Caen.

Cais. *See* Caster.

Cald, Calde, Caldi *E.* from *ceald,* cold, indicating a bleak site. Ex.: Cald-beck (Cum.) cold brook; Calde-cott, 6 places, and Caldi-cot (Mon.), cold hut.

Calling, Calne *B.* from *celyn,* the holly-tree. Ex.: Calling-ton (Cornw.), holly town; Caln-e (Wilts), holly water or brook.

* There was a Cedda bishop of Hereford in A.D. 752.

D. Old Danish. *G.* Greek. *L.* Latin. *N.F.* Norman French. *N.* Norse. *qu. v.* which see.

CALLOW *E.* from *ceald* and *hlæw.* Ex.: Callow (Heref.), cold hill, the place facing the north and east.

CAM *E.* anciently *cwat*,* from *hwatu*, an omen. Ex.: Cwatbridge, now Cambridge (Glouc.), the bridge of omens.

CAMEL, *E.* from *gafel*, a tax or toll.† Ex.: Camel-ford (Cornw.), the ford of the tax, or the ford where toll was levied.

CAMLAS *B.* standing or sluggish water. Ex.: Aber-camlas (Glam.), the estuary of the sluggish stream.

CAMP. *See* Champ.

CAND *E.* from Cendred or Guendred, a man's name. Ex.: Candover (Hants), Cendred's hills.

CANEWDON, from the name of King Canute, and *don*, a hill. Ex.: Canew-don (Ess.), Canute's hill, he having kept his court there.

CANN *B.* from the Cangi, a Brit. tribe,‡ so named from Cen-ga, the head or chief place, and therefore applied to the principal tribe. Ex.: Cann (Dorset), Can-wg, now Cannock (Staff.), the district of the head or hill.

CANON *N. F.* a member of a cathedral chapter; indicating, when part of the name of a place, one of the estates of the capitular body. Ex.: Canon-bury (Midd.), the canon's fortified town; Norton Canon, Canon Froome (Heref.).

CANONICORUM *L.* of the canons. Ex.: Whitchurch Canonicorum (Dorset), the Whitchurch which belonged to a chapter of canons.

CANTREF *B.* the town of the cantred or hundred. Ex.: Cantref (Brecons.).

CANWYLLARN *B.* from *canwyll*, a candle or light, and *carn*, a heap of stones. Ex. Twyn-y-canwyllarn (Mer.), the curved bank of the candle-heap of stones, *i.e.* beacon. *See* Twyn, *infra.*

CAP, COP *E.* a head or hill, allied to the Latin *caput* and French *chef.* Ex.: Capler (Heref.), from *cap* and *le*, hill place; Cop, frequent in the names of streets in Shrewsbury, owing to that town being situated on a hill with many small summits.

CAPEL, CAPLE *B.* a chapel, from the low Latin *capella.* Ex.: Capel, 6 places; How-caple (Heref.), the chapel in the hollow.

CAPLER *B.* and *E.* from *cop*, a summit, and *le*, place. Ex.: Capler camp (Heref.).

* Bosworth. † Idem. ‡ Camden.

CAR, CARE, a pool. Ex.: Car-ton (Linc.), pool town; Care-by (Linc.), pool abode.

CARDIFF *B.* corrupted from Caer-taff, the camp on the bank of the Taff.

CARDING *E.* probably from Cerdic, king of Wessex, and *incga*, descendants. Ex.: Carding-ton, 2 places, the town of Cerdic's descendants.

CARE. *See* Car.

CARISBROOK *E.* from *gara*, a promontory, and *byrg*, a fortification. Ex.: Garasbyrg (now Carisbrook), the fortified promontory.

CARL *E.* from *ceorl*, a husbandman. Ex.: 38 places in midland and southern counties.

CARN, GARN, CARNEDD, plural carneddau, garneddau *B.* a monumental or sepulchral heap of stones. Ex.: Carn-dafydd (Merion.), David's carn; Garn-fach (Monm.), the little carn; Carnedd Llewelyn (Merion.), Llewelyn's carn.

CARREG, GARREG *B.* a rock, answering to Carrick in Ireland and Scotland. Ex.: Carreg-y-drudion (Flints.), the rock of the daring ones; Llanbadarn-y-garreg (Angl.), St. Padarn's church on the rock.

CASTER, CAISTOR, CASTOR, CESTER, CHESTER *E.* from *cestre*, a corruption of *castrum* (Lat.), a camp and afterwards a fortified town. Ex.: Caster-ton (Linc.), camp town; Caistor, the camp; Castor, 2 places; Don-caster (Yorks.), the camp near the river Don; Al-cester (Warw.), the old camp; Chester, the camp; Cissa-chestre (Suss.), now Chichester, Cissa's camp, from the Saxon king so named.

CAT, CATER, CATES, CATTIS, CATS *E.* from Catta, a cat, also a man's name. Ex.: Cater-ham (Surr.), Catta's home; Catesby (Hants), Catta's abode; Cat-thorp (Leic.), Catta's farm; Catti-stock (Dorset), Catta's station; Cats-field (Suss.), Catta's field.

CATTERICK *L.* and *E.* from Cataractonium, the name of a Roman station at that place.* Ex.: Catterick (Yorks.).

CAUN *B.* from *cawn*, reed-grass. Ex.: Cawn-lle, now Caundle (Dorset), the place of reed-grass; Caun-ton (Notts), the town of the same.

CAVEN, CHEVEN, CHEVING *N. F.* from the *chevin* or chub, adopted

* Bede.

as a man's name. Ex.: Caven-ham (Suff.), Chevin's home; Cheven-ing (Kent), Chevin's meadow; Cheving-ton (Suff.), Chevin's town.

CAVER, CHEVE, CHEVER *B.* from *gafr*, a goat, adopted as a man's cognizance and name. Ex.: Cavers-ham (Kent), Caver's home; Cheve-ley (Camb.), Chever-hill (Wilts).

CAWK *E.* from *cealc*, chalk, still called *cawk* in Scotland. Ex.: Cawk-well (Linc.), the chalk well.

CAWS *E.* from Caver. Ex.: Caws-ton (Norf.); Caw-thorp (Linc.), Caver's village and farm.

CAYO *B.* from Caius, the name of some Roman officer. Ex.: Conwyl Gayo (Card.), Caius's muster-place.

CEFN *B.* a ridge. Ex.: Cefn-llys (Rad.), palace ridge.

CEL *B.* from *cil*, a retreat or cell of a hermit. Ex.: Cel-lan (Card.), the church of the hermit's cell; Cil-y-cwm (Carm.), the cell of the dingle.

CELLI, GELLI *B.* the hazel-tree. Ex.: Pencelli (Brec.), hazel hill; Tre-gelli, now Hay (Brec.), hazel town.

CELYN *B.* holly-trees. Ex.: Cwm-celyn (Monm.), holly dingle.

CEMAES, CEMMES *B.* from *cemp-maes*, the field of the circle, perhaps a Druidical circle of stones. Ex.: Cemaes, corrupted to Kemeys (Monm.); Cemmes (Mont.).

CENNIN *B.* a leek. Ex.: Carreg-cennin, the rock of the leeks. [Allium ursinum grows freely among rocks in various parts of Wales.]

CERNE, CERNEY *E.* from *ciern*, a churn, indicating a place where cheese-making was carried on. Ex.: Cerne (Dorset), Cerney (Glouc.).

CERRIG *B.* plural of carreg, *q. v.*

CETHIN *B.* dark. Ex.: Bryn-cethin, dark hill.

CEUGH, a form of *cleugh* or *clough*, a valley. Ex.: Middle-ceugh (Cumb.). *See* Clough, *infra.*

CHACE. *See* Chad.

CHAD, CHADDES, CHADS *E.* from Ceadda or Chad, A.D. 665, the first bishop of Lichfield. Ex.: Chad-well (Ess.), St. Chad's well; Chaddes-den (Derb.), St. Chad's valley; Chad's-hunt (Warw.), St. Chad's forest; Chace-ley (Glouc.), Chad's meadow.

CHADDLE, CHEDDLE, CHETTLE, CHIT, CHITTLE *E.* from Chetel, the owner's name. Ex.: Chaddle-worth (Berks), Chetel's estate; Cheddle-ton (Staff.), Chetel's town; Chettle (Dorset); Chitt-ern (Wilts), Chetel's place; Chittle-hamp-ton (Devon), the town of Chetel's home.

CHAL, CHALLA, CHALLOCK *E.* from *cealc*, chalk. Ex.: Chal-grove (Bedf.), the chalk entrenchment; Challa-comb (Devon), chalk dingle; Challock (Kent), chalk town.

CHAMP *N. F.* a field or plain. Ex.: Beau-champ, beautiful plain.

CHAMPFLOWER *N. F.* from Champfleur, the name of the Norman lord. Ex.: Huish Champflower (Somers.), the Huish which belonged to a lord of that name, as distinguished from the bishop's possession, which was called Huish Episcopi.

CHAR, CHARD *E.* from Cerdic king of West Saxons.* Ex.: Cardre, now Chard (Som.), Cerdic's hill; Chard-stock (Dorset), Cerdic's station; Cerdices-ford, now Char-ford (Hants), Cerdic's ford; Charring (Kent), and Charing (Mid.), Cerdic's meadow.

CHARL *E.* from *ceorle*, a husbandman. Ex.: 24 places, of which 14 are Charl-ton, husbandman's town; Charlinch (Som.), ceorl's *lenes*, that is, husbandman's land held on fee farm.

CHAT *E.* from Chetel, the owner's name. Ex.: Chat-ham (Kent), Chetel's home; Chats-worth (Derb.), Chetel's estate †; Chat-moss (Lanc.), Chetel's morass.

CHEARD *E.* from Cerdie. Ex.: Chardes-ley (Bucks), Cerdic's land.

CHED, CHEDDING, CHEDIS *E.* *See* Chad.

CHEDDAR *E.* anciently Ceordre, probably from Ceordric or Cerdic, king of Wessex. Ex.: Cheddar (Som.).

CHEDZOY *E.* Chad's *ey*, or water. Ex.: Chedzoy (Som.).

CHEL, CHOL *E.* from *ceol*, a keel or ship. Ex.: Chels-ea (Midd.), the port of the ships ‡; Chols-ey (Berks).

CHELTENHAM *E.* the village on the river Chelt.

CHEP, CHEAP, CHIPPIN, CHIPPEN *E.* from *ceap*, a market. Ex.: Chep-stow (Mon.), the palisaded market; Cheap-side, the broad market; Chippen-ham, the market village; Chipping Norton (Oxf.), the market Norton, in distinction from other Nortons.

CHER, CHERI, CHERRY (doubtful), but perhaps from the cherry-

* Camden. † Idem. ‡ Somner.

tree. Ex.: Cher-hill (Wilts), cherry hill; Cheri-ton, 5 places; Cherry-hinton (Camb.).

CHERTSEY *E.* anciently Ceorotsei,* from the owner's name, and *ig*. Ex.: Chertsey (Surr.).

CHESIL, CHISEL, CHISLE, CHIS, CHESSING *E.* from *ceosel*, a sand-bank. Ex.: Chesilhurst (Kent), sand-bank wood; the Chesil bank (Dorset); Chisel-borough (Som.), the fortified sand-bank; Chisl-ett (Kent), the hut on the sand-bank; Chisle-don (Wilts), sand hill; Chiswick (Midd.), sandy abode; Chessing-ton (Surr.), sandbank town.

CHESTER. *See* Caster.

CHESWARDIN *E., B.* from Chad's-dwr-din, *i. e.* Chad's camp by the water. Ex.: Cheswardin (Salop).

CHET, CHETTLE. *See* Chaddle and Chat.

CHEVEN, CHEVING. *See* Caven.

CHEVER. *See* Caver.

CHI *E.* from Cissa, king of the South Saxons, A.D. 500. Ex.: Chi-chester (Suss.), Cissa's fortification. *See* Caster.

CHID *E.* from Cedda, a man's name. Ex.: Chid-ham (Suss.), Cedda's village.

CHIDDING, CODDING *E.* from Cedda and *incga*. Ex.: Chidding-fold (Suss.), and Chiddings-ton (Kent), the fold and the town of the descendants of Cedda; Coddington, 3 places.

CHIL, CHILT *E.* from *ceald*, cold. Ex.: Chil-ham (Kent), cold village, *i. e.* a village on a bleak site; Chilt-ern (Bucks), cold place.

CHILD, CHILDER, CHILLES *E.* perhaps from *cild*, a child, a term applied in old ballads to a young chief, as in the ballad of "Child Waters." Ex.: Child's Ercal (Staff.); Child-Oke-ford (Dorset), the young chief's Okeford; Childer-ditch (Ess.), the young chief's entrenchment; Chillesford (Suff.), the young chief's ford.

CHILLING *E.* from *cild*, adopted as a name, and *incga*, descendants. Ex.: Chill-ingham, now Chillingham (Northum.), the home of the descendants of a chief called Cild.

CHIN, CHINE *E.* a cleft, or a piece cut out. Ex.: Chinn-ock (Som.), the oak in the cleft or gap of a range of hills; Chine (Isle of Wight), frequent, as Black-gang Chine, etc.

* 'In Ceorotsei, that is, the island of Ceorot.'—*Bede*.

B. British. *C.* Celtic. *E.* The Old English, commonly known as Anglo-Saxon.

CHIPPEN, CHIPPING. *See* Chep.

CHIR *E.* from *cyrc* or *circ*, a church. Ex.: Chir-bury (Salop), church fortification.

CHIRK *B.* from Ceiriog, its ancient name. Ex.: Chirk (Denb.).

CHISEL, CHISLE. *See* Chesil.

CHIT, CHITTLE. *See* Chaddle.

CHIVEL *E.* a man's name. Ex.: Chivel's-ton (Devon), Chivel's town.

CHOLSTREY *E.* and *B.* from Ceolred, king of Mercia, A.D. 709, and *tref*, town. Ex.: Ceorlestre, now Cholstrey (Heref.).

CHURCH, CHUR, CHURS *E.* from *cyrc*, a church, indicating church property as distinguished from that of king and baron.

CIL *B.* a cell. *See* Cel.

CIRENCESTER *E.* anciently Cissan-cestre, the fortified town of Cissa, one of the lieutenants of Ælla, founder of the kingdom of Sussex. The local name of the town is Cisseter, manifestly a corruption of Cissan-cestre.

CLAP, CLIPPES, CLIPS *E.* from Clappa, the owner's name. Ex.: Clap-ham (Surrey), Clappa's home, Clippes-by (Norf.), Clippa's abode; Clips-ton (North. and Notts), Clappa's town.

CLARE *N. F.* from the knightly family of that name. Ex.: Clare-borough (Notts), Clare's fortified town.

CLAS, CLOS *B.* a cloister. Ex.: Clas-Garmon (Radn.), St. Germanus's cloister; Clos-worth (Som.), the cloister or monks' estate.

CLAT *E.* from *glat*, a gap. Ex.: Clat-ford (Hants), the ford near the gap; Clat-worthy (Som.), the water-farm near the gap.

CLAWDD *B.* a dike or earthen rampart. Ex.: Clawdd Offa, Offa's Dike; Tre-'r-clawdd, now Knighton (Radn.), the town on Offa's Dike.

CLAWRPLWYF *B.* from *llawr* and *plwyf*, the people's cleared spot. Ex.: Clawrplwyf (Monm.), which was probably surrounded by forest.

CLAY, CLEA, CLE *B.* from *clai*, clay. Ex.: 12 places, among which are Clay-hanger (Devon), the clay hill; Clea-tor (Cumb.), the tower on the clay, or the clay hill; Cle-honger (Heref.), the clay hill.

CLE. *See* Clay.

CLEE *B.* from *lle*, a place. Ex.: Clee hills (Salop), *the* place, by way of eminence.

CLEEVE, CLEVE, CLIVE, CLIFFE *E.* from *clif*, a steep bank. Ex.:

Cleeve, 3 places; Cleve-don (Som.), cliff hill; Clive (Salop), the cliff; Clif-ton, 14 places, cliff town; Clif-ford, 3 places; Cliffe, 3 places.

CLEO *E.* from *hlaew*, a hill. Ex.: Cleo-bury (Salop), the fortified hill.

CLERE *E.* clear, indicating a cleared place in a forest. Ex: High-clere and King's-clere, both in Hants.

CLIPPES, CLIPS. *See* Clappa.

CLITHEROE *B.*, *D.* from *llethyr*, a precipice, and *hoe* a hill. Ex.: Clitheroe (Lanc.).

CLODOCK *B.* from *clawdd-wg*, the place fortified by an earthen rampart. Ex.: Clodock (Heref.).

CLOP. *See* Clap.

CLOS. *See* Clas.

CLOUGH, CLAUGH, from *clough*, a valley, a word still used in Cumberland. Ex.: Claugh-ton (Lanc.), valley town.

CLOVELLY *B.* from *clos-belis*, the enclosure of thatched cottages. Ex.: Clovelly (Devon).

CLUN *B.* perhaps from *celyn*, the holly. Ex.: Colun, now Clun (Salop); Clun-ga-ffordd, now Clungunford (Salop), the station on the road near the Clun river.

CLWYD *B.* from *llwyd*, brown, or from Clwyd, son of Cunedda Wledig, who conquered the Gwyddel or Irish settlers in North Wales, and gave name to the river and vale of Clwyd.*

CLYDACH, CLYDAWG, CLYDEY, CLYDOG *B.* a warm or sheltered place, or from St. Clydawc, a son of King Brychan Brycheiniwg. Ex.: Clydach (Brec.); Clydey (Pemb.), etc.

CLYTHA *E.* from Cil-Ithan, St. Ithan's cell. Ex.: Clytha (Monm.)

COATES *E.* from *cot*, a hut. Ex.: Coates, 5 places, the huts.

COB *E.* perhaps from Cebba, the chief's name. Ex.: Cob-ham (Kent), Cebba's village.

COCH, GOCH *B.* red, from the colour of the rock or soil. Ex.: Ty-coch, red house; Carn-goch, red heap of stones.

COCK *E.* little. Ex.: Cock-shott (Heref. and Yorks.), little shoot or spur from a hill.

COCKAYNE, COCKERING, COCKER, COCKING *E.* from Cuccwin or Cocwin, the cock of battle, a man's name. Ex.: Cockayne (Bedf.); Cockering-ton (Linc.), Cocwin's town; Cockerham

* Iolo MSS.

(Lanc.), Cocwin's village; Cocking-ton (Devon), Cocwin's town.

CODDEN, CODI, CODS *E.* from Ceddan, possessive of Cedda, a man's name. Ex.: Codden-ham (Suff.); Codi-cote (Herts), Cedda's hut; Cods-all (Staff.), Cedda's hall. *See* Cad.

COED, GOED *B.* a wood. Ex: Coed-Arthur, Arthur's wood; Ar-goed, woodland.

COGAN, COGEN, COGGES, COGGS *B.* from Gwgan, a man's name. Ex.: Cogan (Glam.); Cogen-hoe (Northamp.), Gwgan's hill; Cogges-hall (Ess.), Gwgan's hall; Coggs (Oxf.).

COLCHESTER *E.* from *ceol-cestre,* the camp of the ships. Ex.: Colchester (Ess.), or from Coln-cestre, the camp near the Coln river.

COLD, COLE, COL *E.* from *cele,* cold, from its position on a bleak hill. Ex.: Cold-ast-tun now Coldaston (Derb.), the high situated kiln town; Cold-field Sutton (Warw.), the Sutton on the bleak field; Cole-orton (Leices.), the bleak hill town; Col-ton (Lanc.), cold town; Colewelle, now Colwall (Heref.), the cold well.

COLLUMP *E.* from *collum,* Lat., a hill. Ex.: Collump-ton (Devon), the hill town.

COLN, *E.* from *colonia,* a Roman colony. Ex: Lindum Colonia, now Lincoln; Coln river (Ess.), perhaps from its flowing past a Roman station; Colne, 6 places.

COLVA *B.* from *coll-fa,* the place of the hazel-tree. Ex: Colva (Radn.).

COMBE, the Saxon form of *cwm* (*B.*), a dingle.

COMP *E.* from *comp* or *camp,* a field of battle. Ex.: Comp-ton, 23 places, camp town.

CONGER, CONGRES E. from *cyninga,* belonging to the king. Ex.: Congers-ton (Leices.), Congres-bury (Som.), the king's town and fortification.

CONGLE B. from *congl,* a corner. Ex.: Congle-ton (Ches.), the town at the corner or bend of the ridge. [Wencel, in Saxon, has the same meaning.]

CONINGS, CONIS *E.* from *cyning,* a king. Ex.: Conings-by (Linc.), the king's abode; Conis-borough (Yorks.), the king's fortification.

COOMBE. *See* Combe and Cwm.

COP *E.* a head or hill. *See* Cap.

D. Old Danish. *G.* Greek. *L.* Latin. *N. F.* Norman French. *N.* Norse. *qu. v.* which see.

Cor, Core *B.* from *corwg,* a wicker boat or coracle. Ex.: Corbridge (Northamp.); Core-ley (Salop).

Corfe *B.* either from *gorfa,* a high place, or *corr-wy,* a dwarf stream. Ex.: Corfe river (Salop and Hants).

Cors, Cos B. from *cors,* a marsh. Ex.: Cors-ton (Som.), a marsh town; Cos-ton, 3 places, the same.

Cot, Cote, Cotten, Cottes *E.* cottage or shepherd's hut. Ex.: Cot-grave (Notts), the entrenched hut; Bram-cote (Notts), the hut among the broom; Cotten-ham (Camb.), the village of cottages; Cottes-wold (Glouc.), the wild place of huts.

Cotter *E.* from *cottar,* a kind of tenant belonging to an estate. Ex.: Cotter-stock (Northamp.), the cottar's station.

Court, Cwrt *N. F.* from *cwrt,* a court or enclosed place, pointing out the residence of the feudal lord. Ex.: Court, frequent in Heref. and other counties; Cwrt, common in South Wales.

Cove *E.* from *cof,* a small bay or recess. Ex.: Cove-hithe (Suff.), harbour cove.

Coven, Coving *E.* from *cofan,* roofed or covered. Ex.: Coventry, the covered or protected town; Coven-ey (Camb.), the covered pool; Coving-ton (Hants), covered town.

Cow *E.* indicating a pastoral site. Ex.: Cowley (Midd.), the cows' place.

Cowarn *B.* from *cae-warn,* marshy hollow. Ex.: Cowarn (Heref.).

Coy *B.* from *coed,* a wood. Ex.: Coed-ty, now Coyty (Glam.), wood house; Coy-church (Glam.), the church in the wood.

Cradley *E.* in Domesday Book called Credelai, *i.e.* Creda's place; probably from Crida or Creoda, king of Mercia. Ex.: Cradley (Heref. and Worces.). *See* Credenhill, *infra.*

Crake, Craik *E.* from *cricca,* a creek or stream. Ex.: Crakehall and Craik (Yorks.).

Cran *E.* a crane, and also a man's name and cognizance. Ex.: Cran, 21 places, all in N., E., and Mid. counties, among which is Cran-oe (Leices.), Crane's-hill.

Craw *E.* the crow. Ex.: Crawley, 3 places, Crow's place.

Cray *E.* from the Cray river, anciently *cricca,* or the creek. Ex.: Cray, 4 places; Crayford (Kent).

Creak, Crick *E.* from *cricca,* a creek. Ex.: Crick-lade (Glouc.).

Credenhill *E,* the hill of Crida, probably named from Crioda, who overcome the Silures in A.D. 586, and founded the kingdom of

Mercia. Ex.: Credenhill (Heref.), at the foot of which stood the Romano-Silurian city of Magna Castra.

CREDITON *E.* the town near the Credan river.

CREECH, CRICH, CRITCH *B.* from *crûg*, a hill. Ex.: Creach (Som.); Crich (Derb.); Critch-hill (Dorset).

CRESSAGE *E.* The local tradition explains the word as 'Christ's Oak,' but it is not known how the name originated.

CRICK, in Wales, a corruption of *crûg*. Ex.: Crick-howel (Brec.), Hywel's hill; Crick-adarn (Brec.), Cadarn's hill; Cricciaeth (Glam.), anciently Crûg-caeth,* the narrow hill.

CRIDDESHO *E.* and *D.* Crida's hill, the name of a place in Worcestershire, not now to be identified.

CROCK *B.* the Herefordshire corruption of *crûg*, a hill or heap.

CROES, GROES B. cross. Ex.: Croes-bychan (Mon.), little cross; Wern-y-groes, the alder grove of the cross, probably alluding to the crossing of two roads.

CROFT *E.* a field or appropriated land; applied also in Yorkshire to streets or roads passing through fields. Ex.: Croft, 4 places; Croft-ton (Yorks.).

CROOM *B.* from *crom*, arched or covering; hence a *crom-lech*, or covering stone. Ex.: Croome, three places in Worc., which may have been the sites of cromlechs in Druidical times.

CROS, CROSS *B.* from *croes*, a cross, from two roads intersecting each other. Ex.: Cros-by (Westm.), the abode at the cross; Cross-thwaite (Cumb.), the cleared land at the cross; Cross-twight (Norf.), the same.

CROW. *See* Craw.

CROX, CRUX, *L.* the cross or crucifix, called in Saxon the rood. Ex.: Croxton, 5 places, crucifix town; Crux-easton (Hants), crucifix Easton. [Perhaps these places were the depositaries of some of the so-called 'pieces of the true cross,' which were so highly prized in the crusading ages.]

CROZEN *E.* from *croft's end*, the termination of the appropriated land, and the beginning of the folc's land or common. Ex.: The Crozen (Heref.).

CRÛG *B.* pronounced *creeg*, a hill. Ex.: Dan-y-crûg (Brec.), under the hill; Crûg-cadarn (Brec.), the hill of Cadarn, perhaps Hu Cadarn, a famous British chief.

* Einion ap Madawc, thirteenth century.

D. Old Danish. *G.* Greek. *L.* Latin. *N.F.* Norman French. *N.* Norse. *qu. v.* which see.

CRYSE *E.* from *æc* and *rise.* Ex.: Green-cryse (Heref.), the green ascent of the oaks. *See* Acryse.

CUBI *B.* St. Cybi. Ex.: St. Cubi (Cornw.). *See* Gybi.

CUCKAM *E.* corrupted from Cwicchelm, the owner's name.* Ex.: Cuckams-ley (Berks), Cwicchelm's place.

CUSOP *B.* probably from St. Cewydd and *hwpp,* a sloping plain. Ex.: Cusop (Heref.), St. Cewydd's slope, called in Domesday Book 'Cheweshope.'

CWM *B.* a dingle or small valley in a range of hills; Greek *κόμβος*, hollowed out. In Gloucester, Wilts, Dorset, Somerset and Devon, the word occurs frequently in the Saxonised form of Comb or Combe. In the pure form, frequent in Wales and the marches.

CWN *B.* plural of *ci,* a dog. Ex.: Pwll-y-cwn (Brec.), the dogs' pool.

CWRT *B.* a mansion, the residence of the feudal lord. Ex.: Cwrt-y-gollen (Brec.), the court among the hazel-trees.

CYFARTHFA *B.* contracted from Cyfarwydd-fa, the place of Cwtta Cyfarwydd, one of the heroes of Welsh legend. Ex.: Cyfarthfa (Monm.).

CYMMAR *B.* the confluence of two streams. Ex.: Coed-cymmar (Glam.), the wood of the confluence.

CYNOG *B.* a saint's name. He was brother of Tydfil, A.D. 400.

CYNTAF *B.* St. Cyntaf, a companion of Brân the blessed, father of Caractacus.

* Cwicchelm was King of Wessex in A.D. 625.

B. British. *C.* Celtic. *E.* The Old English, commonly known as Anglo-Saxon.

D

DAD, DADL, DIDDL *E.* probably from Dodda, a famous Earl of Mercia. Ex.: Dad-lene-tun, now Dadlington (Leices.), the town of Dodda's fee-farm land; Did-lene-tun, now Diddlington (Norf.), the same.

DAG *D.* from Degga or Dagga, the owner's name, probably derived from *daeg*, the day.* Ex.: Dag-worth (Suff.), Dagga's estate; Dagen-ham (Ess.), Dagga's home; Daggan-aelh, now Dagnell (Bucks), Dagga's hall.

DAL, DALE *N.* from *dalr*, a broad valley, common in the northern counties. Ex.: Dal-ton, 14 places, dale town; Dal-bury (Derb.), the fortification in the dale; Dals-cote (Northamp.), the shepherd's hut in the dale.

DAN *B.* under. Ex.: Dan-y-parc (Brec.), under the park.

DAN, DANE, DEN *E.* forms of the word *Daene*, a Dane, and indicating Danish settlements; found almost wholly in the Danelagh or Danish England. Ex.: Dan-by (Yorks.), the Dane's abode; Dane-thorp (Camb.), the Dane's farm; Den-ton, 16 places in north-east counties, the Dane's town; Dens-hanger (North.), the Dane's hill.

DANWG *B.* from St. Tanwg. Ex.: Llan-danwg (Merion.), St. Tanwg's church.

DAR, DART *B.* a corruption of *dwr*, water. Ex.: Dar-ley (Derb.), *i.e.*, dwr-lle, the place by the water; Dar-wen (Lanc.), bright water; Darent-ford, now Dartford (Kent), the ford of the Dwr-gwent or Darent, *i. e.* the water of Gwent, a name applied to the downs of Hampshire and the neighbouring district; Dar-las-ton (Staff.), the town of the gray water, the coal shale probably giving the water its characteristic hue.

DARLIN *B.* from *dâr*, oak, and *llain*, a patch. Ex.: Darlin (Mon.), the oak patch.

DARREN *B.* a small rocky hill. Ex.: Darren-hall (Yorks.), now Darnall, the hall of the rocky hill; Darren-ton, now Darrington (Yorks.), the town of the same; Pen-y-darren (Glam.), the head of the rocky hill.

* The Danish name Dagmar, day-spring, is a parallel case.

D. Old Danish. *G.* Greek. *L.* Latin. *N.F.* Norman French. *N.* Norse. *qu. v.* which see.

DARRING. *See* Darren.

DAVEN, DAVING *B.* from *dwy-afon*, two rivers. Ex.: Daven-tre, now Daventry (Northamp.), Daven-ham (Ches.), Davington (Kent).

DAW, DOW *E.* a doe, answering to *Stag*-batch, etc. Ex.: Daw-ley (Salop), the doe's place; Doe-lis,* now Dawlish (Devon), the doe's meadows; Dow-lish (Som.), the same.

DAYLES. *See* Degley.

DDAU, TAU *B.* two. Ex.: Llan-ddau-sant (Radn.), the church of two saints; Cwm-tau-ddwr (Radn.), the dingle of two waters.

DDEINIOL *B.* St. Deiniol or Daniel. Ex.: Llan-ddeiniol (Card.), St. Deiniol's church.

DDU *B.* dark or black. Ex.: Pwll-ddu (Radn.), black pool.

DEAN, DENE *E.* a hollow; Celtic, *Den*, a small valley; Brit., *Denau*, the hollows.† Ex.: frequent in midland and south-east counties, but not found north or east of Ches. and Lanc. Ex.: Dean Forest (Glouc.), the forest of the hollows; Rotting-dean (Suss.), the hollow of Hrotan, a chief; Hasling-dene (Kent), hazel meadow hollow.

DEE *B.* from *du-wy*, dark water. Ex.: the river Dee.

DEEP *E.* deep, or low-lying. Ex.: Market-deeping (Linc.), the market town in the low-lying meadow; Deep-dale (Cumb.); Deep-ford, now Dept-ford (Kent).

DEER *E.* from *deor*, a wild animal. Ex.: Deer-hurst (Kent), the wild animals' wood.

DEGAI, *B.* from *ty*, house and *Gai*, the saint's name. Ex.: Llan-degai (Carm.), St. Gai's church house.‡

DEGFAN *B.* St. Tegfan. Ex.: Llan-degfan (Angl.), St. Tegfan's church.

DEGLEY, DAYLES *B.* from Tegla, or Thecla, a saint. Ex.: Llan-degley (Radn.), St. Thecla's church; Dayles-ford (Worc.), St. Thecla's ford.

DEGWEN *B.* from *ty*, house, and *Gwen*, the saint's name. Ex.: Llan-degwen (Mer.), St. Gwen's church-house.

DEILO *B.* from Teilo, saint and bishop. Ex.: Llandeilo-fawr (Carm.), the great church of Teilo.

* Domesday Book.

† Dean Forest is so called in the Iolo MSS.

‡ Gai is named as a companion of King Arthur.—*Lives of British Saints.*

B. British. *C.* Celtic. *E.* The Old English, commonly known as Anglo-Saxon.

DELPH, *E.* from *delfan*, a ditch. Ex.: Delph (Yorks.), the King's Delph, a raised causeway and ditch extending from Peterborough to Ramsey, the work of King Canute, A.D. 1035.

DEN. *See* Dan.

DERBY *E., D.* from *deor*, a wild animal, and *by*, an abode. Ex.: Deora-by, now Derby, the wild animals' abode, the county being mostly forest in Saxon and Norman times.

DERNDALE *E., D.* from *deoran*, of a deer, and *dalr*, a broad valley. Ex.: Derndale (Heref.), the deer's vale.

DERRY *B.* from *deru*, the oak. Ex.: the Derry hill (Monm.), oak hill; Nant-y-derry (do.), oak brook.

DERWENT *B.* probably from *dwr-gwent*, the water of 'Gwent,' or of the high lands, to which that term seems to have been generally applied. Ex.: Derwent rivers in Yorkshire and Derbys.; Derwent, Darent, or Dart, rivers in Kent and Devon.

DEVIZES *L.*; the word occurs in old writers as Devisæ, Divisæ, Devies, and Divisio, and is locally corrupted to The Vies. It is traditionally explained as arising from the division of the land between king and bishop. Ex.: Devizes (Wilts).

DEVON *B.* from *dwfn*, deep valley, plural *deifneint*, the British name of Devonshire.

DEW, DDEWI *B.* from St. Dewi or David, the apostle of Wales, sixth century. Ex.: Dew-church (Heref.), St. David's church; Dews-bury (Yorks.), St. David's fortification; Llan-ddewi, 8 places (all in Wales), St. David's church.

DIALS *B.* St. Tyeull. Ex.: St. Dial's (Monm.).

DIDDLING. *See* Dad.

DIFF *B.* from Taff, the river. Ex.: Caer-daff, now Cardiff, the Roman camp near the Taff.

DIGANWY *B.* St. Tegonwy, one of the founders of the college of Bardsey. Ex.: Diganwy (Carm.)

DRAETH, TRAETH *B.* from *traeth*, a sea-shore. Ex.: Tref-draeth (Ang.), the town or village on the sea-shore; Traeth-bach (Merion.), the little shore, being the shore of a small bay.

DYKE *E.* properly dike, an entrenchment or wall. Ex.: Offa's Dike; Foss-dike (Linc.), the entrenched wall.

DIL, DILLI, DILW, DILLING *B.* from *delw*, an idol, probably indicating ancient sites of idol-worship. Ex.: Dil-ton (Wilts), idol-town; Delw-car, now Dilliker (Westm.), the idol's pool;

Dilw-yn * (Heref.), the idol's place; Dilan-tun, now Dillington (Norf.), the idol's town; Dil-horn, *i. e.* Delw-warn (Staff.), the idol's marsh.

DIN *B.* a camp, answering to the Latin *dunum*, the Celtic *dun*, and the Saxon *tun*. Ex.: Din-mawr, now Dinmore (Heref.), great camp; Din-dwr, now Dinedor (Heref.), water camp; Din-der (Som.), the same.

DINABO *B.* St. Dinebo. Ex.: Llan-dinabo (Heref.)

DINAS *B.* a fortified hill. Ex.: Dinas-fawr (Carm.), now Dynevor, the great or chief fortified hill, being the abode of the kings of South Wales.

DINGA, DINGAT *B.* St. Dingat. Ex.: Dinga-stow (Monm.), St. Dingat's station; Llan-dingat (Carm.), St. Dingat's church.

DISCOED *B.* below a wood. Ex.: Discoed (Radn.).

DISSERTH *B.* a desert. Ex.: Disserth (Radn.).

DIT *E.* a place enclosed by an entrenchment or ditch. Ex.: Ditton, 8 places; Ditter-idge (Wilts), ridge enclosure; Dittesham (Devon), enclosed village.

DITCH *E.* an entrenchment, answering to Foss (*ffos*, *B.*), all places in both classes lying on or near a Roman road. Ex.: Ditch, 7 places.

DIX *E.* from *dic*, a dike or wall. Ex.: Dix-ton (Mon.), the town of the dike.

DOCK *E.* the dock or docken, *Rumex* of botany, still a common wild plant. Ex.: Dock-low (Heref.), dock hill; Dockan, now Docking (Norf.), the place remarkable for the abundance of dock.

DOD, DODDEN *E.* from Doddo, Earl of Mercia. The name still survives as Dodd. Ex.: 23 places, all in Mercia. *See* Dad.

DOGMAEL *B.* a saint. Ex.: St. Dogmael's (Pemb.).

DOGO *B.* St. Oudoceus, died A.D. 620. Ex.: Llan-dogo (Monm.), St. Oudoceus's church.

DOL *B.* a bend of a stream.† Ex.: Dolwyddelan (Carn.), St Gwyddelan's bend.

DON, DUN *C.* a hill; *dunum*, *L.* Ex.: frequent as a suffix, as in London, Swindon, Maldon, etc., *qu. v.*

DON, DUN, water or a river; a word belonging to the language of the Ossetians, a people of the Caucasus. The Don river, in

* In Domesday Book called Dilge, *i.e.* Delw-ga, the idol's place.

† Dr. Owen Pughe.

the country of the Don Cossacks. *Donau*, German, the Danube.* Ex.: the Don or Dun river (Yorkshire and Aberdeenshire).

DONNINGTON *E.* from Donna, a man's name, still preserved in the surname Donne. Ex.: Donnington (Heref.), Donna's town; Donnington (Leices. and Berks), the same.

DORE *B.* from *dwr*, water. Ex.: Dore (Derb. and Heref.); Dorchester (Dorset), the Saxon fortified camp on the Roman site by the Briton's water.

DORMINGTON *E.* from Dorma, the chief's name, still preserved in the surname Dormer. Ex.: Dormington (Heref.).

DORSET *E.* the *setu* or station of the Dor tribe, or the tribe that dwelt by the water.

DOVER *B.* from *dwfwr*, water. Dover (Kent); Condover (Salop).

DOUGH *B.* from St. Docheu. Ex.: Llan-dough (Glam.), St. Docheu's church.

DOW *E.* the doe. *See* Daw, *supra.*

DOWN *E.* from *dune*, a grassy hill, answering to *weald* in Kent, and *wold* in Glouc., Linc., and Yorks. Ex.: frequent in Sussex, Hants, and Wilts.

DRILLO *B.* St. Trillo. Ex.: Llan-drillo (Merion.), St. Trillo's church.

DRINDOD *B.* the Trinity, from *trinitas*, Lat. Ex.: Llan-drindod (Radn.), Trinity church.

DRINIO *B.* St. Trinio. Ex.: Llan-drinio (Mont.), St. Trinio's church.

DRUGARN *B.* from *derwydd* and *garn*, the Druid's heap. Ex.: Drugarn (Brecons.).

DUDLEY *E.* anciently Dodda-lege, or Dodelege, Dodda's land. Ex.: Dudley (Worc.).

DUDNO *B.* St. Tudnof. Ex.: Llan-dudno (Carn.), St. Tudnof's church.

DULAS *B.* anciently Duneleis,† from *dun*, a hill, and *llys*, a palace. Ex.: Dulas (Heref.), palace-hill.

DUM, DUN. *See* Don and Din.

DUR *E.* corrupted from *deor*, a wild animal. Ex.: Dur-ham, the wild beast's home.

DUTTON *C.* and *E.* from *dun*, a hill, and *tun*, a fortification. Ex.: Dutton (Ches.), anciently Duntune,‡ the fortified hill.

* Philological Proofs of the Unity of the Human Race. By A. J. Johnes.
† Domesday Book. ‡ Ibid.

DWR *B.* water. *See* Dor.

DWRWG *B.* St. Twrwg. Ex.: Llan-dwrwg (Carn.), St. Twrwg's church.

DY *B.* a house. Ex.: Dy-moch, now Dymock (Glouc.), the swine's house. *See* Ty.

DYFAN *B.* St. Dyfan, the first baptizer of the Cymry, A.D. 154.* Ex.: Merthyr Dyfan (Glam.), the martyr Dyfan's church.

DYFFRYN *B.* a river valley. Ex.: Dyffryn-clwyd (Denb.), the valley of the Clwyd.

DYFODWG *B.* from *ty*, a house, and Bodwg or Fodwg. Ex.: Llan-dy-fodwg (Glam.), St. Fodwg's church-house.

DYFRYDDWG, DYFRIWG *B.* St. Fryddwg. Ex.: Llan-dy-fryddwg (Angl.), Llan-dy-friwg (Card.), St. Fryddwg's church-house.

DYKE. *See* Dike.

DYSILIO, DYSSUL *B.* St. Silio or Sul. Ex.: Llan-dy-ssilio and Llan-dy-ssul (Mont.), St. Silio's church-house.

* Iolo MSS.

E

E, contracted from *ea* or *ey*, water. E-withington (Heref.), water withing-ton, in distinction from Church Withington; E-ton (Bucks), water town.

EA, EY, EI, IG, I *E.*; *aa*, *D.*, water, indicating the sites of places once surrounded by pools or marshes, which in many instances have now become dry land, owing to the cutting down of the forests and the drainage of the soil in agriculture. Ex.: Ea-ton, 10 places; Ey-ton, 2 places, water town; Ey-ham, now Eyam (Derb.), water village; Ey-worth (Bedf.), water estate; Ey-wick, now Eyke (Suff.), the Norseman's village by the water. As a suffix, Ea occurs in 60 places, and Ey in 4. Ex.: Ports-ea (Hants), the water port; Swans-ea (Glam.), Sweyn's water; I-field (Kent), water field; Ig-borough (Northamp.), the fortified town by the water.

EAD, ID *E.* possession; in combination forming many personal names, as Ead-win, Ead-mond, &c., in which cases it means the fortunate warrior, the fortunate protection, &c. Ex.: Eades-burh, now Eddisbury (Ches.), Ead's fortification; Iddes-leigh (Devon), Ead's place; Id-borough (Oxf.), Ead's fortification.

EAGLE, EGLE, E. the eagle, also adopted as the name of a man. Ex.: Eagle's-cliff (Dur.); Egle-ton (Rut.). *See* Ayl.

EAL, EL *E.* from *ealh*, a hall or palace. Ealhing, now Ealing (Midd.), the hall in the meadow; Eling (Hants), the same.

EAR *E.* the sea, or a large body of water. Ex.: Ears-don (Norf.), the hill near the sea; Ear-mouth, now Yarmouth (Norf. and Isle of Wight), the sea-mouth or estuary. *See* Yar.

EARDIS *E.* from *herd*, a tender of cattle. Ex.: Herdis-lege, now Eardis-ley, and Herdis-len, now Eardis-land (Heref.), the herd's meadow and *len*, or fee-farm land.

EARL *N.* *jarl* (pron. yarl), the only Norse title of nobility, meaning leader, which superseded the Saxon title *thegn*, and still remains as the third rank of the peerage; the only title in England which is earlier in date than the Norman conquest.

D. Old Danish. *G.* Greek. *L.* Latin. *N.F.* Norman French. *N.* Norse. *qu. v.* which see.

Ex.: 8 places, all in midland counties, except Earl-ham (Norf.), the earl's dwelling.

EARN *E.* a name for the eagle, and thence a chief's name. Ex.: Earn-ley (Suss.), eagle's meadow; Earns-hill (Som.), eagle's hill.

EAST *E.* the eastern of two places with similar root names in the same district. Ex.: 36 places, of which 13 are East-on, east town.

EASTER, EOSTR *E.* from the Saxon goddess Eostre, whose festival was, it is said, changed by the Christian missionaries to the commemoration of the Resurrection. The places thus named were probably the sites of the worship of the goddess. Ex.: Easter-ey, now Eastrey (Kent), Eostre's pool; Eastr-op (Hants), Eostre's thorp or farm.

EBB, EBBE, EBBER, EBR *E.* Ebbe, a female saint.* Ex.: St. Ebbe (Glouc.); Ebben-ey, now Ebony (Kent), St. Ebbe's pool; Ebbes-bourn (Wilts), Ebbe's brook; Ebbers-ton (Yorks.), Ebbe's town; Ebring-ton (Glouc.), the same. *See* Abb.

EC, ECK *E.* from Ecca, a man's name.† Ex.: Ec-ton (Northam.), Ecca's town; Eckley, Ecca's meadow.

ECCLES *G.* from ἐκκλησία, a place of assembly, afterwards a church. Ex.: Eccles (Lanc.); Eccles-field (Yorks.).

ECHING *B.* the narrow places. Ex.: The islands anciently so called in the Bristol Channel, now known by the Norse names of Steep and Flat Holmes.

ECKING *E.* from Ecca and *incga.* Ex.: Ecking-ton (Derb.), the town of Ecca's children.

ED *E.* *See* Ead.

EDBUR *E.* from Eadburh, feminine Eadburghu, the happy fortress, a personal name. Ex.: Edbur-ton (Suss.), Eadburh's town.

EDDLE, EDDLES *E.* cor. from *æthel,* noble, a man's name. Ex.: Edlas-ton (Derb.), Æthel's town; Eddles-borough (Bucks), Æthel's fortified town. *See* Æthel.

EDEN, EDING *E.* from Edwin, king of Northumbria. Ex.: Edens-or (Derb.), Edwin's over or hill; Eding-all (Staff.), Edwin's hall.

EDEYRN *B.* founder of a college of 300 'saints' at Llan-edeyrn (Glam.), Edeyrn's church.

* Ebbe was daughter of King Ethelfrid, A.D. 660.—*Bede.*

† Ecca was Bishop of Hereford, A.D. 747.

EDG, EDGE *E.* from *ecg*, a ridge. Ex.: Edg-cott (Northam.), the shepherd's hut on the ridge; Blackston-edge (Yorks.), the ridge of black rock.

EDMON *E.* corrupted from Ædelmen, belonging to Ædelm. Ex.: Edmon-ton (Midd.), called Ædelmentun in Domesday Book.

EDMUND *E.* happy protection, the name of the famous king of the East Angles, afterwards canonised. Ex.: St. Edmund's-bury (Suff.), Edmund's fortified town; Edmund-thorp (Leic.), Edmund's farm.

EDVIN *E.* anciently Gedefen.* Ex.: Edvin Ralph and Edvin Loach (Heref.). *See* Ged, *infra.*

EDWIN *E.* the happy victor. *See* Eden.

EFFINGHAM *E.* from *Effa* and *incgaham*, meaning the home of the children of Effa or Uffa. Ex.: Effingham (Surrey). *See* Uffa.

EG, EGG, EGGIN, EGRE *E.* from *æge*, water. Ex.: Eg-dean (Suss.), water hollow; Egges-ford (Devon), the ford of the stream; Eggin-ton (Derb.), water town; Egre-mont (Cumb.), the mount by the water.

EGLWYS *B.* from ἐκκλησία, a church, indicating a church built on a site *not* sacred in heathen times. Ex.: Eglwys-cymin (Carm.), the church on the common hill.

EGWAD *B.* a saint. Ex.: Llan-egwad (Carm.), St. Egwad's church.

EINION *B.* a king's name. Ex.: Llan-fair-caer-Einion (Mont.), St. Mary's church in Einion's camp or town.

EL *E.* *See* Ayl.

ELBER *E.* *See* Albur.

ELDER *E.* the elder, *Sambucus* of botany; or from Aldred, a Saxon saint.

ELIAN *B.* a saint. Ex.: Llan-elian (Angl.), St. Elian's ch.

ELIW *B.* a saint. Ex.: Llan-eliw (Brec.), St. Eliw's ch.

ELLER, ORL *E.* from *aler*, *alr*, or *orl*, the alder-tree, still called orl in Herefords. Ellerton (Northum.), Orleton (Heref.), the town among the alders.

ELLES *E.* from King Ella. *See* Alling.

ELLY *B.* St. Elli, sixth century. Ex.: Llanelly (Brec. and Carm.), St. Elli's church.

* Domesday Book.

ELM *E.* the elm-tree, *Ulmus* of botany. Ex.: 23 places.

ELS *E.* from king Ella. *See* Alling.

ELT *E.* from *eald*, old. Ex.: Elt-ham (Kent), old home.

ELVA, ELVAN, ELVE, ELVIS, ELVING, *E.* from St. Elvan. Ex.: Elvas-ton (Derb.), Elvan's town; Elve-den (Suff.), Elva's hollow; St. Elvis (Pemb.); Elvan-ton, now Elving-ton (Yorks.), Elvan's town. Perhaps Elvan is only an Anglicised form of Elwedd or Elwy, a British saint's name.

ELWEDD *B.* a saint. Ex.: Llan-elwedd (Rad.), St. Elwedd's church.

ELY *E.* from *eel* and *ey*. Ex.: Ely (Camb.), the island of eels.

EM *E.* from Emma. *See* Am.

EMBER, from King Ambrosius. *See* Amber.

EMBLE, EML, *N.* from *embla*, the alder-tree. Ex.: Emble-ton (Durham), alder-town; Emley (Yorks.), alder place.

EMMING *E.* from Emma and *incga*. Ex.: Emming-ton (Oxf.), the town of Emma's descendants.

EMNETH *E.* from the name of Edmund king of East Angles and a martyr, and *hythe*, a harbour. Ex.: Emneth (Norf.), Edmund's harbour.

END, EN *E.* the end of an estate or a ridge of hills. Ex.: End, frequent in Worc.; En-field (Midd.), the end of the open country or field, or En-fen, the end of the fen or marsh.

ENDER *E.* perhaps from King Penda. Ender-by (Leic. and Linc.), Penda's abode.

ENGLE *E.* English. Ex.: Englefield (Berks), the scene of the great battle in A.D. 871, in which the men of Wessex defeated the Danes with great slaughter.

EP, EPS *E.* from *æps*, an aspen tree. Ex.: Ep-worth (Linc.), aspen estate; Eps-om (Surr.), æps ham, or aspen village.

EPPES *E.* from *æps*, an aspen.

EPPING *E.* from Gippan, possessive of Gippa, a man's name. Ex.: Epping-forest, Gippa's forest. *See* Ips.

ERDING *E.* from Cerdic, a man's name. Ex.: Erdington (Warw.), Cerdic's town.

ERMING *E.* *See* Irming.

ERVAN *B.* *See* Irfon.

ERWOOD *B.* *recte* Erwd, the ploughed land in the wood. Ex.: Erwd (Brec.).

EVANJOBB *B.* anciently Evanchop, or *Evan's cop*, i. e. Evan's hill-top. Ex.: Evanjobb (Rad.)

EVE, EVEN, EVES, EVING, HEVEN, HEVER, HEVING *E.* from *efes*, brink or margin. Ex.: 17 places, all in midland counties; Eve-don (Linc.), the brink of the hill; Even-load (Worc.), the brink of the way; Ever-ton (Lanc.), the town on the brink; Eves-ham (Worc.), the home on the brink (of the Avon); Eves-batch (Heref.), the path on the brink; Evington (Leic.); Hever (Kent), the brink.

EW, EWELM, from *æwelm*, the fountain-head of a stream. Ex.: Ewell (Surr.); Ewelm (Oxf.).

EWIN *B.* from St. Ieuan or John. Ex.: St. Ewin (Glouc.).

EWYAS *B.* anciently Euas, perhaps from *yw ys*, the place of the yew trees. Ex.: Ewyas (Heref.); the adjoining district of Crickhowell was called Ystradyw, yew valley.*

EX *E.* from *acs*, an ash tree. Ex.: the river Exe (Devon); Exan-cestre, now Exeter, the fortified town by the Exe; Ex-minster, the monastery by the Exe.

* Iolo MSS.

F

In British words, the single *f* is always sounded as *v* in English; the double *ff* as *f*.

FA, MA, *B.* a place. Ex.: Bleddfa. (Radnors.), Bleddyn's place*; Gwydd-fa (Carnarv.), conspicuous place; Ma-llwyd (Merion.), the brown or gray place.†

FABON *B.* St. Mabon. Ex.: Llan-fabon (Glam.), St. Mabon's church.

FAC, FAKEN. *See* Fax.

FAES *B.* a field. Ex.; Llan-faes (Brec.), church-field.

FAGAN *B.* St. Fagan. Ex.: St. Fagan's (Glam.).

FAIR, MAIR *B.* the Virgin Mary. Ex.: 14 places, all in Wales and Mon., except Llan-fair-gadr-din (Salop), now Llanfair-waterdin, St. Mary's church at the camp, seat, or station. Ex.: Llan-fair-ar-y-bryn (Carmar.), St. Mary's church on the hill.

FAITH *E.* a female saint. Ex.: St. Faith (Midd.).

FAL. *See* Fell.

FALKEN, FAULK, FALCON, FAWK *E.* from the possessive case of Falk, Foulk, or Fulke, a man's name, the *falcon* being his cognizance. Ex.: Falken-ham (Suff.); Faulk-bourn (Ess.), Falk's brook; Falcon-bridge; Fawk-ham, Folkes-ton (Kent). Thence also the surnames Fawkes, Vaux, and Ffoulkes. *See* Folk.

FALKING *E.* from Falk and *incga*. Ex.: Falking-ham (Linc.), the home of Falk's descendants.

FAN *B.* high. *See* Ban.

FAPLEY *B.* from St. Mabli. Ex.: Llan-fapley (Mon.), St. Mabli's church.

FAR, FARE, FAIR *E.* from *faer*, a way. Ex.: 10 places in Mid. and S. counties. Ex.: Far-leigh (Kent), way-side place; Fare-ham (Hants), the home by the way; Fair-field (Kent), the field by the way.

* Bleddyn was the name of several bards, A.D. 1090–1260.
† Richards' Welsh Dictionary.

B. British. *C.* Celtic. *E.* The Old English, commonly known as Anglo-Saxon.

FARM *E.* from *feorm*, a farm. Ex.: Farm-borough (Som.), the fortified town of the farm.

FARING, FARN, FERRING *E.* from *fearn*, a fern, the *Filix* of botany. Ex.: 22 places, of which there are—Faring-don, 3 places, ferny camp *; Farn-hurst (Suss.), ferny wood; Ferring (Suss.), the ferny place.

FARTHING *E.* from *feording*, the fourth part. Ex.: Farthing-hoe (Northam.), the hill portion of an estate which was divided among four persons; Win-farthing (Norf.), victory fourth part, the estate having probably been won in a battle.

FAVERS, FEVERS *E.* perhaps from Fava or Fyva, a man's name. Ex.: Favers-ham or Fevers-ham (Kent), Fyva's home.

FAW, FOW, VOW *B.* from *ffau*, the den of a wild beast. Ex.: Faw-le, now Fawley (Heref.), the place of the den; Faw-wy, now Foy (ditto), the water near the den; Fow-ey (Cornw.), the same; Fown-hope (Heref.), the slope of the den; Vow (ditto), the den.

FAWK. *See* Falken.

FAX, FAC, FAKEN, FECKEN *E.* from *feax*, hair. Ex.: Hali-fax (Yorks.), holy hair; Fac-comb (Hants), hair dingle; Faken-ham (Norf.), Fecken-ham (Worc.), hair village. The allusion is probably to some forgotten legend of the hair of a saint working miracles.

FEATHER. *See* Fether.

FECHAN *B.* little, the feminine of *bychan*.

FECKEN. See Fax.

FEDW *B.* the birch-tree. *See* Bedw.

FEDWY *B.* St. Medwy. Ex.: Llan-fedwy (Glam.).

FELIS, FELS, FELIX, FLIX *L.* from St. Felix, first bishop of the East Angles, A.D. 636. Ex.: Felis-kirk (Yorks.), Fels-thorp (Norf.), Felix-stow (Suff.), Flix-borough (Linc.), respectively the church, farm, station, and fortified town of Felix.

FELL, FAL *D.* from *fjeld*, a range of hills. Ex.: frequent in N. Yorks., Camb., and S. Scotland.

FELP *E.* from Philip. Ex.: Felp-ham (Suss.), Philip's home.

FELT *E.* from *feltan*, a garden or inclosure. Ex.: Felt-ham (Midd.), the home in the garden; Felt-ton (Heref.), the town in the garden.

* Anglo-Saxon Chronicle.

D. Old Danish. *G.* Greek. *L.* Latin. *N. F.* Norman French. *N.* Norse. *qu. v.* which see.

Fen, Fenny, Fins *E.* from *fenn,* a fen. Ex.: Fen-ditton (Camb.), the enclosure in the fen; Fenny Stratford (Bucks), the ford of the fen on the Roman road; Fins-bury (Midd.), the fortification in the fens.

Ferri *E.* from *feran,* a ferry. Ex.: Ferri-by (Lincolns.), the abode at the ferry.

Festiniog *B.* perhaps from *mesen,* an acorn, and *wg,* a district. Ex.: Festiniog (Merion.), the district of acorns.

Feth, Feath *D.* from Feada, a man's name.* Ex.: Fetherstonhaugh (Northum.), Featherston (Yorks.), Feth-ern (Glouc.). *See* Haugh and Ern.

Ffili *B.* a saint. Ex.: Caer-ffili (Glam.), Fili's Roman camp.

Ffin *B.* a boundary; *finis,* Latin. Ex.: Capel-y-ffin (Brec.), the chapel on the boundary, between Heref. and Brec.

Ffordd *B.* a road. Ex.: Pen-y-gau-ffordd (Brec.), the hill of the woodland road.

Ffraed, Ffread *B.* St. Bride or Bridget. *See* Bride.

Ffraw *B.* fair or gentle. Ex.: Aber-ffraw (Angl.), the estuary of the gentle river, answering to *garw* or *arrow,* rough or impetuous. *See* Arrow.

Ffrwd *B.* a stream. Ex.: Gwaun-ffrwd (Brec.), the moor near the stream.

Ffynnon *B.* a spring or well. Ex.: Ffynnonau (Brec.), the wells.

Fi, Fife, Five, *See* Fy.

Field. *E.* or *N.* from *feld,* the open country; or *felde,* grassy land. Ex.: Field Dalling (Norf.), Dalla's field; Merri-field (Warw.), St. Mary's field; Brad-field (Yorks.), the broad field.

Figan *B.* from *mign,* a bog, or from St. Meigan. Ex.: Llan-figan (Brec.).

Fihangel *B.* from *mihangel,* the archangel Michael. Ex.: Llanfihangel, 35 places, St. Michael's church.

Fil *E.* from *feld,* a field. Ex.: Fil-by (Norf.), field abode.

Fin. *See* Fen.

Finch *E.* from *finc,* the linnet. Ex.: Fincan-field, now Finchingfield (Ess.), linnet's country; Finch-ham (Norf.).

Firth *D.* from *fiord,* an arm of the sea. Ex.: the Solway Firth, corrupted to Frith; and frequent in Norway.

Fis, Fish, Fisher, *E. fisc,* a fish, indicating fishing stations. Ex.: Fis-gard (Pemb.), fishing inclosure; Fish-bourn (Suss.), fishbrook; Fisher-ton (Wilts), fisher's town.

* Feada, a Dane, an officer of Hardicanute, was killed at Worcester, A.D. 1042.

B. British. *C.* Celtic. *E.* The Old English, commonly known as Anglo-Saxon.

FLAD, FLED *E.* from *flede*, a flood, or a site liable to be flooded. Ex.: Flad-bury (Worc.), flood fortification; Fled-borough.

FLAM, flame, hence a beacon or lighthouse. Ex.: Flamburgh,* now Flamborough (Yorks.), beacon fortress; Flamstead (Herts), beacon station.

FLAN *E.* an arrow, and also a man's name. Ex.: Flanesborough (Northam.), Flan's fortified town.

FLAX *E.* from Flecc or Flacc, a man's name, still preserved in the surname Fleck. Ex: Flax-ley (Glouc.), Flacc's land.

FLED. *See* Flad.

FLEET *E.* from *fleot*, a naval station. Ex.: 3 times as a prefix; 4 times as a suffix; Herring-fleet (Suffolk), Swine-fleet (Yorks.), Sweyn's naval station; By-fleet (Surr.), the naval station near the Danish village.

FLETCH *N. F.* from *fleche*, an arrow. Ex.: Fletching (Surr.), arrow-meadow, or bowman's place.

FLET, FLIT *E.* from *flet*, a cottage. Ex.: Flet-ton (Hants), cottage town; Flit-wick (Bedf.), cottage village.

FLIX. *See* Felis.

FOCHRHIW *B.* anciently Bochrhiw-carn, which is translated, in the *Lives of British Saints*, 'the check on a stony road.' Ex.: Fochrhiw (Glam.), the scene of a combat in which King Arthur fought.

FOIST *B.* St. Fwyst. Ex.: Llan-foist (Mon.), St. Fwyst's church.

FOLD, FOLE *E.* from *folde*, a fold. Ex.: Deer-fold (Heref.), now Darvel, the enclosure for deer; Folds-hill, now Foleshill (Warw.), the folds on the hill.

FOLK, FOLKES *E.* from Falk or Foulk, a Norman chief's name. Ex.: Folk-ton (Yorks.), Folkes-ton (Kent), Folke (Dorset), &c.

FOLLY *E.* from *folc-ley*, the people's or public land, held by all persons in common on paying chief rent to the king. Ex.: Folc-ley, now Folly, a common name of a piece of land near a town.

FONT *L. fons*, a fountain or spring. Ex.: Font-hill (Wilts), spring hill.

FORCE *D.* from *fors*, a waterfall. Ex.: Only in Cumb. and West., and sometimes corrupted into Foss.

* Traditionally said to be named from Ida the flame-bearer, a Norse chief.

D. Old Danish. *G.* Greek. *L.* Latin. *N. F.* Norman French. *N.* Norse. *qu. v.* which see.

Ford *E.* a shallow part of a river where a road crosses. Ex.: 10 places as a prefix, and frequent as a suffix, all in Mid., E. and S. counties. Ex.: Ford-ham, 3 places, the home or village at the ford; Bath-ford (Som.), the ford by the bathing-place; Rom-ford (Ess.), the ford of the Romans.

Ford, from *ffordd,* Brit., a road. Ex.: rare; Haverford-west, *i.e.* Gafr-ffordd-gwest, the inn on the goat's road.

Fore *E.* in front of. Ex.: Fore-mark (Derbys.), in front of the boundary.

Forn. *See* Farn.

Foss *B.* from *ffoss,* a ditch or entrenchment. Ex.: occurs only in Yorks., Linc., Camb., and Oxf.; Foss-dyke, the road defended by a ditch and a mound; Foss-town, now Foston, ditch town.

Fown *B.* *See* Faw.

Fox *E.* from *folces,* belonging to the people. Ex.: Fox-ley (Heref.), the folk's land. *See* Folly. (*Tod* is the Saxon word for a fox.)

Foy *B.* *See* Faw.

Frais, Fries, Fris, Frys, *E.* from Freya or Friga, the Saxon Venus, to whom Freya's daeg, or Friday, was dedicated. Ex.: Frais-thorp (Yorks.), Freya's farmhouse; Fries-thorp (Linc.), the same; Fris-by (Leic.), Freya's abode; Frys-ton (Yorks.), Freya's town.

Framp, Framling, Freming *E.* from *frem,* foreign. Ex.: 9 places, all probably the settlements of foreigners, among which are—Fram-field (Suss.), the foreigner's field; Framling-ham (Suff.), the foreigner's village, *ling* meaning state or condition, as in weak-ling, found-ling, etc.; Fremingham (Yorks.), the home of the children of the stranger.

Frensham *D.* and *E.* from *Frene* and *hám.* Ex.: Frenes-ham, now Frensham (Surr.). (Frene is mentioned as one of the chiefs of the invading Danes in A.D. 871.—*A. S. Chronicle.*)

Frethorn *E.* anciently Fethan-lea,* Feada's meadow. Ex.: Frethorn (Glouc.).

Friday *E.* from Fridu or Frideswide, a king's daughter and saint, A.D. 740. Ex.: Friday-thorp (Yorks.), St. Frida's farmhouse.

* Anglo-Saxon Chronicle, A.D. 584.

B. British. *C.* Celtic. *E.* The Old English, commonly known as Anglo-Saxon.

FRITH, corrupted from *firth*, *qu. v.*

FRITH, *B.* said by Camden ('Magna Britannia') to mean a wood. Ex.: Chapel-en-le-frith (Derb.), chapel in the wood.

FROME, FROOM *B.* from *ffraw*, fair. Ex.: Frome river (Som.); * Froom river (Heref.).

FROTHER. *See* Brother, *supra.*

FRYERN *E.* belonging to Friars. Ex.: Fryern Barnet (Midd.), the friar's Barnet, in distinction from East and Chipping, *i. e.* Market Barnet.

FRYNACH, *B.* St. Brynach.† Ex.: Llan-frynach (Brec.), St. Brynach's church.

FRYS. *See* Frais.

FUL, FULLAN *E.* foul or dirty. Ex.: 10 places, among which are Ful-brook (Oxf.), and Ful-beck (Linc.), the dirty brook; Fullan-ig (Yorks.), now Fulneck, the dirty water; Fullan-ham (Midd.), now Ful-ham, the village in the dirty place.

FULMODESTAN *E.* the rock of Fulmod. Ex.: Fulmodestan (Norf.).

FUNDEN, FUNTING *E.* perhaps a corruption of fountain. Ex.: Funden-hall (Norf.), fountain hall; Funting-ton (Suss.), fountain town.

FY, FI, FIVE, FIFE *E.* from Fyva, the owner's name. Ex.: Fy-field (Berks) and Fi-field (4 places), Fyva's field; Five-head (Som.), Fyva's hut or hill; Fife-head (Dorset), the same.

* Asser the monk, quoted by Richards. † Rees' Lives of British Saints.

D. Old Danish. *G.* Greek. *L.* Latin. *N. F.* Norman French. *N.* Norse. *qu. v.* which see.

G

GA *B.* from *gwi*, water. Ex.: Aber-ga-venny (Monm.), the estuary of the Fenni, or of the mountain water. *See* Venny.

GAD, GADE, GADDES *B.* from *gâd* or *câd*, a battle. Ex.: Gads-hill (Kent), battle hill; Gade river (Leic.); Gaddes-by, an abode by that river.

GADFAN *B.* St. Cadfan, of Britanny, A.D. 524, a companion of Padarn. Ex.: Llan-gadfan (Mont.), St. Cadfan's church. *See* Badarn.

GAFFO *B.* St. Gafo. Ex.: Llan-gaffo (Angl.)

GAIN *B.* from St. Cain (Cornish, Keyn). Ex.: Llan-gain (Carm.), the church of St. Cain. *See* Cain, *supra.*

GALLT *B.* a steep wooded place. *See* Allt.

GAMBLE, GAMLIN *E.* from *gamel*, old; Danish, *gamle*, also a man's name. Ex.: Gamble-by (Cumb.), Gamel's abode; Gamelsthorp (Cumb.), Gamel's farm; Gamelan-hay, now Gamlinghay (Cumb.), Gamel's enclosure. Hence the Scotch surname Gemmel.

GAMMARCH *B.* St. Cammarch. Ex.: Llan-gammarch (Brec.), St. Cammarch's church.

GAN *B.* from *genau*, a mouth or opening of a pass. Ex.: Llangan (Carm.), the church in the opening; Llan-ganna (Glam.), the same; Gana-rhiw, now Ganarew (Heref.), the sloping path in the opening. Or it may be from Gunna *N.*, and *rhiw B.*, indicating the settlement among the Britons of some Norse rover, bearing a name which variously appears as Gun, Gunn, Gunnr, and Gunna. *See* Gun, *infra.*

GAP *E.* an opening.

GAR *E.* from *gara*, a promontory. Ex.: Gar-forth (Yorks.), the road by the promontory.

GARBOLD *E.* bold in war, a man's name, still preserved in the name Garrold. Ex.: Garbold's-ham (Norf.), Garbold's home.

GARD *D.* from *gaard*, an enclosure, hence garden. Ex.: Fisgard (Pemb.), the fishery enclosure.

GARMON *B.* St. Germanus. Ex.: Clas-garmon (Rad.), St. Germanus's cloister.

GARMOND *D.* a man's name. Ex.: Garmonds-hay (Dur.), Garmond's enclosure.*

GARNONS *N. F.* from Robert de Garnon, the first Norman lord.† Ex.: Garnons (Heref.).

GARS *E.* from *gers*, grass. Ex.: Gars-ton (Berks), grass town; Gars-don (Wilts), grassy-hill; Garsan-tun, now Garsington (Oxf.), grass town.

GARTH *B.* a hill or promontory. Ex.: Garth-brengig (Brec.), the Frenchman's hill.

GARTH *N.* from *gardr*, a field or enclosure. Only occurs in Yorkshire and the Norse-colonised districts. Ex.: Ays-garth (Yorks.), the field of the gods, or the hedged field. *See* Ais, Hag, Hay.

GARVES *N. F.* from Gervase, the lord's name. Ex.: Garves-ton (Norf.), Gervase's town.

GARWAY *E.* from *gyrwe*, a marsh. Ex.: Garway (Heref.), the marsh; or from *garw* (*B.*), a rough place.

GAT, GATE *B.* from *gadr*, a seat or a high hill. Ex.: Gat-comb (Glouc.), the dingle by the high hill; Gate-le (Norf.), the hill place, the hill top.

GATES *E.* from *gaet*, a goat. Ex.: Gates-head (Dur.), called by Flor. Wig. 'caput capræ.'

GATHAN *B.* St. Cathan. Ex.: Llangathan (Carm.), St. Cathan's church.

GATTERTOP *E.* and *B.*; anciently Gatterede-hope,‡ probably from Guthred, the owner's name, and *hope*, a sloping plain. Ex.: Gattertop (Heref.).

GATTOC *B.* from Cattwg, saint and bishop. Ex.: Llan-gattoc (Mon.), St. Cattwg's church.

GAY. *See* Ged.

GAY, suffix, *N. F.*, a form of *haie*, or enclosure. Ex.: Gamlin-gay (Suf.), Gamelin's entrance; Shin-gay (Camb.), Sheen's enclosure. *See* Shin.

GED, GAY, as prefix, *E.* from *gaed*, a goad, also a man's name. Ex.: Gaedan-ey, now Gedney (Linc.), Gaeda's water; Gede-fen, now Edvin (Heref.), Gaeda's fen; Gay-ton, 6 places.

* Gurmundus, a Norse captain, in A.D. 590, overcame Careticus in battle.—*Galfridus Monm.*

† Domesday Book.

‡ Domesday Book; and Dugdale's Monasticon.

D. Old Danish. *G.* Greek. *L.* Latin. *N. F.* Norman French. *N.* Norse. *qu. v.* which see.

GEDDING, GIDDING *E.* from *gaed*, a man's name (Geddes is still a surname in Scotland), and *incga*, children. Ex.: Gedding-ton (Northam.), and Gidding (Hants), the town and the possession of Gaed's children.

GEDWYN B. from St. Caedwyn. Ex.: Llan-gedwyn (Denb.), St. Caedwyn's church.

GEINWYN *B.* St. Heinwyn. Ex.: Llan-geinwyn (Angl.), St. Heinwyn's church.

GELE *B.* the river Gelau, *i. e.* of horse-leeches. Ex.: Aber-gele (Denb.), the estuary of that river.

GELLI *B.* *See* Celli.

GENAU *B.* a mouth, or opening between hills. Ex.: Llan-fihangel-Genau-'r-glyn (Mont.), St. Michael's church in the mouth of the glen.

GENNY *B.* St. Cannau. Ex.: Llan-genny (Glam.), St. Cannau's church.

GENYDD *B.* St. Cenydd. Ex.: Llan-genydd (Glam.), St. Cenydd's church.

GERSEG *B.* *See* Cerseg.

GIDDING. *See* Gedding.

GILL, a narrow glen, perhaps from *gyll*, *B.*, the hazel tree, which grows in such places. Ex.: common in Cumberland and Westmoreland.

GILLING *B.* from Gelinga, a man's name. Ex.: Gilling (Yorks.), from Gelingan, belonging to Gelinga; Gilling-ham, 3 places, anciently Gelinge-ham,* Gelinga's home.

GILMOR *C.* a man's name, and still a surname in the Scottish low-lands. Ex.: Gilmor-ton (Leic.), Gilmor's town.

GILS, GILES, GILLI *E.* from St. Giles. Ex.: 7 places, among which are Gils-ton (Herts), Giles's-town; Gilli-gate (Durh.), Giles's gate; Giles-ton (Glam.), Giles's town; Gil-crux (Cumb.), Giles's cross.

GLADES *B.* from St. Gwladys, daughter of King Brychan Bry-cheiniog. Ex.: Glades-tre (Radn.), Gwladys' town.

GLAIS, *B.* from *glâs*, blue or green. Ex.: Glais-dale (Yorks.), the green dale.

GLAMORGAN *B.* from *glann*, a bank, *môr*, sea, and *ga*, place: the place at the sea-shore.

* Domesday Book.

B. British. *C.* Celtic. *E.* The Old English, commonly known as Anglo-Saxon.

GLAN, GLAND *B.* from *glann*, a river's bank. Ex.: Glan-grwyney (Brec.), the bank of the Grwyney; Gland-ford (Norf.), the way (ffordd) on the bank.

GLASBURY *B.* and *E.* probably a corruption of Gwladys-burh, the Saxon station named from the British saint, a daughter of Brychan Brycheiniog, the king of the district.

GLASTON *E.* anciently Glaesting, from the British word *glâstennen*, the holm oak. Ex.: Glaesting-burh, now Glastonbury (Som.), the fortification of the holm oak, or of the place named from that tree by the Britons. St. David retired hither A.D. 530.

GLEM *E.* from St. Clement. Ex.: Glem-ham (Suff.), the home of Clement.

GLEN *E.* from *glynn B.*, or *gleann C.* a narrow valley. Ex.: 2 places, Glen-field and Glen-magna (Leic.).

GLEWS *B.* from St. Glewis. Ex.: Glews-ton (Heref.), St. Glewis' town.

GLODDFA *B.* from *cloddfa*, an excavation. Ex.: Pen-y-gloddfa (Card.), the head of the excavation.

GLOU *B.* from *gloyw*, bright or clear. Ex.: Glou-cester, anciently Caer-gloyw, the fortress near the clear water.

GLYN, GLYNDE *B.* from *glynn*, a narrow valley. Ex.: Glyn-nedd (Glam.), the narrow valley of the river Nedd; Glynn, now Glynde (Suss.).

GOAD, GOD, GODE, GOODER, GOS *E.* from Godu or Godgifu, God's-gift, a woman's name. Ex.: Goad-by (Leic.), Godu's abode; God's-hill (Wight), Godu's hill; Godu-rich, Good-rich (Heref.), Godu's *ric* or rule *; Gooders-ton (Norf.), Godu's town; Godu's-well, now Gos-well (Midd.).

GOAT, GOT *E.* from *gaet*, a goat, probably the cognisance of the owner. Ex.: Goat-hurst (Som.), the goat's wood; Got-ham (Notts), the goat's village.

GODDARD *E.* from Godred, good in counsel, a man's name.

GODDING, GOODNES *E.* from Godwin, the good victory, a famous name among the Saxons. Ex.: Godwin's town, now God-dington (Oxf.); Goodnes-ton (Kent), the same.

GODMAN, GOODMAN *E.* from Godmund, one whose protection is good, a man's name. Ex.: Godman-chester (Hunts), God-

* The manor belonged to Godu, sister to Edward the Confessor.

mund's fortification; Goodman-ham (Yorks.), Godmund's home.

GOF *B.* from *gof*, a smith, or from *gogof*, a cave. Ex.: Pwll-y-gof (Denb.), the smith's pool, or the pool near the cave.

GOLD *E.* the metal. Both Britons and Saxons wore golden ornaments, probably formed from the gold found in the streams; and it may be that the sites of some of these gold-washings are indicated by the names. Ex.: Gold-cliff (Monm.).*

GOOD. *See* Goad.

GOP. *See* Copp.

GOR *B.* a choir or cathedral. Ex.: Ban-gor, 2 places, the high choir.

GORLLWYN *B.* probably from *cors*, a bog or marsh, and *llwyn*, a copse. Ex.: Gorllwyn (Monm.), the copse in the marsh.

GOS *E.* the gorse, *Ulex* of botany, still a common plant. Ex.: Gos-field (Ess.), Gos-beck (Suff.). Or it may be a contraction of Goda's. *See* Goad.

GOT. *See* Goat.

GOUD *E.* perhaps from the woad, *Isatis* of botany, a plant used by the Britons in the production of the blue dye wherewith they stained their bodies.† Ex.: Goud-hurst (Kent), woad wood.

GOWER *B.* from *gwyr*, crooked, probably in allusion to the line of coast. Ex.: Gower (Glam.).

GOY *B.* corrupted from *coed*, qu. v.

GRABAN *B.* a man's name, perhaps the herald to King Maelgwn, mentioned in the life of St. Padarn.‡ Ex.: Llandilo-Graban (Radn.), the church of St. Teilo, built by Graban.

GRAFF, GRAF, GRAVEN, GRAVES *E.* a ditch or moat.§ Ex.: Graff-ham (Suss.), the moated home: Graf-ton (Heref.), the moated town; Graven-ey (Kent), the moated place by the water or river; Graves-end (Kent), the end of the ditch or moat, or the fortified end of the cultivated land. *See* End, *supra.*

GRAIN, GRENO *D.* from Grena or Grana, a man's name. Ex.: Grain-thorp and Grains-by (Linc.), the farm and the abode of Grena; Greno-side (Yorks.), Grena's *hide* (a measure of land), *i.e.* estate.

* 'So called,' says Giraldus Cambrensis, 'because the cliff is golden-hued from the reflection of the sun on it, and the peasantry believe that the rock contains gold.'

† Cæsar's Commentaries.

‡ Rees' 'Lives of Cambro-British Saints.'

§ Lord Clarendon.

B. British. *C.* Celtic. *E.* The Old English, commonly known as Anglo-Saxon.

GRAMPOUND *N. F.*, *D.*, and *B.*, locally derived from *grand pont*, great bridge, in support of which derivation the bridge on the arms of the borough is quoted; but the analogy of Grandborough and other names suggests rather a Dano-British etymon, *quasi* Granda's pont. *See* Grand and Pont *infra*.

GRAND, GRANT *E.* from the owner's name. Ex.: Granda's burh, now Grand-borough (Bucks and Warw.); Grandison Stretton (Heref.), Granda's street-town; Grant-chester (Camb.), Granta's fortified Roman town.

GRANGE *E.* the farm-house of a monastery. Ex.: Wigmore-grange (Heref.), the grange of Wigmore monastery. The word always indicates the neighbourhood of ancient monastic houses.

GRANNOG *B.* from St. Crannog, a contemporary of St. Patrick. Ex.: Llan-grannog (Card.), St. Crannog's church.

GRAT *E.* great. Ex.: Grat-wick (Staff.), great village.

GRAVEN, GRAVES. *See* Graff.

GREAT, GREET *E.* great. *See* Grat.

GREEN, GREN, GRIN *E.* green. Ex.: Green-wich (Kent), the green *wich* or village in the verdant spot; Gren-don (Heref.), anciently Grenedene,* the green *dene* or hollow; Grin-stead (Suss.), the verdant station.

GRES, GRAZE *E.* from *gres*, grass, whence *grese*, deer in grass-time, *i.e.* fat deer.† Ex.: Gres-ham (Norf.), grass farm; Gres-ley (Derb.), grass land; Gressen-ham, now Gressingham (Lanc.), grass farm; Gressen-hall (Norf.), the hall in the pastures; Graze-brook, etc.

GRESFORD *B.* originally Croes-ffordd, the way of the Cross. Ex.: Gresford (Denbighs.).

GRET *E.* great. *See* Grat.

GREY *N. F.* from the name of the chief, De Croi, Anglicised to Grey. Ex.: Grey-stoke (Cumb.), Grey's palisade; Grey-stead (Northum.), Grey's station.

GREYTREE *E.* anciently Greitrewes, from Grey, and *treow*, a tree. Ex.: Grey-tree (Heref.), Grey's trees. The Lords Grey of Wilton held land in the hundred of Greytree.

GRIMS, GRIMALDS, GRIMES *D.* from Grimald, the terrible ruler, the chief's name. Ex.: Grims-by and Grimalds-by (Linc.),

* Domesday Book.

† 'A hart of grese.'—*Old Ballad*.

D. Old Danish. *G.* Greek. *L.* Latin. *N.F.* Norman French. *N.* Norse. *qu. v.* which see.

Grimald's abode; Grimes-thorp (Yorks.); and the surname Grimes.

GRIN. *See* Green.

GRO *B.* gravel or coarse sand. Ex.: The Gro, a riverside pleasure ground at Builth (Brec.).

GROS *N. F.* broad. Ex.: Gros-mont (Mon.), the broad hill.

GRUNDIS *D.* from Grunda, the chief's name, whence the surname Grundy. Ex.: Grundis-burgh (Suff.).

GUA *B.* from St. Gua or Gulan. Ex.: Llan-gulan,* now Llangua (Monm.), St. Gulan's church; Gue-graze (Cornw.).

GUILD *E.* an incorporation. Ex.: Guild-ford (Surr.), the corporate town at the ford; Guilds-borough (Northam.), the fortified corporate town.

GUILSFIELD, perhaps St. Gulan's field. Ex.: Guilsfield (Mont.).

GUIS *N. F.* from Gui or Guy, the owner's name. Ex.: Guisborough (Yorks.), Guy's fortified town.

GUM *E.* excellent or distinguished. Ex.: Gum-ley (Leic.), the land of the distinguished man, or the land of a chief named Gum.

GUMFRES *E.* from Humphrey. Ex.: Gumfres-ton (Pemb.), Humphrey's town.

GUN *D.* from Gunna, the name of a chief, and still, contracted into Gunn, a common surname in the Norse part of Scotland.† Ex.: 14 places, all in Danish England; Gun-fleet, Gunna's harbour; Gun-thorp, Gunna's farm; Gunna's-by, now Gunnersby, Gunna's abode.

GURIG *B.* from St. Curig or Cyricus. Ex.: Capel-gurig (Carn.), St. Curig's chapel.

GWAETHIR *B.* land alienated to make compensation for bloodshedding, from *gwaeth*, blood, and *tir*, land.

GWARTHA *B.* from Gwynn Gwarther, an early British king mentioned by Merddyn.‡ Ex.: Maes-y-Gwartha (Glam.), Gwarther's-field.

GWAUN *B.* a mountain field, or down. Ex.: Gwaun-ddwr. (Brec.), water field; Pen-y-waun (Glam.), the head of the field.

* Wakeman's Notes to the Liber Landavensis.

† Dio. Cassius (lxvii. 5) mentions a prophetess named Ganna among the Germans, worshipped temp. Domitian.

‡ Stephens's 'Literature of the Kymry.'

GWEN *B.* feminine of *gwyn*, white or fair. Ex.: Gwen-hwpp, now Gwennap (Cornw.), the fair slope.

GWENT *B.* bright or elevated tract, the ancient name of Hampshire, and also of Monmouthshire.

GWERN *B.* the alder, *Alnus* of botany. Ex.: Gwern-y-bwlch (Mont.), the alders in the pass; Llan-y-wern (Brec.), the church among the alders.

GWEST *B.* a resting-place. Ex.: Gwest-ydd (Mont.), from gwest-ty-ddin, the camp resting-place.

GWIC *British* and *Breton*, a town or village. Ex.: Llan-gwic (Glam.), the village church.

GWILI *B.* from *gwill*, a swift.* Ex.: the river Gwili (Carm.).

GWM a form of *Cwm*, qu. v.

GWNOG *B.* a saint's name. Ex.: Llan-gwnog (Mont.), St. Gwnog's church.

GWORLOD *B.* from *gweirglodd*, a meadow. Ex.: frequent in South Wales.

GWRLE *B.* from *gwr* and *leng*. Ex.: Caer-gwrle (Denb.), the camp of the legion of the Gwr, a tribe who seem to have called themselves *the* men.

GWRON *B.* a hero or worthy.

GWY, WY, WYE *B.* from *gwy*, water. Ex.: Gwy-ddaren (Denb.), the water near the rocky hill; the rivers Wye (Heref., Derb., Kent).

GWYDDEL *B.* a man of the woods, or savage, applied to the Irish. Ex.: Gwyddel-wern (Merion.), the alders of the Irish, probably indicating the place where a band of invading Irishmen were defeated.

GWYN, WYN *B.* white or fair; when it is a prefix it is a man's name. Ex.: Gwyn-fa (Carm.), Gwyn's-place; Ber-wyn (Mont.), the white boundary, perhaps from the snow covering it in winter.

GWYTHIAN *B.* from *gwydden*, a tree. Ex.: Gwythian (Corn.), the place of trees. The name Gwyther is probably from the same root, and (like savage) originally meant a dweller in the woods.

GYBI *B.* from St. Cybi. Ex.: Llan-gybi (Monm.), St. Cybi's church.

* Richards, in Welsh Dict.

GYFELACH *B.* from Cyfelach, bishop of Llandaff. Ex.: Llangyfelach (Glam.), St. Cyfelach's church.

GYNLLO *B.* St. Cynllo. Ex.: Llan-gynllo (Rad.), St. Cynllo's church.

GYNOG *B.* from St. Cynog, a son of king Brychan, A.D. 400. Ex.: Llan-gynog (Mont.), St. Cynog's church; Merthyr Cynog (Brec.), the church of the martyr Cynog.

GYNWYD *B.* from St. Cynwyd. Ex.: Llan-gynwyd (Glam.), St. Cynwyd's church.

H

Often takes the place of *g* at the beginning of British words, and at the end of Old English words; omitted from Old English words where it precedes *r* and *w*; and often prefixed, in the midland and eastern counties, to words originally beginning with a vowel, a peculiarity still marking the speech of those districts.

HA, HEAGE, HA *E.* from *heag* or *heah*, high. Ex.: Ha-burh, now Habrough (Linc.), the high fortification; Heage (Derb.), the high place (Yorks., Ess., Norf.), the high camp; Ha-burh-ham, now Habergham (Lanc.), the village of the high fortification.

HABBER. See Abber.

HAC, HACCON, HACKN, HAX *N.* from the possessive case of Haco, the name of a Norse king. Ex.: Haccon-by (Linc.), and Hax-ty (Yorks.), Haco's abode; Hackn-ey (Midd.), Haco's marsh or pool; Hack-ness (Yorks.), Haco's promontory; Hac-comb (Devon), Haco's valley.

HACKING, HECKING *N.* and *E.* from Haco and *incga.* Ex.: Hack-ing-ton (Kent), Haco's children's town; Hecking-ham (Norf.), the home of the same.

HAD, HADDIS *E.* from Hadda, or Adda, or *Ættor*, an adder, the chief's name. Ex.: Had-don (Hunts), Hadda's camp or hill; Haddisor, now Hadsor (Worc.), Hadda's boundary. *See* Adder.

HAFOD *B.* a booth or summer hut. Ex.: Hafod (Card.); Bryn-hafod, etc.

HAG, HAGUE, HAIGH, HAY, HEY, HEYS *E.* from *haga*, enclosed land. Ex.: Hag-bourn (Berks), the enclosure near the brook; Haigh, Hague (Lanc.), the enclosure; The Hay (Brec.), ditto; Uris-hay (Heref.), the enclosure of Uris, a Norman knight of the eleventh century; Northern and Southern Hay (Devon), Round-hay (Som.); Harpur-hey and Green-heys (Lanc.). Hence also haw-thorn, the thorn of which hedges were composed. The Hague in Holland, and La Haye Sainte, the holy enclosure, in Belgium.

HAIGH. *See* Hag.

HAIL, HAILE, HALES, HAYLE, HEAL *N.* from *haela*, a hero, assumed as a man's name. Ex.: Hail-weston (Hunts), Haela's waest-town, in distinction from other waest-towns, or towns built on the waste; Hailes (Glouc.), Haela's estate; Hales-owen (Worc.), Haela's own; Heal-haugh (Yorks.), Haela's grassy hill; Hayle (Cornw.).

HAL, HALL *E.* from *hal*, or *alh*, a hall or palace. Ex.: 30 places, in which the suffix is ford, ham, ing, low, stead, stow, ton, or well, *qu. v. singulatim.*

HAM *E.* a home or a village. Ex.: 17 places as a prefix, and frequent as a suffix. Ham-stead and Ham-ton are corruptedly written Hamp-stead and Hamp-ton. Hence also the word homestead.

HAMBLE, HAMIL, from Gamel, *q. v.* Ex.: Hamble-den (Bucks), Gamel's valley; Hamil-ton, Gamel's town, also a surname, from Hambledon, the seat of Sir Gilbert de Hambledon, the founder of the Scotch ducal family of Hamilton, in the thirteenth century.

HAMNISH *E.* from *ham*, a home, and *naess*, a promontory, or jutting hill. Ex.: Hamnish, anciently Hamenessa * (Heref.), promontory home.

HAN, HEAN, HENN *E.* from *hean*, high, a form of *heah*. Ex.: 29 places, among which are Han-bury (Worc.), high fortification; Hean-or (Derb.), the high boundary; Henn-ey (Ess.), the high place near the water.

HAND *E.* the owner's name. Ex.: Hand-borough (Oxf.), Hand's fortified place; Hands-worth (Yorks.), Hand's estate.

HANGER, HONGER *E.* a hill. Ex.: Pans-hanger (Herts), Penna's or Panna's hill; Cle-honger (Heref.), the clay hill.

HAR *E.* gray or hoary.† Ex.: Har-borough (Warw.), the gray fortification; Har-by (Leic.), the gray abode; Har-grave (Norf.), the gray entrenched fortress.

HARBER *E.* from arbour. Ex.: Harber-ton (Devon), the town of the arbour, or the retreat.

HARD, HARDEN *E.* from *heord*, a shepherd, possessive *heordan.* Ex.: 13 places, the most common form being Hard-wick, the shepherd's village or living place.

HARDING, a famous Norse rover. Ex.: Hardings-ton (Northam.),

* Dugdale's Monasticon.

† 'An old har hoar.'—*Shakspere*: Romeo and Juliet.

Harding-ton (Som.), Harding's town; Harding-ham (Norf.), Harding's village.

Hare, Hares *E.* from *hara*, a hare, perhaps assumed as a name to imply swiftness of foot, as in the case of King Harold Harefoot. Ex.: Hare-wood (Yorks.), the hare's wood; Hares-field (Glouc.).

Harg *E.* from *hearg*, an idol's temple. Ex.: Harg-ham (Norf.), temple village.

Hargest *B.* perhaps from *garw*, rough, and *gist*, clay or earth. Ex.: Hargest (Heref.), the rough earth hill.

Harl *N.* from *jarl*, a leader or earl. Ex.: Harls-ton (Norf.), the leader's town. Or it may be a contraction of Harold's town.

Harling. *See* Arling.

Harm, Harmon, Harmonds *B.* from Garmon, the British form of the name of St. Germanus of Troyes in France. Ex.: Harms-ton (Linc.), St. Germanus' town; Harmonds-worth (Midd.), St. Germanus' estate; St. Harmon (Rad.).

Harold *E.* from King Harold II., to whom Ewyas Harold (Heref.), belonged. Mab-harold was the British name of a castle built in that district by the illegitimate son (*mab*) of that king. Ex.: Harold (Bedf.), etc.

Harp, Harpen *E.* from *hearp*, a harp, and perhaps marking the abodes of harpers, who held land on the tenure of doing service as such to the king. Ex.: 9 places. The surnames Earp and Harper probably had the same origin.

Harrai *B.* from St. Garrai. Ex.: Llan-harrai (Glam.), St. Garrai's church; common in Ireland in the form of Garry, as Garryowen, etc.

Harring *E.* from Hara, and *incga*. Ex.: Harring-ton (Linc.), the town of Hara's descendants; Harring-worth (Northamp.), the estate of the same.

Harro. *See* Harrow.

Harrolds. *See* Harold.

Harrow *E.* from Hara, the owner's name. Ex.: Harrow-den (Northam.), Hara's dene or valley; Harro-gate (Yorks.), Hara's way.

Hars *E.* from *Er*, the Saxon Mars. Ex.: Harsley (Yorks.), Er's place; Hars-well (Yorks.), Er's well; Harston (Leic. and Camb.), Er's town. *See* Erming.

Hart, Hert *E.* from *heorot*, a hart. Ex.: 23 places.

Hartle *E.* perhaps from *wyrtl*, a diminutive of *wyrt*, a plant or herb, from whence we have *whortle* or *hurtle*, the little herb, *Vaccinium myrtillus* of botany. Ex.: Hartle-bury (Worc.), the fortification among the whortles. The plant is common on the hills of the district.

Hartlip *E.* from *hart* and *leap*. By old law, the owner of a park or forest was entitled to the land beyond its boundary as far as a deer could leap. When the land was disafforested, the deer's leap was still claimed. In Derbyshire, it is called the 'buck leap,' and the claim was allowed in an action for trespass, tried at the assizes in 1844. Ex.: Hart-lip (Kent), Potes-lepe, now Putley (Heref.).

Harw *B.* from *garw*, rough. Ex.: Harw-ar-din, now Harwarden (Flints.), the camp on the rough land.

Hasel, Hasling, Hesling, Hessle *E.* from *haesl*, the hazel-tree. Ex.: Hasel-ey (Warw. and Oxf.), the hazel water or marsh; Haeslan-den now Haslingden (Lanc.), hazel hollow; Hesling-ton (Yorks.), the town among the hazels; Hessle (Yorks.), the hazel.

Hasting, *N.* the name of a noted sea-king. Ex.: Hastings-leigh (Ess.), Hasting's meadow or place.

Hat *E.* from *haeth*, a heath. Ex.: Hethfield,* now Hatfield (Heref.); Hatfield (Herts and Yorks.).

Hatch, Haches *E.* from *hæca*, a bar or bolt, hence a dwelling. Ex.: Hatch Beauchamp (Som.), Beauchamp's dwelling; Colney Hatch (Midd.), Colney's dwelling; Haches-ton (Suff.), the barred town.

Hather, Heath *S.* from *haeth*, a heath. Ex.: Hather-leigh (Devon), and Hather-ley (Glouc.), the heathy meadow or place; Hathers-age (Derb.), the edge of the heath; Heath-or, now Heather (Leices.), the boundary of the heath.

Haugh *N.* from *haughr*, a green hill or bank. Ex.: Haugh-ley (Suff.), the meadow by the green hill.

Haughmond. *See* Almond, *supra*.

Haven *E.* from *hæfen*, a port. Ex.: Hæfenan-ham, now Haven-ing-ham (Suff.), the home of or by the port.

* Dugdale's Monasticon.

HAVER, HEVER, AVER *E.* perhaps from *efe*, the brink. *See* Even, *supra.*

HAVER *B.* from *gafr*, a goat. Ex.: Haver-ford-west, called Hawr-ffordd by Llywarch Hên,* thirteenth century, *i.e.* the resting-place by the goat's path.

HAWK, HAUK *E.* a hawk, probably the cognisance of the chief, afterwards adopted as a name. Ex.: Hawks-worth (Notts), Hawk's watered estate; Hauks-well (Yorks.), Hawk's well.

HAX *E.* Haco's. *See* Haccon, *supra.*

HAY. *See* Hag, *supra.*

HAY *N.F.* from *haie*, Saxon *haga*, a hedge. Ex.: Idridge-hay (Derb.), Eadred's enclosure; Fothering-hay (Northam.), the enclosure of Feada.

HAYLING. *See* Hail, *supra.*

HAYLING, HEALING *E.* from Haela and *incga*. Ex: Hayling (Hants), and Healing (Linc.), the possession of Haela's descendants.

HAZLE. *See* Hasel, *supra.*

HEADING, HEADEN, HEDING *E.* probably from Edwin. Ex.: Heading-ley (Yorks.), Edwin's meadow or place; Heden-ham (Norf.), and Heding-ham (Ess.), Edwin's home.

HEALING. *See* Hail, *supra.*

HEANOR *E.* from *hean*, high, and *ofre*, a ridge. Ex.: Heanor (Derb.).

HEARN, HERN, *E.* the heron, called also the heronshaw. Hence the old proverb 'He does not know a hawk from a heronshaw,' corrupted into 'a handsaw.' The name Hearnshaw preserves the Saxon word for the bird. Ex.: Hern-hill (Kent), the heron's hill.

HEATH. *See* Hat, *supra.*

HECKING *E.* *See* Haccon, *supra.*

HECKMOND *E.* either from *heah-mond*, high protection, or from *ege-mond*, the protecting eye, name of a chief. *See* Almond, *supra.*

HED *E.* from *heder*, a covering or hiding place, thence a house. Ex.: Hed-don (Northum.), and Hedon (Yorks.), the house; Heds-or (Bucks), boundary house.

HEIGH, *E.* from *heah*, high. Ex.: Heigh-ton (Suss.), high town; Heigh-ham (Norf.), high home.

* Stephens's 'Literature of the Kymry.'

Hel, Helles. *See* Els, *supra.*

Helen, probably from the Empress Helena, mother of Constantine the Great, a favourite saint among the Britons. Ex.: 12 places, 8 of which are styled 'St. Helen's.'

Heli *B.* salt. Ex.: Pwll-heli (Carn.), the salt pool.

Helling *E.* from Ælla, and *incga,* descendants. Ex.: Helling-ley (Suff.), the place of Ælla's descendants; Helling-bury (Ess.), the fortification of the same.

Helm *E.* an elm tree, also a man's name. Ex.: 6 places.

Helming *E.* from Helm, and *incga.* Ex.: Helming-ton (Devon), the town of Helm's descendants.

Helper *E.* perhaps from the name of Ulfa or Wulfhere, King of Mercia A.D. 674. Ex.: Helper-thorp (Yorks.), Ulfa's farm; Wolferlow (Heref.), Ulfa's hill; Wolver-ton (Bedf.), Ulfa's town; Wolverhamp-ton (Staff.), the town of Ulfa's home.

Helsborough *E.* from Ælla, and *burh.* Ælla founded the South Saxon kingdom, A.D. 477. Ex.: Helsborough (Devon), Ælla's fortification.

Helygen *B.* the willow. Ex.: Llanfihangel Helygen (Radn.), St. Michael's church among the willows.

Hem, corrupted from Emma. *See* Am, *supra.*

Heming *D.* from the leader of the Danish fleet A.D. 1007. Ex.: Hemings-ton, now Hemingstone (Suff.), Heming's town.

Hemp *E.* probably the same as Hamp, a corruption of Ham, *q. v.*

Hen *B.* old. Ex.: 25 places; Hen-llan, now Hentland (Heref.), old church; Hen-llys (Monm.), old palace. Where it occurs in words evidently Saxon, as Henthorp, Henley, Henney, etc., it is probably a contraction of *hean,* high. *See* Han, *supra.*

Hengst *E.* from Hengist, the Saxon chief. Ex.: Hengst-ton, Hengist's town.

Hennor *E.* from *hean,* high, and *ofre,* ridge. Ex.: Hennor (Heref.).

Hereford *B.* Some antiquarians explain the name Hereford as a Saxon word meaning army-ford, forgetting that the Saxons called the place Fern-lege, *i. e.* the meadow of fern. One of its British names was Hen-ffordd, *i. e.* the old way. Probably the true etymology is from the other British name (*see* Iolo MSS.), Caer-ffawydd, corrupted by the Saxons to Harford, and thence to Hereford. This etymology is supported by Shakspere's accenting the word as two syllables,

'Harry of Hereford, Lancaster, and Derby.'

Some old writers, too, spell the word 'Hariford.'

HERRING *E.* from *haring*, the fish so called. Ex.: Haring-fleot, now Herring-fleet (Suff.), the port of herring-fishers.

HERST, HURST *E.* from *hyrst*, a wood. Ex.: Herst-monceau (Suss.), Monceau's wood; Billings-hurst (Suss.), Belin's wood. In 7 places hurst is a prefix; in 64 it is a suffix.

HERT *E.* from *heorot*, a hart. Ex.: Hert-ford, the hart's ford.

HESEL, HESSLE. *See* Hasel, *supra*.

HETH. *See* Hat, *supra*.

HETHEL. *See* Adl, *supra*.

HETTY *B.* from Esther. Ex.: Llanthetty (Brec.), St. Esther's church.

HEVEN, HEVER, HEVING. *See* Even, *supra*.

HEX *E.* contracted from *Heagstealde*, high station. Ex.: Hexham (Northum.), the home of the high station.*

HEY *E.* *See* Hay, *supra*.

HEYTESBURY *E.* anciently *Hegtredes-byrig*, the high path fortification. Ex.: Heytesbury (Wilts).

HICK, HICKS, HIG, HITCH, IC, ICKEN *E.* probably from the personal name Hugh. Hick's Hall (Midd.), Hitch-ham (Bucks), Hugh's home; Ic-comb (Glouc.), Hugh's dingle; Ickles-ham (Suss.), ditto.

HICKLING *E.* from Hick and *len*, fee-farm land. Ex.: Hickling (Norf. and Notts), Hick's land which was farmed out.

HIDE, perhaps from the Saxon *hida*, a measure of land. Ex. West-hide (Heref.), the measured out or cultivated spot on the waste; Trent-hide (Dorset). *See* Hyde, *infra*.

HIGH *E.* from *heah*, high, indicating a hill-site. Ex.: 12 places.

HILL, HIL *E.* from *hyl*, a hill. Frequent.

HILLS, HILS *E.* from Ella, king of Mercia and Northumbria. *See* Alling, *supra*.

HIMBLE. *See* Kimble, *infra*.

HIN, HIND *E.* from *hine*, the female deer. Ex.: Hin-ton, 12 places in the south-west counties, the hind's town; Hind-ley (Lanc.), the hind's place.

* Bede: 'Ecclesiastical History.'

D. Old Danish. *G.* Greek. *L.* Latin. *N.F.* Norman French. *N.* Norse. *qu. v.* which see.

HINCK, HINKS, HINX *E.* from Hinck, which is still a personal name. Ex.: Hinck-ley (Leices.), Hinck's place; Hinks-ey (Berks), Hinck's marsh; Hink-worth (Herts), Hinck's watered estate.

HINDER *N.* perhaps from Hyndla, a prophetess mentioned in the Edda. Ex.: Hinderwell (Yorks.), the well of Hyndla.

HING *N.* from Hingwar, a Norse chief, brother of Hubba (*see* Hubber), who was one of the leaders in the overthrow of the East Anglian monarchy, temp. Edward A.D. 870.* Ex.: Hing-ham (Norf.), Hingwar's home.

HIPPER. *See* Ep, *supra.*

HIR *B.* long. Ex.: Hir-nant (Mont.), long brook; Abbey-cwm-hir (Radn.), the abbey in the long hollow; Hir-waun (Glam.), the long meadow (given by King Gwrgan to poor Welshmen, *circa* A.D. 900).

HITCH *E.* *See* Hick, *supra.*

HITCHEN, HITCHING, from Hitch and *incga.* Ex.: Hitchen, now Hitching (Herts), the place of Hitch's descendants.

HITHE, HYTHE, *E.* from *hyth*, a port or small haven. Ex.: Queen-hithe (Kent), the queen's port; Rother-hithe (Surr.), the port on the boundary (*yr odar*, Brit.), Hythe (Kent), the port.

Ho, HOE, HOO, HOW *D.* a hill. Ex.: Ho-by (Leices.), the hill abode; Wiven-hoe (Ess.), Wiva's hill: Hoo (Suff.), the hill; How Caple (Heref.), the chapel on a hill.

HOCK *E.* from *heah*, high. The anniversary of a victory over the Danes was a Saxon festival or high-day, and was called 'Hock-day.' Ex.: Hock-cliff (Beds), high cliff.

HOF, HOVE, HOUGH *E.* a hut, hence hovel, a little hut. Ex.: Hove (Suss.), the hut; Hove-ton (Norf.), hut town; Hough-ton (14 places).

HOG, HOGGES, HOX, UG, UGGES, probably from some Norse chief called Ugga. Ex.: Hogs-thorp (Linc.), Ugga's farm; Hog-ston (Bucks), Ugga's wood; Hogs-den, now Hox-ton (Midd.), Ugga's valley; Ug-byryg, now Ugborough (Devon), Ugga's fortress; Ugges-hall (Suff.), Ugga's hall.

HOL *E.* a hole or low place. Ex.: Hol-deira-ness,† now Holder-ness (Yorks.), the promontory of the low-lying part of the kingdom of Deira; Hol-land (Linc.), the low land.

* Anglo-Saxon Chronicle.

† Somner's Anglo-Saxon Dict. *in voce.*

B. British. *C.* Celtic. *E.* The Old English, commonly known as Anglo-Saxon.

Holles, Hollin, Holn, Holly *E.* from *holegn*, the holly-tree. Ex.: Holles-ley (Suff.), the place of the holly; Holling-ton, (Suss.), holly town; Holne (Devon), the holly.

Holm, Hulm *N. holmr*, a grassy hill by the water, or an island. Holm occurs in 30, and Hulm in 8 places. Ex.: Holm Lacy (Heref.), Lacy's holm; Priest-holm (Angl.), the priest or bard's home.

Holmer *E.* the mere of the hollow. Ex.: Hole-mere,* now Holmer (Heref.).

Holt *E.* a wood, or hold of wild animals. Ex.: Burh-holt, now Berg-holt (Essex), the fortress in the wood.

Honddu *B.* the name of two small rivers in South Wales, from *Afon-ddu*, black or dark-hued river. Ex.: The Honddu (Breconshire and Monmouthshire).

Honey *E.* from Hunna, the chief's name. Ex.: Honey-bourne (Worc.), Hunna's brook; Honi-ley (Warw.), Hunna's place or meadow. *See* Hunning, *infra.*

Hook *E.* the mallow (*Malva*), and probably afterwards adopted as a personal name. Ex.: Hocke-mere-tun,† now Hook Norton (Oxf.), the town of the mallow pool, or Hocke's town by the pool.

Hook. *See* Hock, *supra.*

Hooper *E.* a wild swan, named from its cry.

Hope *B.* corrupted from *hwpp*, a sloping place between hills. Frequent in the Welsh marshes and in Derbyshire. When it occurs as a suffix, as in Bacup, Burrup, etc., it is often corrupted into *up.* Ex.: Hope-say (Salop), the slope belonging to the Norman family of Say; Long-hope (Glouc.), the long slope.

Hor, Hoar, Hore *E.* from *hor*, gray. Ex.: Hor-burh, now Horbury (Yorks.), the gray fortress; Hoar-withy (Heref.), the place of the gray willows.

Hord, Horn *E.* a storehouse or cattle-shed, 41 places. Ex.: Horder-ley (Hants), storehouse land; Hord-aern, the place of the storehouse or barn; Hornan, now Horning (Norf.), the store-house; Hornan-hold, now Horninghold (Leices.), the fortified store-houses.

Hornsea *E.* from *haran-ey*, the pool of the hares. Ex.: Hornsea (Midd.).

* Domesday Book *in loc.*

† Bromtonus, *fl. circa* 1330.

D. Old Danish. *G.* Greek. *L.* Latin. *N. F.* Norman French. *N.* Norse. *qu. v.* which see.

HORS *E.* probably from Horsa, one of the Saxon chiefs; 20 places. Ex.: Horsen-den (Bucks), Horsa's hollow; Hors-ted (Suss.), Horsa's station.

HORSING *E.* from *Horsa*, and *incga.* Ex.: Horsing-tun, now Horsington (Som.), the place of Horsa's descendants.

HOUNS *E.* from *hund*, a hound. Ex.: Houns-low (Midd.), the hound's gentle rising ground.

HOW. *See* Ho, *supra.*

HUBBERS *E.* from Hubba, a Norse king, killed in battle, temp. Alfred. Ex.: Hubbers-ty (Derb.), Hubba's stow or station.

HUCK, HUCKEN *E.* from Hucc, the owner's name, and *incga*, descendants. Ex.: Hucken-hall (Notts), now Hucknall.

HUDDERS *E.* from Uther, a British king. Ex.: Hudders-field (Yorks), probably the battle-field of Uther.

HUDDING, ODDING *E.* from Oddo or Uddo, the name of a Saxon earl of Mercia, and *incga*, descendants. Ex.: Hudd-ing-ton and Odd-ing-ley, now Huddington and Oddingley (Worc.), the town and the land of Oddo's descendants.

HUL *E.* from *hyl*, a hill. Ex.: Hull, a river in Yorkshire, which descends from the hills to the Humber; Hul-cot (Bucks), the shepherd's hut on the hill.

HULM. *See* Holm, *supra.*

HUMBER *B.* from *hymyr*, the gathering of waters. Ex.: the river Humber, which is formed by the union of the Ouse, the Don, and the Trent.

HUMBER *E.* from *hám*, a dwelling, and *burh*, hill. Ex.: Humber (Heref.), hill dwelling.

HUMBERS *E.* from Humba, the name of the chief. Ex.: Humbers-ton (Lincolns.), the town of Humba.

HUNGER *D.* from Hingwar, the companion of Hubba, A.D. 866. Ex.: Hungerston (Pemb.).

HUNNING *E.* from Hunna, a chief's name, and *incga*, descendants. Ex.: Hunning-ham (Warw.), Hunna's descendants' home.

HUNS, from Hunna. Ex.: Huns-ton (Suff.), Hunna's town; Huns-worth (Yorks.), Hunna's watered estate; Huns-den (Herts), Hunna's hollow.

HUNT *E.* from Hunta. Ex.: Hunt-ley (Glouces.), Hunta's land, or land for hunting, being on the edge of Dean Forest.

HUNTING *E.* from *hunta*, a hunter, also a man's name, and *incga*, descendants. Ex.: Huntington (Heref.), the hunter's town; Hunting-don, the hunter's hill.

HURST *E.* from *hyrst,* a wood. Ex.: Hurst (Kent and Berks), the wood; Deer-hurst (Glouces.), the deer's wood. In 7 instances it is a prefix; in 64 it is a suffix. *See* Herst, *supra.*

HUT *E.* a hut. Ex.: Hut-ton (10 places), the town of huts.

HYDE, *E.* from *hida,* a measure of land, equal to 120 acres; hence a farm or small estate. Ex.: Hyde (Ches.); Trent-hyde (Dorset), Trant's estate.

HYNT *B.* a street.

HYTHE. *See* Hithe, *supra.*

I, J.

I. *See* Ea, *supra.*

JARROW *E.* from *gyrwe,* a marsh. Ex.: Jarrow (Durham), anciently Gyrwe, the marsh.*

IB, IBBER, IBS *E.* from St. Ebbe. *See* Ebb and Abb, *supra.*

ICKEN, ICKLING, IX *E.* from *Hick* and *len,* fee-farm land. Ex.: Icken-ham (Midd.), Hick's home; Ickling-ham (Suff.), Hick's land farmed out; Ix-worth (Suff.), Hick's well-watered estate.

ID, IDDES. *See* Ead, *supra.*

IDAN *B.* St. Nidan. Ex.: Llan-idan (Anglesey), St. Nidan's church.

IDLE *E.* from *ig,* water, and *dale.* Ex.: Idle (Notts and Yorks.), the watery dale.

IDLOES *B.* St. Idloes. Ex.: Llan-idloes (Mont.), St. Idloes church.

IDRIDGE *E.* Eadred's, marking the estate of some chief so named. Ex.: Idridge-hay (Derbys.), the enclosure or fortified estate of Eadred.

JEFFERIES, the possessive of Jeffery or Geoffrey, apparently a Norman corruption of Godfred, the good peace, or God's peace. Ex.: Moreton Jefferies (Heref.); Jeffrieston (Pemb.).

IESTYN *B.* from Iestyn, the builder.† Ex.: Llan-iestyn (Carnarv.), Iestyn's church.

IFF *E.* corrupted from *efes,* the margin or edge of anything; hence the edge of a roof is called the eaves. Ex.: Iff-ley (Oxf.), the meadow on the edge of a wood or a stream.

IGHT *E.* eight. Ex.: Ight-ham (Kent), traditionally said to be so named because the parish contained eight hamlets or hams.

IL *B.* from Ivel, name of the river. Ex.: Ivel-cestre, now Ilchester; Ivel-mynstre, now Ilminster (Som.), the Saxon camp and monastery on the Ivel.

ILAR *B.* St. Hiliary. Ex.: Llan-ilar (Card.), St. Hilary's church.

* Girwy, now Jarrow.—*Camden.*

† Iestyn ap Gwrgan was lord of Glamorgan, in the twelfth century.

ILDER *E.* from Hilda. Ex.: Elder-ton (Northam.), Hilda's town

ILEY *E.* from *ig*, water, and *lea*, land. Ex.: Iley (Bedf.)

IIFRA *E.* from Ælfric, name of a chief. Ex.: Ilfra-comb (Devon), Ælfric's valley.

ILID, ULID *B.* St. Ilid, or Juliot. Ex.: Llan-ilid (Monm.), St. Ilid's church; Llan-ulid (Brecons.).

ILK, ILKES, ILKETS *E.* from Elcha or Elchat, a chief. The surname Halket is probably a corruption of the same name. Ex.: Ilk-ley (Yorks.), Ilkes-ton (Derbys.), Ilkets-hall (Suff.), the land, town, and hall of Elcha. Hence the name Elkington, *i. e.* the town of Elcha's *incga*, or descendants.

ILL, ILLING *E.* from Ella, and *incga*, descendants. Ex: Ill-mere (Bucks), Ella's pool; Illing-ton (Norf.), the town of Ella's descendants.

ILLTYD *B.* blameless, the name of St. Illtyd, or Iltutus, called "The Knight." * Ex.: Llan-illtyd, now Llantwis (Glam.), Llan-tood (Pemb.), St. Illtyd's church.

INCE *B.* from *ynys*, an island or a piece of land surrounded by marsh, answering to *inch*, in Celtic. Ex.: 3 places in Cheshire and Lancashire.

ING, *E.* Where it immediately precedes *ham, ton, don, dean, ley, thorp, worth*, or *hurst*, it is in nearly all cases a contraction of *incga*, children or descendants. Ex.: Huntingdon, *qu. v.*

ING. Where it forms the first root of a word, it means a meadow. Ex.: Ing-ham, 3 places, meadow home; Ing-grove (Yorks.), the entrenched meadow.

INGATESTONE *E.* the town of Ingat, the chief's name. Ex.: Ingatestone (Suff.).

INGLE, INGOLD *D.* from Ingold, name of a chief.† Ex.: Ingoldsthorp (Norf.), Ingold's farm; Ingolds-by (Linc.), and Ingleby (Yorks.), Ingold's abode.

INGLEBOROUGH *E.* from Angle-byryg, the English fortified town. Ex.: Ingleborough (Notts), which was situated in a district conquered by the Danes, who seem to have herded together, and whose example was naturally followed by the Angles for the same object, mutual defence.

INGLI *B.* from *engylion*, angels. Ex.: Carn Ingli (Pemb.), the angels' carn or heap of stones.‡

* Iolo MSS.

† Ingold headed the first colony to Iceland, A.D. 874.—*Mackenzie's Iceland.*

‡ Rees' 'Lives of the Welsh Saints.'

INGR, *E.* from Ingra, a chief. Ex.: Ingra-ham, now Ingram (Northum.), Ingra's home.

INGSTONE *E.* the town of Inga or Ingat. Ex.: Ingstone (Heref.).

INK *E.* probably a corruption of Ing, *q. v. supra.* Ex.: Ink-pen (Berks), the meadow sheep-fold; Ink-berrow (Worces.), the meadow beorh, or camp.

INNIS *B.* the Cornish form of *ynys*, an island. Ex.: Innis-vean, *i.e. ynys faen*, stone island.

IP *E.* *See* Epping, *supra.*

IPPLE, IPPOLITS *E.* from St. Hypolitus. Ex.: Ipple-pen (Devon), St. Hypolitus' hill; Ippolits (Herts), St. Hypolitus's church.

IPS *E.* from *æps*, an aspen tree.

IR, IRE *E.* perhaps from *irf*, property; a cognate word with *ar* (Brit.), land. The occurrence of Ir and Ire, in conjunction with *thorp*, *by*, and *stead*, lead to the supposition that they are contractions of the name of some Danish chief.

IRMING, ERMING *E.* corrupted from Ermundsul, *i. e.* the image of Er, the defender, which was erected on the line of one of the four great military roads made by the Romans; hence called Ermund or Erming-street.* St. Erme (Cornw.), and Ermington (Devon), may have had the like origin.

IRTHING, IRTHLING *E.* from *yrthling*, child of the earth, *i. e.* a farmer. Ex.: Irthington (Cumb.), the farmer's town; Irthling-borough (Northam.), the farmer's fortified town.

IS, ISSA, ISAF *B.* low, lower, lowest; the first properly *ys*. Ex.: Bangor Yscoed (Flints.), the high choir below the wood; Pentre-issa (Denbighs.), lower village.

ISHEN *B.* St. Isan. Ex.: Llan-ishen (Glam.), St. Isan's church.

ISIS, corrupted from Ouse, the ancient name of the river.†

ISLE, ISLAND *E.* indicating places which were once, if they be not now, environed by water or marsh.

ISLINGTON *E.* in Domesday Book, Isendune, Isendon, and Iseltone, from *isil*, or *isen*, a small stream which flows through the parish, and *dune*, a down or broad hill.‡

ITCHING *E.* from *yting*, a way. Ex.: Itching-ford, anciently Ittinga-ford,§ the ford where several ways met.

* Saxon Chronicle. † Somner's Anglo-Saxon Dictionary.

‡ Sharon Turner.

§ Saxon Chronicle. The place was noted as the scene of a peace between Saxons and Danes.

ITHEL *B.* the king of Gwent, slain in battle A.D. 846. Ex.: Mynydd Ithel (Monm.), Ithel's mountain.

ITHON *B.* the fifth king of Britain, from Annyn or Æneas.* Ex.: the Ithon river, and Llanfihangel-rhyd-Ithon (Radn.), St. Michael's church at the ford of Ithon.

JULIOT *B.* St. Juliot or Ulid. Ex.: St. Juliot's (Cornw.).

IVER *E.* from St. Ive, and *ofer*, a brink. Ex.: Iver (Bucks), Ive's brink.

IVES, IVING *E.* from St. Ive, and *incga.* Ex.: St. Ive's (Hunts.); Iving-hoe (Bucks), the hill of Ive's descendants.

IWADE *E.* from *iw* and *wædo*, the ford of the yew. Ex.: Iwade (Kent).

IWERN *E.* from *iw ærn*, the place of the yew. Ex.: Iwern (Dorset).

IWRCH *B.* a roebuck. Ex.: Bryn-iwrch, Ffynnon-iwrch, Llwyn-iwrch, the hill, the fountain, and the hedge or copse of the roebuck.

IX. *See* Iccen, *supra.*

* Iolo MSS.

K.

Neither the Britons nor the Anglo-Saxons had this letter, which is represented in their languages by *c*.

KEA *B.* from *ci* (pron. kee), a dog; Greek, *κύων*. Ex.: Kea (Cornw.).

KEAL, KEEL, KEL *E.* from *ceol*, a ship, still in Northumberland called a keel.* Ex.: Keal (Linc.); Keel (Staff.); Keel-by (Linc.), the abode of some Danish sea-king; Kel-marsh (Northam.); Kell-ey (Devon), keel-water or port. *See* Chel, *supra*.

KEDDING *S.* perhaps from Cedda, bishop, A.D. 703, and *incga*, descendants. Ex.: Kedding-ton (Suff. and Linc.), Cedda's descendants' town. *See* Cad.

KEDL *B.* from Cadell, a British chief.† Ex.: Kedles-ton (Derb.), Cadell's town.

KEG, KEIGH, KEY *E.* perhaps from *caeg*, a key; hence a place locked up, or a dwelling. Ex.: Keg-worth (Leices.), the dwelling on the well-watered estate; Keigh-ley (Yorks.), the meadow-dwelling; Key-mere (Suss.), the dwelling by the pool. For a similar metonymy, *see* Hatch, *supra*.

KEM, KEMPS *E.* from Cynmære, a Saxon land. Ex.: Kemer-ton (Glouc.), Cynmære's town; Kemps-ford (Glouc.), Cynmære's ford; ‡ Kemp-ley (Glouc.), Cynmære's land; Kemps-ey (Worc.), etc. Bosworth translates Cynmære as 'famous royal,' but the presence of the *s* seems to show that it is a *name* in the possessive case.

KEMEYS *B.* from Cemaes, name of a chief. Ex.: Kemeys, 2 places (Monm.).

KEN *B.* from *cen*, a head, and hence a headland. Ex.: Ken-arth (Carm.), the farm on the headland.

KENCHESTER *E.* perhaps from Cenred, king of Mercia, and *cestre*, the Roman town of Magna Castra, which is near to Kenchester.

* Hence the fisherman's song, 'Merry may the keel row.' † Iolo MSS.

‡ Anglo-Saxon Chronicle, which records a great battle there A.D. 800, between the West Saxons and the Wiccii.

B. British. *C.* Celtic. *E.* The Old English, commonly known as Anglo-Saxon.

KENDER *E.* from Quendreda, a Saxon saint. Ex.: Kenderchurch (Heref.).

KENIL *E.* from Kenelm or Kenulph, a chief who first built a castle at the place, thence called Kenil-worth (Warw.), Kenelm's well-watered estate.

KENNING *E.* from *cyn*, royal, and *incga*, children; pointing out either the seat of a tribe which called itself the king's children, or the actual abode of some of the Saxon princes. Ex.: Kenn-ington (Surr.), the town of the king's children; Kenning-hall (Norf.), the hall of the same.

KENSING *E.* from *cynes*, of a tribe, and *incga*, the children. Ex.: Kensing-tun, now Kensington (Midd.), the town of the children of *the* tribe or family *par eminence*.

KENT, a word of frequent occurrence but uncertain etymology. Ex.: Kent-church (Heref.), seems to come from Gwent, the British name of the district adjoining; Kentish-town (Midd.), is said to be from St. Thomas de Cantalupe; Kent, a river in Westmoreland, Kent (the county), Kentisbere (Devon), Kentford (Suff.), are doubtful. Perhaps the true etymon in all these cases is *cain* (*B.*), fair or bright.

KERDIS, *E.* from Cerdic, the first king of Wessex. *See* Chard, *supra*. Ex.: Cerdices-ford (Suss.), the scene of one of Cerdic's great battles.*

KERRY *B.* from Ceri, one of the early kings of Britain. Ex.: Porth-kerry (Glam.), Ceri's port.

KES *E.* or *N.* probably from Kessa, or Cissa, from whom Cissacestre, now Cirencester, is named. Ex.: Kessan-ham, now Kessingham (Suff.), Cissa's home; Keston (Kent), Cissa's town; Kes-wick (Cumb.), Cissa's dwelling.

KET, KETTIS *E.* from Kitt. Ex.: Ket-ton (Rut.), Kitt's town; Kittis-ford (Som.), Kitt's ford.

KETTERING, KETTERINGHAM *E.* perhaps from the name Kitt, or Christopher, and *incga*, descendants. Ex.: Kettering (Northam.), Kettering-ham (Norf.).

KETTLE *E.* or *D.* from Chetel, name of a chief. Ex.: Kettle-burh now Kettleborough (Suff.), Chetel's fortified town; Kettle-by (Linc.), Chetel's abode; Chetel's-worth,† now Chatsworth (Derb.), Chetel's well-watered estate.

* Anglo-Saxon Chronicle.

† Lysons' 'Magna Britannia.'

D. Old Danish. *G.* Greek. *L.* Latin. *N. F.* Norman French. *N.* Norse. *qu. v.* which see.

KEW *B.* from St. Cewydd. Ex.: St. Kew (Corn.); Kew (Midd.).

KEY *E.* from *caeg*, a key. *See* Keg, *supra.*

KEYING, KEYNE, from the name of Cain, a female British saint. Ex.: Keying-ham * (Yorks.), St. Cain's home; St. Keyne (Corn.); Keyn's-ham (Som.), etc. *See* Cain, *supra.*

KIDDER *B.* from *cae-dwr.* Ex.: Kidderminster (Worc.). The local tradition † is that Kidder-minster was founded by a King Cadder; but as all the other 'minsters' bear descriptive names—Bed-minster, *i. e.* St. Peter's minster, being the only exception—it is probable that Kidder is corrupted from the British *cae-dwr*, enclosure by the water.

KIDLING *B.* and *E.* from Cadell, name of a British chief, and *incga*, descendants. Ex.: Kidling-tun (Oxf.), the town of Cadell's descendants. *See* Kedl, *supra.*

KIL *B.* a cell or retreat. Ex.: Kil-gwrwg (Mon.), the cell of Gwrwg. Very frequent in Scotland and Ireland.

KILD *D.* equivalent to the Saxon *cild*, a young chief, and also a man's name. Ex.: Kild-wick (Yorks.), Kild's village.

KILLA *E.* corrupted from Cynwald, the Saxon or Anglian lord's name. Ex.: Killa-marsh, anciently Cynwold's maresc (Derb.), Cynwold's marsh.

KILN *E.* a kiln, or it may be a contraction of some chief's name. There are but three examples, viz. Kilns-ea and Kilnwick (2 places), all in Yorkshire.

KILPECK, anciently Kilpedec, *B.* the cell of St. Badawe.

KIMBER, CUMBER, KIMMER *E.* perhaps from a chief or thegn named Cymba or Gumba. Ex.: Kimber-ley (Norf.), Kimber-worth (Yorks.), Cumber-worth (Linc.), Kimmer-idge (Dorset), the place, estate, and ridge of Gumba. Cumberland is Cymry (*i.e.* Britons') land.

KIMBLE, KIMBOL, HIMBLE, the former is traditionally said ‡ to be from Cunobeline, a British king, who was defeated by the Romans at Kimble (Bucks), Kimbol-ton (Hunts and Heref.), and Himble-ton (Worces.), seem to be from the same derivative.

KIN, KINE. *See* King, *supra.*

KING *E.* from *cyning*, a king. Occurs in the names of 64 places,

* The British name adopted by the Saxons, and receiving a Saxon possessive form; not an unfrequent occurrence.

† Nokes's 'Notes for Worcester.' ‡ Lewis's 'Topographical Dictionary.'

most of which are known to have been the residences or property of Saxon monarchs. The most common forms are: King-ton, King's town, of which there are 29 instances; King's-wood, 6 instances; Kings-bury, 3; Kingsby, 3; and King-thorp, 2. Kin-fare (Staff.) seems to be 'The King's Way.'

KINGER, from the Saxon *cyn*, tribe, and *incga*, children. Ex.: Kinger-by (Linc.), probably the *by* (abode) of the family of a Danish king or chief.

KINNERSLEY *E.* anciently Chinardeslege, and probably from Cenred and *lege.* Cenred was the name of one of the early kings of Mercia. Ex.: Kinnersley (Heref.), Cenred's land or place.

KIR, KIRK, KIRT *E.* from *ciric*, a church. Ex.: Kirby (14 places), all in the Danish district, church abode or village; Kirk-bride (Cumb.), St. Bride's church; Kirk-by (22 places), all in the Danish district; Kirk-ham, etc., 18 places; Kir-ton, 3; Kirtling and Kirkland, etc. *See* Chir, *supra.*

KITTIS. *See* Ketter, *supra.*

KNAP *B.* from *cnap*, a protuberance, and thence a round isolated hill. Ex.: Knap-toft (Leices.), the grove hill.

KNEB, KNIP. *See* Knap, *supra.*

KNEE, KNIVE *E.* from *cyne*, royal. Ex.: Cynes-aelh, now Knees-all (Notts), the hall of royalty; Knee-ton (ditto), the royal town; Knive-ton (Derb.), ditto.

KNIGHT, from the Saxon *cniht*, a servant. Occurs in two places as Knight-ton, and one as Knight-wick, meaning knight town and knight's village; probably indicating estates held on the feudal tenure of knightly service.

KNOCK *B.* from *cnwcc*, a bunch or swelling, in allusion to the form of the hill. Ex.: Cnwcc-ynn, afterwards Cnuckin, now Knockin (Salop), the bunchy hill of the ash-trees (ynn); Knock-holt (Kent), the wood of the bunchy hill; Knook (Wilts), etc.

KNOLL *E.* from *cnoll*, a round smooth hill. Common in Yorkshire as a word with that meaning. Ex.: Knowle (Warw.); Knowlton (Kent), the town on or near the knoll.

KNOTT, KNUT *D.* from King Canute or Knut, who won a battle at Knuts-ford (Ches.) Ex.: Knuttan-lege, now Knotting-ley (Yorks.), Knut's place.

D. Old Danish. *G.* Greek. *L.* Latin. *N.F.* Norman French. *N.* Norse. *qu. v.* which see.

KYLOE *E.* from *cy*, cattle, and *hlaew*, a hill. Ex.: Kyloe (Northum.), cattle hill.

KYMIN, from *cyd*, common, and *min*, the brow of a hill. Ex.: the Kymin (Mon.); Eglwys Kymin (Carm.), the church on the common hill.

KYNANCE *B.* from the name of St. Keyne, and *innis*. Ex.: Kynance (Cornw.), St. Keyn's island. *See* Innis, *supra*.

L.

LACH *B.* corrupted from *llwch*, dusty. Ex.: Ty-lach (Mont.), the house in the dusty place.

LACK *E.* in one instance apparently a corruption of *lark*. Ex.: Lack-ford (Suff.), the ford of the river Lark.

LACKING, LAKEN, LAX, *E.* or *D.* from Lacca, the chief's name, and *incya*, descendants; or from *lachs*, Danish for a salmon, which may have been adopted as a name. Ex.: Lacking-ton (Som.); Lax-ton; Lakenham (Norf.), the home of Lacca's descendants.

LACY *N.* the name of a powerful family in the eleventh and twelfth centuries, many of whose possessions still bear its name. Ex.: Holm, Stoke, and Mansel Lacy (Heref.), Stanton Lacy (Salop), etc.

LAD, LADE, LODE *E.* from *ladan*, to pour; a canal or stream, or its junction with another, or sometimes a path. Ex.: Ladbrook (Warw.); Leach-lade (Glouc.), the junction of the Leach with the Thame; Even-lode (Worc.), the edge of the way, or roadside station.

LAMBER, LAMS *E.* from Lamba, a chief's name, still remaining as the surname Lambe. Ex.: Lamb-hithe, now Lambeth (Surrey), Lamba's port; Lamber-hurst (Kent), Lamba's wood; Lamb's-ton (Pemb.), Lamba's town; Lam-bourn (Berks), Lamba's brook.

LAN, the cornish form of Llan (*B.*), an enclosure, and thence a church. Ex.: Lan-dulph, St. Dilpa's church; Llan-hydrock, St. Hydrock's church.

LAN *E.* corrupted from Lon or Lune, the name of the stream on which the Roman station of Alauna was situated. Ex.: Loncestre, now Lancaster, the camp on the Lon.

LAND, LYNN *E.* corruptions of *len* or *laen*, land let out, or what was legally called fee-farm land. Ex.: Kings-len, now Kingsland (Mid. and Heref.); Kings-lynn (Norf.). *See* Len and Lynn, *infra*.

LANE *D. laan,* a lane or by-road. Ex.: Lane-stoke (Som.), the palisaded dwelling on the by-road.

LANER *L.* and *B.* from Amboglana, the Roman station at that place, which was probably derived from the British *am* and *glann,* meaning the high bank of a river. Ex.: Laner-cestre, now Lanercost (Cumb.), Laner-castrum, or Glana camp.

LANG *E.* long, still used in the north of England and in Scotland. Occurs in 38 instances, chiefly in the midland and eastern counties.

LANT, from St. Lanty. Occurs only in Cornwall. Ex.: Lant-eglos, St. Lanty's church.

LANTWIT *B.* from Llan-Iltutus (Glam.), St. Iltutus's church; Lantood (Pemb.), ditto. *See* Illtyd.

LAP *N.* from Lappa, the Laplander, the name of a chief. Ex.: Lap-worth (Warw.), Lappa's well-watered estate.

LAR *E.* the Herefordshire pronunciation of lower. Ex.: Lar-port, lower gate.

LAS, LASSING, LESSING *E.* from Lassa, the owner's name, and *incga,* descendants. Ex.: Las-burh, now Las-borough (Glouc.), Lassa's fortification; Lassing-ton (ditto), the town of Lassa's descendants; Lessing-ham (Norf.), the home of the same.

LATCHING *E.* from Lecha, a man's name, and *incga.* Ex.: Latch-ing-don (Essex), the hill of Lecha's descendants.

LAT, LATH, LATHE, LEAT, LET *E.* from *leth,* now *lathe,* a division or district, still used in that sense in Kent. Ex.: Lath-bury (Bucks), the fortified place of the district; Lat-ton (Essex), the town of the district; Long-leat (Wilts); Let-ton (Heref.), etc.

LAUGHARNE *B.* corrupted from Leucarum, its Roman name. Ex.: Laugharne (Carm.).

LAUGHTON *E.* perhaps from *hlaew,* hill, and *ton,* town. Occurs in 5 instances.

LAUNCESTON *E* corrupted from Llan-stephan's town, *i.e.* the town of St. Stephen's church.

LAVEN, LAVING *E.* from St. Levan. Ex.: Laven-don (Bucks), St. Levan's hill; Laving-ton (Wilts), St. Levan's town.

LAVER, LEVER *E.* from *hlaford,* lord. Ex.: Laver-stoke (Wilts and Hants), the lord's palisaded dwelling; Laver-ton (Som.), the lord's town; Lever-ton (Notts).

B. British. *C.* Celtic. *E.* The Old English, commonly known as Anglo-Saxon.

LAVERING *E.* from *hlaford* and *incga.* Ex.: Lavering-ton (Cam.), the town of the lord's descendants.

LAW *E.* from *hlaew*, a hill. Ex.: Law-ford (Essex), the ford near the hill. *See* Low, *infra.*

LAWRENCE, the saint of that name, from whom 7 places are named.

LAY, LE, LEA, LEE, LEES, LEIGH, LEIGHS, LEG, LEY *E.* from *lege*, meadow land. Very frequent both as prefix and suffix. The word lay is still used in agriculture, *e. g.* 'lay for cattle,' 'clover-lay,' etc.

LEACH, LECH *E.* from *leced*, dead. Ex.: the river Leach in Gloucester, perhaps named from the slaughter in a battle fought on its banks. The name Lechmere (dead or stagnant pool) has a like etymology.

LEAK, *E.* perhaps from *llech* (*B.*), a broad flat stone, supposed to have been used for sacrifices; hence cromlech and llech-faen.

LEAMING, LEMMING *E.* from the river Leam, *lim*, mud or lime; or the word may be a form of the Brit. *llam*, stepping-stones in a stream. Ex.: Leaming-ton (Warw.), the town by the Leam. The neighbouring river Afon still retains its British name in the form of Avon, which renders the derivation of Leam from the same language more probable.

LEASOWE *E.* from *læs*, a pasture. Ex.: Leasowes (Worc.).

LEATHER *E.* from *hleothor*, an oracle. Ex.: Leother-stede, now Leatherstead, the place of the oracle; Leather-head (Surr.), oracle hill, probably named from some sorcerer or witch who lived there.

LECH. *See* Leach, *supra.*

LECK, LEXING *E.* or *D.* from Lacca, the owner's name, and *incga*, descendants, or from *lecks*, a salmon. Ex.: Leckhampton, Lexington, etc.

LECKHAMPTON *E.* anciently Lechantun,* *i. e.* the town of Lecha, the owner of the estate. The name still survives in surnames, *e. g.* Letcher, Latcham, etc.

LEDBURY *E.* from Lede, now Leddon, the name of a small stream, and *beorh*, fortified place. Ex.: Ledbury (Heref.), the fortified place on the bank of the Leddon.

LEDDON *E.* from *ladan*, to pour. Ex.: Leddon river (Heref.).

LEE. *See* Lay.

LEEDS *E.* the instance in Kent is said to be derived from Ledian, counsellor to Ethelred II., A.D. 978.

* Domesday Book.

LEEDS *B.* corrupted from Loidis, still the local pronunciation, *i. e.* Llwyd-ysg, brown water. Ex.: Leeds (Yorks.), which was the capital of Cadwallo, king of the Brigantes.

LEES. *See* Lay.

LEG. *See* Lay.

LEICESTRE *E.* from Ligera-cestre, afterwards Leir-cestre, and Leycester, the camp on the river Ligera,* which is probably a corruption of the British 'Llœgr,' the name of the midland Britons. Leire (Leices.) preserves the second Saxon form of Llœgr.

LEIGH. *See* Lay.

LEIGHTON *E.*, in one case a corruption of Lygean-burh.† At that place, now Leighton Buzzard, the Britons were defeated in A.D. 571, by Cuthwulf, brother of Ceawlin, king of Wessex.

LEINT *B.* from *llain*, a patch or fragment. Ex.: Llain-dwr-din, now Leintwardin (Heref.), the water-camp on the separated plot of ground. The river Teme there separates a portion of low land which is enclosed between it and the Welsh border.

LEMMING. *See* Leaming, *supra.*

LEN, LENA, LEEN *E.* land held in fee ‡ or farmed out. Ex.: Kings-len, now Kingsland (Heref.), the king's farm. Lena, now Haylane (Heref.); the Leen (ditto); Len-ham (Kent), the home on the farm, *i. e.* the tenant's dwelling; Len-ton (Notts), the town on the farm.

LENBURY *E.* anciently Lygean-birg, § Lyge's hill.

LENCH, LINCH *N.* from *hlinc*, an enclosure.‖ Ex.: Rouse-lench (Worc.), Rouse's enclosure; Linch (Suss.).

LEOMINSTER, the minster of nuns, from *lleian* (*B.*), a nun, and *mynstre* (*E.*), a monastery.

LESSING. *See* Las, *supra.*

LET. *See* Leat, *supra.*

LETHERING *E.* from *leoda*, a band, and *incga*, children. Ex.: Lethering-sett and Lethering-ham (Norf.), the station and the home of the children of the band.

LEVEN, LEVING, LEVAN, LEVIS, LEWIS, from Lefan, a British saint. Ex.: Levens (West.); Leven (Yorks.); St. Levan's (Cornw.); Levens-holm, now Levenshulme (Lanc.);

* Wright. † Anglo-Saxon Chronicle, ‡ Spelman.
§ Anglo-Saxon Chronicle, anno 571. ‖ Professor Munch, Copenhagen.

Levan-ton, now Levington (Suff.); Levis-ham (Yorks.); Leves-ham (Kent), now Lewisham, St. Levan's home.

LEVER. *See* Laver, *supra.*

LEWES *E.* probably from *lege* or *lea*, a meadow, and *waes*, water. Ex.: Læ-wes,* now Lewes (Suss.), the water meadow. The adjoining river is still called the Ouse, a word which seems to describe a gentle stream flowing through muddy soil. Hence the verb to ooze.

LEWISHAM. *See* Leven, *supra.*

LEWK *E.* from Lucan, St. Luke's. Ex.: Lewknor (Oxf.), St. Luke's *over*, or brink.

LEY. *See* Lay.

LICH *E.* from *leced*, dead.† Ex.: Lich-field (Staff.), the field of the dead, so called from 1,000 Christians having been martyred there in the persecution under Diocletian, *circa* 304.

LIDNEY *B.* and *E.* from *llid*, district, and *ig*, water. Ex.: Lidenege, now Lidney (Glouc.), the district by the water.

LIFT *E.* the highest part of a range of hills. Ex.: Ladylift (Heref.), the highest part of a range called Maryhill, the connexion of names showing that the word 'lady' here means 'Our Lady.'

LIL, LILLES *E.* from Lilla, the name of the Saxon lord. Ex.: Lil-bourne (Northam.), Lilla's brook; Lilles-hall (Salop), Lilla's hall.

LILLINGS *E.* from Lilla and *incga*, descendants. Ex.: Lillingston (Oxf.), the town of Lilla's descendants.

LIN, LYN *E.* from *hlynna*, a brook. Ex.: Lin-ton, 9 places; Lynton, Lyn-mouth, and the East and West Lyn rivers, in Devon.

LINCH. *See* Lench, *supra.*

LINCOLN *E.* from Lindum Colonia, the Roman name. Linds-ey, the water of Lindum. The latter word was probably a Romanised form of Lliant-din, the camp by the stream or flood.

LIND, LYND *E.* the linden or lime-tree. Ex.: Lind-ridge (Worc.), the ridge of the lime-tree; Linds-hall, now Lind-

* Laws of Athelstan, Wilkins *passim.*

† The covered gate of a churchyard is still called the lich-gate, or gate of the dead.

sell (Ess.), the hall among the limes; Lynd-hurst (Hants), the wood of limes.

LING, LYNG *E.* the *Calluna* of botany, still a common plant on hills in England. Ex.: Ling-ham, now Lingen (Heref.), the home among the ling; Lyng (Norf.), etc. Where it occurs in the middle of a name, it is a particle denoting possession. Ex.: Irling-borough (Northam.), the fortified place of the yrthling, or son of the earth, *i. e.* farmer.

LINK *E.* from *hlinc*, or enclosure. Ex.: Malvern Link (Worc.).

LIS, from the British *llys*, a palace. Ex.: Lis-card (Ches.), and Lis-keard (Cornw.), the palace *garth*, or enclosure.

LISLE, LUEL *E.* from the Latin *legiolium*. Ex.: Caer-luel, now Carlisle; Bede says that the former was the corrupt form of the Roman name.*

LIT, LYT *E.* contraction of little, *qu. v.* Ex.: Lyt-ton.

LITHER, a Lancashire word meaning slow, applied to a stream.†

LITTLE *E.* pointing out the less of two places bearing the same name.

LIVER, perhaps from the British *llif*, a flood. Ex.: Liver-pool, the overflowing pool, or that part of the shore of the river which is liable to be inundated; Liver-mere (Suff.), the overflowing pond or lake.

LLAI *B.* brown or dun-coloured. Ex.: Nant-llai (Glam.), the brown brook.

LLAN *B.* originally any enclosure, as for example *cor-llan*, a sheep-fold; afterwards a heathen sacred enclosure, and thence a church. Occurs in 458 places, all in Wales and the marches; generally a prefix to the name of some saint to whom the church was dedicated.

LLECH *B.* a hiding-place; also a large flat stone, which was probably used as an altar or a tomb, as in the word *crom-lech*, covering stone. Ex.: Tre-lech (Monm.), the town of the large flat stone; Llech-rhyd (Brec.), the ford of the flat stone.

LLECHID *B.* name of a saint. Ex.: Llan-llechid (Carnarv.), St. Llechid's church.

LLETH *B.* from *llaith*, dead. Ex.: Machyn-lleth (Card.), the field of the dead by the way-side; Pilleth (Rad.), the dead or stagnant pool.

* T. Wright.

† Llithrig, Brit., gliding or slippery.

B. British. *C.* Celtic. *E.* The Old English, commonly known as Anglo-Saxon.

Llethyr *B.* a precipice. Ex.: Llethyr-neuadd-ucehaf (Carm.), lower court near the precipice.

Llewern *B.* correctly *llewyrn*, the will-o'-the-wisp. Ex.: Llanfihangel-ystrin-llewyrn (Monm.). *See* Ystern.

Llowell *B.* a saint. Ex.: Llan-llowell (Monm.), St. Llowell's church.

Llwchaearn *B.* name of a saint. Ex.: Llan-llwchaearn (Card.), St. Llwchaearn's church.

Llwch *E.* a lake or pond. The word is originally Irish, and occurs almost solely in South Wales, the proper British word being *llyn*. Ex.: Llwch-or, the Roman Leucarum, now Loughor (Glam.), the edge of the lake.

Llwch *B.* dusty. Ex.: Maes-llweh (Rad.), the dusty field.

Llwyd *B.* grey or brown. Ex.: Ma-llwyd (Denbigh.), the brown district, so called probably from the appearance of the mountains.

Llwyn *B.* a hedge or grove. Ex.: Llwyn-onn (Carnarv.), Ash-grove; Llwyn-y-fedw (Glam.), Birch-grove.

Llychau *B.* plural of *llwch*. Ex.: Tal-y-llychau (Carm.), the ends of the lakes.

Llyn *B.* a lake. Ex.: Llyn-safeddan (Brecons.), Safeddan's lake; Aber-glas-lyn (Carnar.), the estuary of the blue lake.

Llys *B.* a palace or court-house. Ex.: Llys-wen (Brecons.), the white palace; Cefn-llys (Rad.), palace ridge.

Llywel *B.* anciently Caer-Lliwelydd,* the camp of the multitude. Ex.: Llywel (Brecons.)

Lo, Low *E.* from *loe* or *hlæw*, a hill; Lo-stock (Lanc.), the hill station. *See* Low, *supra*.

Loc, Lock, Luc *E.* from *loc* or *lucu*, an enclosure; hence lock, a fastening. Ex.: Loa-lege, now Locker-ley (Hants), the enclosed place; Mat-lock (Derb.), the meat enclosure, *i. e.* storehouse; Luçu-tun, now Lucton (Heref.), the town of the enclosure.

Locking, Lox *N.* from *Loki*, the Norse god of mischief, and *incga*, children. Ex.: Lok-ingatun, now Lockington (Yorks.), the town of the children of Loki; Lokis-lege, now Loxley (do.), Loki's meadow.

Lod, Lode *E.* from *ladan*, to pour, and hence *lod*, possessive *loddan*,

* Stephens, 'Literature of the Kymry.'

D. Old Danish. *G.* Greek. *L.* Latin. *N.F.* Norman French. *N.* Norse. *qu. v.* which see.

a canal or stream, or its junction with another; also a way. Ex.: Lod-don (Norf.), the fortified hill by the stream or way; Even-lode (Glouc.), the *efe* or brink.

Lodding *E.* from Lodda or Ludda, the owner's name, and *incga*, children. Ex.: Loddington (Leic.), the town of the children of Lodda.

Lol. *See* Lul, *infra.*

Londes, Londs *E.* probably the possessive of Londa, the name of the founder or lord. Ex.: Londesbrough (Yorks.), Londa's fortified town.

Long *E.* from the shape of the village or town. Ex.: 27 places, nearly all in midland counties.

Looe, *Cornish*, a port, perhaps a form of *llwch*, from the lake-like shape of the port. Ex.: East and West Looe (Cornw.).

Lop *E.* perhaps from *loppe*, a piece of a tree or anything else which is cut off, or from Loppa (*N.*), a man's name. Ex.: Lop-ham (Norf.), the lonely home, or Loppa's home.

Lopping *E.* from Loppa, and *incga.* Ex.: Lopping-ton (Salop), the town of Loppa's descendants.

Lost, Lust, *Cornish*, perhaps from the Saxon *lust*, desire. Ex.: Lost-withiel (Cornw.), Withyel's desire, named from Withyel, a Saxon Earl of Cornwall; Lust-leigh (Devon), the desired place.

Loughor. *See* Llwch, *supra.*

Louth *E.* from the river Luda. Ex.: Louth (Linc.).

Low *E.* from *loe* or *hlæw*, a hill. *See* Lo, *supra.*

Lowestoft *D.* anciently Lothan-wis-toft, a grove or grounds belonging to a house traditionally said to be named from Lothbrock, a Danish rover.

Luc, Lux. *See* Loc, *supra.*

Lud *E.* from *hleod*, people, probably indicating the place where the assembly of the tithing, wapontake, or hundred was held. Ex.: Leod-hlæw, now Ludlow (Salop), the people's hill.

Ludden, Ludding, from *hleod*, and *incga.* Ex.: Luddenham (Kent), the home or village of the children of the people, in distinction from the children of a chief; Luddington (Linc.), the people's town.

Ludgers, from Lutgar, a Danish or Norse rover. Ex.: Lutgar's hall, now Ludgershall (Wilts and Bucks).

Luffen *E.* from *lufan*, possessive of Lufa, the name of the Saxon lord. Ex.: Luffen-ham (Rutl.), Lufa's home; Luf-ton (Som.), Lufa's town.

LUG *B*. name of the neighbouring stream, from *llûg*, light or bright. Ex.: Lug-dwr-dinas,* (Heref.), now Lugwardine, the camp or palace by Lug water.

LUL, LULLING *E*. probably from Lulla, name of the Saxon lord, and *incga*, descendants. Ex.: Lul-worth (Dorset), Lulla's well-watered estate; Lullington, 4 places, the town of the descendants of Lulla.

LUNDY *N*. and *E*. from *Lund*, and *ig*. Ex.: Lundy, the island of Lund. The word island now appended is superflous.

LUST. *See* Lost, *supra*.

LUT, LUTTER *E*. from Lutta, the lord's name. Ex.: Lut-ton (Norf.), Lutta's town; Lutter-worth (Leices.), Lutta's well-watered estate.

LUX. *See* Loc, *supra*.

LYD, LYTCHETT, LID *B*. from *llid*, country or district; *S*., *leod*. Ex: Lyd-byryg, now Lydbury (Salop), the fortified town of the district; Pippan Leod, now Pipe and Lyde (Heref.), the district of St. Pippa; Llid-iart, now Lydeard (Som.), a country gate, and thence a farm house; Lydget, Lytchett, Lydgate, and Liddiard, are corrupt forms of Llidiart.

LYME *E*. anciently Liming, from *lim*, lime or mud. Ex.: Lyme (Dorset), Lyming-ton (Hants), Lymm (Ches.), Lyminge (Kent).

LYN. *See* Lin, *supra*.

LYND. *See* Lind, *supra*.

LYNG. *See* Ling, *supra*.

LYNN *E*. anciently Lena, from *len* or *læn*, land held by tenure of fee.†

LYONSHALL, corrupted from Linhales, the ancient name, which is apparently derived from *len*, land held by tenure of fee-farm, and *aelh* or *ealh*, a hall. It would thus mean the residence of the tenant in fee. King's-lene, now Kingsland (Heref.), is in the neighbourhood.

LYRA *E*. perhaps from the layers (locally called lias) of the rock on which the church stands. Ex.: Duntsborne Lyra.

* Called 'Loghardineys' in Domesday Book.

† Spelman.

M

MA *B.* a place or district. *See* Fa, *supra.*

MABE, MABYN, *Cornish,* St. Mabyn. Ex.: 2 places.

MABLE, MABEL, a female name, from *amabilis* (Lat.), amiable. Ex.: Mable-thorp (Lanc.), Mabel's farm.

MACCLES *E.* from Maegla, the lord's name. Ex.: Maccles-field (Ches.), Maegla's field. [Maegla, the son of Porta, was one of the principal followers of Cerdic, the first king of Wessex.]

MACHEN *B.* probably from *bach,* little, and *ynn,* plural of *onn,* an ash-tree. Ex.: Machen (Monm.), the little ash-trees.

MACK, MAX, MEX *C.* son, probably from Mac or Maccus, some Celtic chief, who formed one of the leaders of the mixed horde called Norsemen. A Danish chief named Maccus or Macwy is mentioned by Matthew of Westminster as having conquered Anglesey: the Welsh chronicles call him Macht ap Harault, *i. e.* Macht the son of Harold. The Scottish name of Maxwell is recorded to have originated from Maccus-vill, *i. e.* Mack's vill or town. So also Mack-worth (Derb.), Macca's estate; Max-ey (Northam.), Maccus's pool; Max-stoke (Warw.), Maccus's station; Mex-borough (Yorks.), Maccus's town.

MAD, MADE *B.* good. Ex.: Mad-le (Heref.), and Made-le (Salop), good or fertile place.*

MADDING, MADE, MAID, MAIDEN *E.* from the Virgin Mary. Ex.: Madding-ton (Wilts), maiden town; Made-hurst (Suss.), maiden's wood; Maid-ford (Northam.), maid's ford; Maiden-Bradley (Wilts). Maidstone is an exception, *qu. v.*

MADOC *B.* from Madog or Badog, a famous British saint. Ex.: Llanmadoc (Glam.), St. Madoc's church.

MADRES *E.* perhaps from St. Matthew. Ex.: Madres-field (Worc.), St. Matthew's field. *See* Matters, *infra.*

* Giraldus Cambrensis.

B. British. *C.* Celtic. *E.* The Old English, commonly known as Anglo-Saxon.

MADRON, *Cornish*, from St. Mathaern. Ex.: St. Madron (Cornw.).

MAEL, MYL *B.* St. Maelor. Ex.: Maelor or Mylor (Cornw.).

MAELOG *B.* name of a saint, the brother of Gildas the historian. Ex.: Gelly-faelog (Glam.), the hazel-trees of Maelog. He had a cell there, whither he retired when he became a hermit, A.D. 603. Also Llandyfaelog (Brecons., Carmar., and Anglesea), Maelog's church house. In some cases, part of the church was fitted up as a house.

MAEN, FAEN, MEN *B.* a stone or rock. Ex.: Maen-dû (Monm.), Black rock; Men-heniot (Cornw.), Heniot's rock.

MAER, *E.* from *mere*, a pool. Ex.: Maer (Staff.), which is situated at the edge of a pool or lake.

MAES, FAES, MAISE *B.* a field. Ex.: Maes-car (Brec.), pool field; Llan-faes (Brec.), church field; Maise-more (Glouc.), *i. e.* maes-mawr, great field.

MAIDENHEAD *E.* corrupted from Maiden-hithe, the Virgin Mary's port.

MAIDSMORTON *E.* so called from the church having been rebuilt *circa* 1400, by two maiden sisters. Ex.: Maidsmorton (Bucks).

MAIDSTONE *E.* originally Medweges-tun, the town on the Medway river.

MAIN, MAYNE *E.* chief. Ex.: Maines-tun, now Main-stone (Salop), the town of Main; Mayne (West.).

MAIR. *See* Fair, *supra.*

MAISE. *See* Maes, *supra.*

MAL *N. F.* bad. Ex.: Malvoisin Castle (Yorks.), the bad neighbour; Mal-pas (Ches.), the bad or difficult road.*

MAL, MAUL *E.* from *mal*, a place of meeting. Ex.: Mal-ton (Yorks.), Maul-den (Bedf.), etc.

MALDON *E.* from Camalodunum, the Roman name of the place.

MALMESBURY *E.* anciently Meald-helms-byryg, from Mældulf and Aldhelm, its founders.

MALT, MAUT *E.* from *malt*, and apparently designating places where the maltster carried on his very ancient trade. Ex. Malt-by (Yorks.), a Danish malting-town; Maut-by (Norf.), ditto.

* Camden.

MALVERN *B.* commonly derived by Welsh antiquaries from *moel-y-barn*, the bare hill of council; but I think rather from *moel-hafren*, the bare hill by the Hafren, now Severn.

MAM *B.* mother. Ex.: Mam-tor (Derb.), mother hill; Mam-hilad (Monm.), mother church of St. Ilid.

MAN, the name of Anglesea and of the Island of Man, both being called Môn by the British. Derivation unknown. *Ma* or *man* means a place, and *maen*, rock, either of which etymologies is suitable.

MANCETTER *E.* from Manduessuedum, its Roman name; and *cestre*, a fortification.

MANCHESTER *E.* called by the Britons Maen-ceinion, the rock of Ceinion (or of gems); by the Romans Mancunium; and by the Saxons Mancestre, hence its present name.

MANGOTS *E.* from the name of the lord. Ex.: Mangot's-field (Glouc.).

MANNING *E.* perhaps from *mannian*, to man or garrison. Ex.: Manning-ham (Yorks), the garrisoned home.

MANNINGTREE, from *manig-treow* (*S.*), many trees.*

MANOR, from the British *maen-or*, a stone wall, hence a house or piece of land so enclosed, and afterwards an estate.

MANS *E.* from the river Maun. Ex.: Mauns-feld, now Mans-field (Notts), the field of or by the Maun.

MAPLE, MAPPLE *E.* from *maapel*, the maple, *Acer* of botanists. Ex.: Maple-beck (Notts), the maple brook; Mapple-ton (Derb.), maple town.

MAR, MER, MERE *E.* from *mere*, a pool or lake. Ex.: Mar-low, anciently Mere-low (Bucks), the hill by the mere; Mer-ton (Surr.), the mere town; Blake-mere (Heref.), the black mere.

MARCH, *E.* from *merc*. Ex.: the Marches of Wales and Scotland, *i. e.* the counties on the boundary.

MARCLE, anciently Marchelaie, from *merc*, boundary, and *hill*, a hill. Ex.: Marcle (Heref.).

MARDEN (Heref.), anciently Marwardin, from Maes-y-dwrdin (*B.*), field of the water camp.

MARGARETTING *E.* from Margarettan, possessive of Margaret. Ex.: Margaretting (Ess.).

* Local tradition.

B. British. *C.* Celtic. *E.* The Old English, commonly known as Anglo-Saxon.

MARKET *E.* denoting a market town.

MARL *E. marl,* from the nature of the soil. Ex.: Merleberge, now Marl-borough (Wilts), the fortified town on the marl.

MARS, MARSH *E.* from *mere,* a marsh or pool. Ex.: Marston, 16 places, the marsh town; Marshwood (Dorset), etc.

MARSTOW *E.* St. Martin's * *stow, i. e.* station. Ex.: Marstow (Heref.).

MART *E.* contracted from market. Ex.: Mart-ock (Som.), the market oak, the market having been held under a great oak-tree at that place †; Mart-ham (Norf.), Market home.

MARTYR *E.* a martyr. Ex.: Martyr-worth-ey (Hants), the martyr's estate by the water.

MARY, from the Virgin Mary. Very frequent.

MAS *E.* in one instance contracted from Mary's. Ex.: Mas-ham (Kent), St. Mary's home.

MASSING *E.* probably from *mæs,* battle, and *incga,* children. Ex.: Massing-ham (Norf.), the home of the children of battle, or warriors.

MAT, MATTERS, MATTIS *E.* from St. Matthew. Ex.: Mats-ton (Glouc.), Matthew's town; Matters-ey (Norf.), Matthew's water; Mattis-hall (Norf.), Matthew's hall.

MATHERN (Monm.), *B.* from St. Mathaern.

MATHON. Ditto.

MATLOCK (Derb.), a food store, from *maet,* meat, and *lucu,* an enclosure.

MAUL. *See* Mal, *supra.*

MAUT. *See* Malt, *supra.*

MAVIS *E.* the thrush. Ex.: Mavis Enderby (Linc.), thrush Enderby, the latter word marking the settlement of a Dane named Ander or Andrew.

MAWDES *E.* Maud's or Matilda's estate. Ex.: Mawdes-ley (Lanc.), Maud's land.

MAWR *B.* feminine of *fawr,* great. *See* FAWR, *supra.*

MAX. *See* Mack, *supra.*

MAY *E.* from Magu, the name of the tribe who settled there.‡ Ex.: May-hill (Glouc.); Magge, Magene, and Magere (Heref.), places mentioned in Domesday Book, as belonging

* Wakeman, in Notes to Liber Landavensis.

† Local tradition.

‡ E. A. Freeman.

D. Old Danish. *G.* Greek. *L.* Latin. *N. F.* Norman French. *N.* Norse. *qu. v.* which see.

to Roger de Lacy, but not now identifiable; May-field (Suss.).

MEARE. *See* Mere, *infra.*

MED *E.* from *mæd,* a meadow. Ex.: Medbourn (Leices.), meadow brook.

MEDMEN *E.* from *madm,* treasure. Ex.: Medmen-ham (Bucks), the treasure house, or place where the king kept his money.

MEDWAY *E.* anciently Medwege, from *mædew,* a meadow, and *ig,* water, the meadow water or river flowing through meadows. Ex.: the Medway (Kent).

MEIFOD *B.* perhaps from *maes,* field, and *fod,** feminine of *bod,* a dwelling. Ex.: Meifod (Mont.).

MEL, from Miln, *qu. v. infra.*

MELK *E.* from *melce,* milk, designating a dairy farm. Ex.: Melks-ham (Wilts), dairy farm home.

MELLING *E.* perhaps from *miln* and *incga,* meaning the posterity of the miller.

MEON *B.* from *mehin,* a place, or from *min,* the brow, applied to a bold eminence. Ex.: only 5 places, all of which are situated on or close to conspicuous hills, viz., Meon Stoke, hill fortification; East and West Meon (Hants), Meon hill and camp (Glouc.).

MEOP, MEP, MEPPERS *E.* from Meopa, the lord's name. Ex.: Meop-ham (Kent), Meopa's home; Mep-ealh, now Mepall (Camb.), Meopa's hall; Meppers-hall (Bedf.), ditto.

MERCIA *E.* the name of the largest of the eight Saxon and Anglian kingdoms, anciently Myrcna-ric, from *merc,* boundary, and *ric,* rule or kingdom, it having been founded by Crida, in the *mercen* or boundary districts now called Herefordshire.

MERRI, MERROW *E.* from *mæra,* a boundary, probably indicating a cultivated spot at the edge or boundary of the waste. Ex.: Meri-dan (Warw.), boundary hollow; Merrow (Surr.), the boundary.

MERS. *See* Mere, *supra.*

MERTHER, MERTHYR *B.* a martyr. Ex.: Merther (Cornw.); Merthyr Tydfil (Glam.), the church of the martyr Tydfil.

MESNE *N. F.* land held of the owner, but sub-let to a third person. Hence the word de-mesne, land not sublet. Ex.: Clifford's

* Names of cities and towns are feminine in Welsh, as in Latin, etc.

Mesne (Glouces.), part of the Forest of Dean, granted to Clifford, but by him sub-granted.

MET, METH, METTING, METHERING *E.* perhaps from *metan*, to measure, or enclose with boundaries. Ex.: Met-field (Suff.), the enclosed field; Meth-ley (Yorks.), the enclosed land; Methering-ham (Linc.); Metting-ham (Suff.), the enclosed home.

MEURIG *B.* name of a king who fought against the Saxons, at the place thence called Pwll-meurig (Monm.), Meurig's pool.

MEX. *See* Mack, *supra.*

MICH, MICKLE, MITCHEL, MUCH *E.* from *mycel*, great, answering to some Little in the neighbourhood. Ex.: Mich-field (Suff.), great field; Mickle-ham (Surr.), great home; Much Birch (Heref.); Mitchel-dean (Glouc.), answering to Little Birch and Little Dean, neighbouring places.

MID *E.* lying between two or more towns, generally of the same root name. Ex.: 11 places.

MIDDLETON *E.* anciently Midatun, probably from *mæd*, a meadow, and *tun*, an enclosed farm-house, afterwards a town. Ex.: 19 places.

MIHANGEL *B.* the archangel. Ex.: Llan-mihangel (Glam.), St. Michael's church. [Probably a corruption, since Llan, being feminine, requires the word which follows to change its radical initial for the corresponding soft consonant. Thus Llan-gynog is the church of St. Cynog.]

MIL, MIL, MILN *E.* from *miln*, a mill; *melin*, *B.* Ex.: 40 places, of which 1 is Miln-thorp (Westmor.), the mill farm; 4 are Mil-den, the mill hollow; 1 is Mill-wick, the mill abode; 19 Mil-ton, mill town.

MILLICHOPE *E.* and *B.* from *mill-edge*, mill-ridge, and *hwpp*, a sloping plain between hills. Ex.: Millichope (Salop).

MIN, MIND, MYNDE, from *min*, *B.* the brow of a hill. Ex.: Min-stead (Hants), the station on the brow; Mind-town (Salop), the town on the brow; Mynde (Heref.), the brow.

MINEHEAD *E.* called in Domesday Book Man-heved, evidently from Maen-hafod (*B.*), the summer residence on or near the rocks.

MINSTER *E.* from *mynstre*, a monastery, hence a cathedral or any other church where monks officiated. None of the cathedrals which were founded at or since the Reformation are called minsters. Ex.: Minster-worth (Glouces.), the estate belonging to a monastery; Westminster, the monastery on the west side of London; Minster-ley (Salop), monastery place.

MISSON, MISSEN *E.* from *mæssen*, possessive of *mæsse*, the mass or Roman service; probably indicating land charged with payment for masses. Ex.: Misson (Notts); Missendon (Norf.), mass-hill.

MISTER *E.* from *mæste*, mast, the fruit of beech and oak-trees, on which swine were fed. Ex.: Mister-ton (Notts), mast-town, or the place where swine were kept.

MOBBER *B.* from *mod*, a ruler, and *her*, a hedge. Ex.: Modberlle, now Mobberley (Ches.), the enclosed land belonging to the ruler.

MOC *B.* from *moch*, a pig. Ex.: Moch-rhos, now Moccas (Heref.), the pig's marshy meadow.

MOEL, MOYL *B.* a bare, pointed hill. Ex.: Mocl Bannau, and many other hills in Wales; Moyl-isker (Westm.), from *moel* and *ysc*, *C.*, the bare hill by the water.

MOIL *B.* from Moil or Macmoil, one of the companions of St. Cadoc, sixth century. Ex.: Pont-y-moil (Montm.), St. Moil's bridge; Maesmoil, now Mamhole (Monm.), the field of St. Moil.*

MOLD *B.* from *mollt*, a wether sheep. Ex.: Mold (Flints.).

MOLE, MOUL *D.* from *mol*, a mole, indicating places where that animal is or was common. Hence the river Mole, from its banks being inhabited by the mole. Ex.: Moles-ey (Surrey), the mole's water; Moles-worth (Hants), the mole's estate; Moul-ton, 5 places, and Mol-ton (Devon), the mole's town.

MON *B.* the river Munnow, from *mynydd*, *B.*, a mountain. Ex.: Mon-mouth, the junction of the Munnow and the Wye.

MONACH, MYNACH *B.*, MONK, MONX *E.* a monk; indicating the site of a monastery, or land belonging to one. Ex.: Monachty (Radnors.), the monk's house; Llan-y-mynach (Salop),

* The land was given to St. Moil by his patron St. Cadoc.—See Rees' 'Lives of the Welsh Saints.'

B. British. *C.* Celtic. *E.* The Old English, commonly known as Anglo-Saxon.

the monk's church; Monk-sylva, now Monksilver (Somers.), the monk's wood, Monx-ton (Hants), monk's town.

MONACHLOG *B.* the monk's place. Ex.: Monachlog-ddu (Pemb.) the place of the black or Dominican monks.

MOND. *See* Mund, *infra.*

MONING, MONNING *S.* from *monec*, a monk, and *ing*, a meadow. Ex.: Monning-ton (Heref.), the town of the monk's meadow.

MONT *N. F.* a mountain or hill. Ex.: Mont-gymry, now Montgomery, the mountain of the Cymry or Britons; Mont-acute (Somers.), the sharp or pointed hill.

MOOR, MORE, MORS *E.* from *mor*, a tract of wild land. Ex.: Moor-by (Linc.), the Danish abode on the moor; Sedge-moor (Somers.), the sedgy or rushy moor; Mor-ton, 9 places; More-ton, 12 places; Mor-peth (Cumb.), the moor path. The word More is sometimes a corruption of *mere*, a pool. Ex: Blake-more (Heref.), anciently Blake-mere, the black pool; Mores-ton (Norf.), the town of the pool.

MORASTON *E.* Meurig's town. Ex.: Moraston (Heref.).

MORFA *B.* a marsh. Ex.: Morfa Rhuddlan (Denb.).

MORRAN *B.* name of a saint. Ex.: Lanmorran (Cornw.), St. Morran's church.

MOSELEY *E.* in Domesday Book called Moles-lage, *i.e.* Mole's land. Ex.: Moseley (Worces.).

MOSS *N.* a bog, a common word in the northern counties and in Lowland Scotland. Ex.: Moss-ton (Lancas.), bog-town; Chat-moss (ditto), St. Chad's bog, or Chetel's bog.

MOT *E.* a boundary. *See* Met.

MOUNT *E.* *See* Mont, *supra.*

MOUTH *E.* the estuary of a river. Ex.: Lyn-mouth (Devon), the estuary of the Lyn.

MUCH, MUCHEL *E.* great. *See* Mich and Michel, *supra.*

MUND, MOND, MUN *E.* a mound, or earthern fortification. Ex.: Mundan, now Munden (Herts), the place of the mound; Healh-mund, now Haugh-mond (Salop), the hall on the mound, or the hall fortified with an earthern rampart.

MUNSLEY *E.* anciently * Moneslai, the monk's land or place. Ex.: Munsley (Heref.).

MUR *E.* a moor. *See* Moor, *supra.*

* Domesday Book.

MYDDFAI *B.* a famous British physician, whose name was derived from *ma*, a cow, and *fa*, a place. Ex.: Mydd-fai (Carm.).*

MYLOR. *See* Mael, *supra.*

MYNACH. *See* Monach, *supra.*

MYNIS *B.* probably from *mynydd*, and *is*, below. Ex.: Maes-mynis (Brecons.), the field below the mountain.

MYNYDD *B.* a mountain. Ex.: Tor-y-mynydd (Monm.), the mountain tower or peak.

* Richards *in voce.*

N

NAC, NACKING, NOC, NOKE, perhaps from the British *cnwch, E. knock,* a bunch or isolated hill. Ex.: Nac-ton (Suff.), the town on or near the isolated hill; Nacen or Nacking-ton (Kent), and Noc-ton (Linc.), the same.

NAFFER *E.* probably from Naffa, the name of the lord. Ex.: Naffer-ton (Yorks.), Naffa's town.

NAILS *E.* from *nægel,* a nail or pin, which became the name of a man, under the form of Nigel. Ex.: Nails-ea (Somers.), Nigel's pool; Nails-worth (Glouc.), Nigel's watered estate; Nails-ton (Leices.), Nigel's town.

NANNERCH *B.* from *nenn,* roof or summit, and *erch,* dark or terrible. Ex.: Nannerch (Denb.).

NANT *B.* a brook. Ex.: Nant-mel (Radnors.), honey brook, from its hue, or from the hives of wild bees in the neighbouring rocks; Nant-wich (Ches.), the dwelling by the brook; Sych-nant (Brec.), a dry brook-course.

NAP *E.* *See* Knap, *supra.*

NAR *E.* *See* Nor, *infra.* Ex.: Nar-burgh, the fortified place on the river Nar.

NARBERTH *B.* perhaps from *na,* not, and *berth,* beautiful. Ex.: Narberth (Pemb.).

NASE, NAZE, NES, NESS *E.* from *næsse,* a promontory or nose of land. Ex.: Nase-by (Northam.), the promontory town of the Danes; Naze-ing (Essex), promontory meadow; Nes-ton (Ches.), the town on the promontory between the Dee and the Mersey; Ness, the name of several promontories in Suffolk, etc.

NASH *E.* from *næsse,* a promontory. Ex.: Nash-scaur (Radnors.), the cliff promontory; Nash (Pemb.), Nash (Monm.). *See* Nase, Ness.

NAUGH, NOW *E.* perhaps from *haugh,* a green hill or bank. Ex.: Naugh-ton (Suff.), the town on the green hill; Now-ton (Suff.), the same.

NAUN, NONING *E.* from *nonne,* or *nunne,* a nun. Ex.: Naun-ton (Glouc.), the nun's town; Naunton Beauchamp (Worces.),

Beauchamp's Naunton; Nonnen-ton or Noning-ton (Kent), nun's town.

NAVEN, NAVES *E.* from *nafa*, or *navu*, the middle; hence the nave of a wheel. Ex.: Naven-by (Linc.), the middle town inhabited by the Danes; Nave-stock (Essex), the middle station.

NAY, NA, NY *E.* from *ey*, water. Ex.: Nay-land (Pemb. and Suff.), land by the water; Na-worth (Cumb.), estate by the water; Ny-land (Somers.).

NEAT, NEOT *E.* St. Neot. Ex.: Neate's-head (Norf.), St. Neot's hill; St. Neot's (Hunts).

NEATH *B.* perhaps from *naid* or *nawdd*, a sanctuary or retreat. Ex.: Nedd, now Neath (Glam.), Cwm-nedd, etc.

NEC, NI, NIGH *E.* from St. Neot. Ex.: Necton (Norf.), Nighton (Cornw.), Niton (Hants).

NEED *E.* perhaps from *snæd*, a fragment, applied to lands separated from the manor belonging to the same lord. Ex.: Need-ham (Norf.), the town of the separated land.

NEMP, NYM *E.* a personal name. *See* Shakspere's 'King Henry IV.'; probably a contraction of Nehemiah. Ex.: Nymen-hut or Nemp-nett (Som.), Nym's hut; Nyms-field (Glouc.), Nym-ton (Devon), Nym-et (Devon), Nym's hut.

NEOT'S *E.* from St. Neot. *See* Neat, *supra.*

NETHER *E.* lower in site than another place of the same root-name. Ex.: Nether and Upper Hallam (Yorks.).

NETS, NETTES *E.* from *næt*, cattle. Ex.: Nets-well or Nettes-well (Essex), the well of the cattle; or it may be St. Neot's well.

NETTLE *E.* from *nædl*, the nettle; or, which seems more probable, from *snidan*, to cut, and *lege*, land, thus indicating a piece of land cut off from the rest of an estate. Ex.: Nettle-comb (Som.), the separated land in the dingle; Nettle-stead (Kent), the station on the separated land. *See* Need and Snead.

NEUADD *B.* a hall. Ex.: Neuadd-felin (Brec.), the hall near the mill.

NEVEN. *See* Naven, *supra.*

NEW, NEWEN, NEWING, NEWN *E.* from *niwe*, new, indicating a town or village which was founded after some neighbouring one of the same name or description. Ex.: 126 places, of

* Bosworth *in voce.*

which *ton* or *town* is the suffix in 45 instances; *castle* in 7; *ham* in 6; *port* in 6; *church* in 5, etc. Thus New-port (Mon.) was so called with reference to Caerleon, the old or Roman port of Isca Silurum; New-burh, now New-bury (Berks), with reference to the ancient town of Speen, etc.

NEWYDD *B.* new. Ex.: Ty-newydd (Brec.), the new house.

NI, NIGH. *See* Nec.

NOKE. *See* Nac.

NOL *E.* a contraction of Oliver. Ex.: Nol-ton (Pemb.), Oliver's town.

NOMANSLAND *E.* a settlement or clearance on a waste. Ex.: Berkshire and other counties.

NONING. *See* Naun.

NONN *B.* a saint, the mother of St. David.* Ex.: Llan-Nonn (Carm.), St. Nonn's church.

NOR, NORTH, NAR *E.* the more northerly of two places. Ex.: 40 places in which Nor is the prefix, 36 of which are Nor-ton; North, 29 places; Nar, 3 places; North-hoe, now Northew (Herts), the north hill.

NORMAN designates towns built by the Normans. Ex.: 10 places, of which Norman-by (3) points out Danish settlements seized by the Normans; Norman-ton, 7 places, built near Saxon towns.

NOT. *See* Nut.

NOTTINGHAM, from the Saxon Snot-incga-ham, the place of the cave dwellers,† or children of the caves.

NUN *E.* from *nunne*, originally an orphan, afterwards a nun. Ex.: 8 places; Nun-eaton (Warw.), the nun's town by the water; Nune-ham (Oxf.), the nun's home.

NUT, NOT *E.* from *hnote*, *hnutu*, *notu*, a nut, probably indicating a site where the nut-bearing hazel was common. Ex.: Nut-field (Surr.), Not-grove (Glouc.), etc.

NYM. *See* Nemp, *supra*.

* Iolo MSS. † Camden.

D. Old Danish. *G.* Greek. *L.* Latin. *N. F.* Norman French. *N.* Norse. *qu. v.* which see.

O

OAD, OD, ODI, probably from the name of the owner; *D. odder*, an otter. A Mercian noble named Oddo is commemorated in Worcestershire tradition. Words compounded of Oad, etc., occur chiefly in counties comprised in the Anglian kingdom of Mercia. Ex.: Oad-by (Leices.), Oddo's abode: Od-comb (Som.), Oddo's dingle: Odi-ham (Hants), Oddo's home.

OAK, OC, OCK, OCKEN, OCLE, OKE *E.* from *æc*, an oak. Ex.: 15 places in which oak has ham, ton, by, or ey appended; Oc-cold (Suff.), *i. e.* oak-holt or oak-grove; Ock, 3 places; Ock-en, from *æcan*, of an oak, 2 places; Ocle (Heref.), oak-hill; Oke-over (Staff.), the oak ridge or boundary.

OARE, ORE, OWR, OWER *E.* from *ora*, a shore; *B. or*, a boundary; Greek ὅρος. Ex.: Oare (Kent and Som.), the shore; Ore (Suss.), the shore; Owers-by (Linc.); Ower-ham, now Ow-ram (Yorks.), etc.

OBORNE *D.* and *E.* corrupted from *hoe-bourn*, hill brook. Ex.: Oborne (Dorset).

OBY *D.* corrupted from *Hoe-by*, hill abode. Ex.: Oby (Norf.).

OC, OCK. *See* Oak, *supra*.

OD. *See* Oad.

ODDING *E.* from Oddo, and *incga*, descendants. Ex.: Odding-ley and Odding-ton (Worc. and Glouc.), the place and town of Oddo's descendants.

OFF, OFFEN, OVEN, OVING, OW *E.* from Offa, king of Mercia. Ex.: Offen-ham (Worc.), Offa's home; Offley (Staff.), Offa's place; Off-ford (Hunts), Offa's ford; Ow-borough (Heref.), Offa's camp;* Ow-thorp (Notts), Offa's farm; Oven-dean (Yorks.), Offa's hollow; Oving-dean (Suss.), the same.

OG *E.* perhaps from Ugga, the lord's name. Ex.: Og-bourne (Wilts), 2 places, Ugga's brook: Og-well (Devon), 2 places, Ugga's well. *See* Ug, *infra*.

OGOF *B.* a cave.

OKE. *See* Oak, *supra*.

* Duncumb's 'Herefordshire.'

B. British. *C.* Celtic. *E.* The Old English, commonly known as Anglo-Saxon.

OLAVE, OLVES, OLIFFE *D.* or *N.* from Olaf, a royal saint. Ex.: St. Olave's, Southwark; Olves-ton (Glouc.), Olaf's town; Ship-ton Oliffe (Glouc.), Olaf's sheep-town.

OLD *E.* contracted from *wold,* wild or uncultivated land. Ex.: Old (Northam.); Old-bærw, or Old-burh, now Oldberrow (Worc.), fortification on the wold; Old-castle (Heref.), wold castle. In some few cases where the name is modern, *old* points out the more ancient of two places. Ex.: Old Sarum, Old Swinford.

OLN, from *olan.* *See* Aln.

OMBERS *E.* probably from Aurelius Ambrosius, the British king. Ex.: Ombers-ley (Worc.), Ambrosius's land; Ombers-lade (Warw.), Ambrosius's brook.

ONGAR *S.* a hill. *See* Anger, *supra.*

ONI *B.* from the river Onny. Ex.: Oni-bury (Salop), the fortification by the Onny.

ONNY *B.* from *onn-wy,* the water near the ash-trees. Ex.: the river Onny (Salop).

ORCHARD, ORCHES *E.* from *orceard,* a garden or orchard. Only occurs in Wilts, Som., and Dorset. Ex.: Orchard-leigh (Som.); Orchards-ton, now Orcheston (Wilts), etc.

ORCOP *B.* and *E.* in Domesday Book called Hercope, *i. e.* long hill, from *hir* (*B.*), long, and *cop,* a hill. Ex.: Orcop (Heref.).

ORD, ORDS *E.* from *ord,* the beginning, point, or extremity; hence a headland or termination of a range of hills; and afterwards a personal name. Ex.: Ord (Northum.), Ord's hall, now Ordsall (Notts), etc. Or from *ord, C.,* a hammer, and afterwards a personal name.*

ORL, ORLES *E.* the alder-tree (*Alnus glutinosa*). Ex.: Orl-ton (Heref.), alder town; Orles-ton (Kent), the same.

ORLING, from *yrthling,* a farmer. *See* Arling, *supra.*

ORMES, ORMS *N.* from *Ormr,* the serpent, also the name of a Norse rover. Ex.: Ormes-by (Yorks.), and Orms-by (Linc.), Orm's abode; Ormes-head (Carnar.), Orm's hill.

OSBALD *E.* from *os,* a hero, or brave, and *bald,* bold; afterwards a man's name. Ex.: Osbald-wick (Yorks.), Osbald's dwelling.

OSBORNE *E.* or *D.* from *os,* brave, and *beorn,* a bear. Ex.: Osborne-by (Linc.), Osbeorn's abode.

* Sir Walter Scott.

Osga *D.* name of the lord, now spelt Oscar. Ex.: Osga-thorp (Leices. and Yorks.), Osga's farm.

Osmas, Osming, Osmother *E.* from Osmund, the lord's name. Ex.: Osmas-ton (Derb.), Osmund's town; Osming-ton (Dorset), the same; Osmunda-lege, now Osmotherley (Yorks.), Osmund's place.

Osmund *E.* from *os*, a hero, and *mund*, protection.

Oswald, Oswes *E.* from Oswald, king of Northumbria, the protector of the British churches against Rome, killed in battle at Oswestry, against Penda, king of Mercia, A.D. 642. Ex.: Oswald-kirk (Yorks.), Oswald's church; Oswald's-tref (Salop), Oswald's town, from a monastery founded there in his honour; St. Oswald (Ches.), etc.

Oswald *E.* from *os*, a hero, and *weald*, the forest.

Oswyth *B.* from *yswydd*, the privet. Ex.: Cae-yswydd (Monm.), privet field.

Osyth *E.* from Osyth or Oswytha, daughter of Redwald, king of East Anglia, who founded a church and a nunnery at the place in Essex afterwards named from her, and was there martyred by the Danes in the ninth century. Ex.: St. Osyth (Ess.).

Ot, Oth, Other *E.* from Otho, name of a leader. Ex.: Otho-lege,* now Otley, (Yorks. and Suff.), Otho's land; Other-ey (Som.), Otho's water or stream; Oth-ham, now Otham (Kent), Otho's home.

Otter, Ottery *E.* from *oter* or *otyr*, an otter, afterwards a man's name. Ex.: the river Otter (Devon); Otter-den (Kent), the otter's hollow.

Ottering *S.* from Oter and *incga*. Ex.: Ottering-ton (Yorks.), the town of Oter's descendants.

Oul, Owl *E.* from *ula*, an owl. Ex.: Oul-ton (Norf. and Suff.), owl-town; Owl-pin (Glouc.), owl-hill.

Ouse *E.* a stream which flows through muddy or sandy soil. Ex.: several rivers, and places on their banks.

Out *E.* out. Ex.: Out-wood (Lanc.), outside the wood or wild land.

Oven, Oving *E.* from Offan, the possessive of Offa. *See* Off, *supra*.

Over *E.* higher, from *ofre*, margin or edge. Ex.: 20 places,

* Domesday Book.

nearly all in midland counties. When a suffix, as in Pe-over (Ches.), Cond-over (Salop), it seems to mean a hill site; when a prefix, it indicates, as in Over-whitacre (Warw.), the higher of two places. Astenofre,* now Eastnor (Heref.), the kiln hill.

OVOR *B.* St. Gofor. Ex.: Llan-ovor (Monm.), St. Gofor's church.

OWSLE, OZLE *E.* the ousel or blackbird. Ex.: Owsle-bury (Hants), the fortification of some chief who assumed the blackbird as his cognizance; Ozle-worth (Glouc.), Ousel's watered estate.

OX, OXEN *E.* from *oxa*, an ox. Ex.: 14 places; Oxen-den (Northam.), oxen hill; Ox-ted (Surr.), the stead or station of the ox; Oxen-ey (Kent), the water of the oxen.

* Domesday Book.

P

PACK, PAKE, PAX, PECK *E.* probably from Pacca, the lord's name. Ex.: Pack-wood (Warw.), Pacca's wood; Pake-field (Suff.), Pacca's field; Pacce-lade,* now Paxton (Hunts), Pacca's path; Peck-ham (Surr.).

PACKING *E.* from Pacca and *incga.* Ex.: Packing-ton (Warw.), town of Pacca's descendants.

PAD, PADI *E.* from Peada, king of Mercia. Ex.: Pad-bury (Bucks), Peada's fortified town; Peada-ham, now Padiham (Lanc.), Peada's home or village.

PADDING *E.* from Peada and *incga.* Ex.: Padding-ton (Midd.), the town of Peada's descendants.

PADSTOW *E.* Petroc's station; a monastery † having been founded there in 432, by St. Petroc. Ex.: Padstow (Cornw.).

PAG, PAGLE *E.* from St. Pega, fl. A.D. 714. Ex.: Pag-ham (Suss.), St. Pega's home; Pag-le-ham, now Pagles-ham (Ess.), the place of Pega's home.

PAIGN, PAIN *N. F.* from Pain or Pagan, the name of a Norman knight. Ex.: Paign-ton (Devon), Pain's town; Pains-wick (Glouc.), Pain's dwelling; Pain's castle (Radn.).

PANCRAS, PANG *E.* from St. Pancratius, a Roman martyr. Ex.: St. Pancras (Midd.); Pancras-wick (Devon), St. Pancras's dwelling; Panx-worth (Norf.), St. Pancras's estate.

PANG *E.* from Panga or Penga, a chief's name. Ex.: Pang-bourn (Berks), Panga's brook.

PANT *B.* a valley or bottom. Ex.: Pant-têg, now Panteg (Monm.), beautiful valley.

PAP, PAPPLE *E.* perhaps from Pappa, the lord's name. Ex.: Pap-worth (Camb.), Pappa's estate; Papp-le-wick (Notts), the place of Pappa's abode.

PARA, PAR, PARN *E.* from *pera,* a pear; *B. ber.* Ex.: Para-comb (Devon), pear valley; Par-ham (Suff.), pear home, or home among the pear-trees; Parn-don (Ess.), pear hill.

* Anglo-Saxon Chronicle.

† Sacked by the Danes in A.D. 981. Anglo-Saxon Chronicle.

B. British. *C.* Celtic. *E.* The Old English, commonly known as Anglo-Saxon.

PARK *E.* from *parruc*, a park. Ex.: Windsor park, Woodstock park, etc. In Scotland, the word means a pasture-field.

PARRET *E.* a river named from Pederida,* king of the West Saxons. Ex.: the Parret (Som.).

PARTH *B.* the floor or ground. Ex.: Deheubarth, the ancient name of South Wales, meaning the southern ground; Parth-y-Syllwr, now Partyseal (Monm.), the ground of the Silurians.

PARTNEY *E.* contracted from *pera-tun-ey*, pear-town by the water. Ex.: Partney (Linc.).

PARTRICIO *B.* (doubtful), but perhaps from Padrig, St. Patrick, and *syw*, wise. Ex.: Partricio (Brecons.).

PAS, PASSING *E.* *See* Pea, *infra.*

PAT, PATCH, PATRING, PATS, PATTING, PATTES, PATTIS *E.* from St. Peter. Ex.: Pat-tun-ey, now Patney (Wilts), St. Peter's town by the water; Pats-hall (Staff.), St. Peter's hall; Pats-ham, now Patcham (Suss.), St. Peter's home; Patring-ton (Yorks.), St. Peter's town; Pattes-ley (Norf.), St. Peter's place; Patting-ham (Salop), St. Peter's home; Pattis-wick (Ess.), St. Peter's abode.

PATH *E.* from *pæth*, a path. Ex.: Ridburn's path (Cumb.).

PATRIX *E.* St. Patrick's. Ex.: Patrix-bourn (Kent), St. Patrick's brook.

PAUL, PAULERS, POUL, POULS *E.* St. Paul. Ex.: Paul-ton (Som.), St. Paul's town; Paulers-burh, now Paulers-pury (Northam.), St. Paul's fortified town; Poul-ton (Kent), Paul's town; Pouls-hot (Wilts), Paul's hut or house. Chaucer speaks of 'Sent Poule's,' meaning St. Paul's.

PAUNT *B.* from *pant*, a valley. Ex.: Paunt-le, now Pauntley (Glouc.), valley place.

PAWLETT *N. F.* from the name of the lord. Ex.: Pawlett (Som.).

PAX. *See* Pack, *supra.*

PAYHAM *E.* from Peada, king of Mercia A.D. 652, and *ham*, home. Ex.: Payhem-bury (Devon). *See* Bury.

PEA, PEASE, PEGS, PIS *E.* from St. Pega, d. A.D. 714, to whom Pea-kirk (Northam.), is still dedicated. Ex.: Pea-over (Ches.), St. Pega's hill; Pease-marsh (Suss.), St. Pega's marsh; Pegs-worth (Leices.), St. Pega's estate; Pis-ford (Northam.).

* Anglo-Saxon Chronicle.

PEATLING *E.* from Peada and *len*, etc. Ex.: Peatling (Leices.), Peada's land let to a tenant. *See* Len.

PEB *E.* from Pebba or Bebba, the lord's name. Ex.: Peb-worth (Glouc.), Pebba's estate; Bab-worth (Notts). the same.

PECK. *See* Pack, *supra*.

PED *E.* from Peada, king of Mercia A.D. 652. Ex.: Ped-more (Berks), Peada's mere or pool.

PEEL, PIL, PILL *B.* from *pill*, a small tower defended by a ditch. Ex.: Peel (Isle of Man); Pil-gwenlli (Monm.), the tower of Gwenlli, a woman's name; Pill (Som.); Pil-ton, 4 places, tower town.

PEM, PEN *B.* from *penn*, a headland or hill. Ex.: Penn-bro, now Pembroke, the head of the country; Pem-bre (Carm.), the head of the promontory; Pen-carreg (Carm.), the rocky hill; Pen-rheidd, now Penrith (Cumb.), the red hill. Pen occurs in 54 instances, and Pem in 5, always as prefixes.

PEND *E.* from Penda, king of Mercia. Ex.: Pendo-mere (Som.), Penda's pool; Pendock (Worc.), Penda's oak.

PENK *E.* a river in Staff.

PENNARTH *B.* from *penn*, a head or hill, and *garth*, cultivated land, meaning a promontory which is not rocky. (*Ard*, *C.*, a promontory.) Ex.: Pennarth (Glam.).

PENRHYN *B.* hill cape. Ex.: Penrhyn (Cornw.), which is situated in the hundred of Pen-wyth, *i. e.* Penn-gwydd, the wild hills overgrown with brambles.

PENSCEL *B.* from *pensel*, a prince. Ex.: Penscel-wood (Som.), the wood which had belonged to a British prince, but was seized by the Saxons.

PENSHURST *E.* perhaps from *pinu*, a pine-tree, and *hyrst*, a wood. Ex.: Pens-hurst (Kent), pine wood.

PENSNETT *E.* perhaps from Penda, king of Mercia, and *snitan*, to excavate. Ex.: Pensnett (Staff.), the cave of Penda.

PENT *E.* a shed or lean-to building. Ex.: Pent-ridge (Derb. and Dorset), the ridge of the pent-house.

PENZANCE, *Cornish*, said to mean the head of the bay.*

PEOPLE *E.* the people, probably indicating a place where the land was held in common. Ex.: People-ton (Worc.), the people's town.

PERRAN, *Cornish*, St. Piran. Ex.: 3 places.

* Lewis's Topographical Dictionary.

PERROT, PETHERTON *E.* from Pederida, king of West Saxons. Ex.: Perrot (Som.); Petherton,* *i. e.* Pederida's town, etc.

PERSHORE *E.* from *pursh,* a willow, and *shore.* Ex.: Pershore (Worc.), willow shore.

PERTH *B.* from *berth,* a hedge. Ex.: Perth-hir (Glam.), the long hedge; perhaps Perth, in Scotland.

PERTHOLY *B.* from porth-halawg, polluted porch. Ex.: Llandeilo Pertholy (Monm.), the church of St. Teilo with the polluted porch, from some crime committed there, the history of which is lost.

PET, PETTIS *E.* from St. Peter. Ex.: Pet-haugh, now Pettaugh (Suff.), Peter's green hill; Pet-worth (Suss.), Peter's estate, called in Domesday Book 'Peteorde,' *i. e.* Peter's land.

PETER *E.* from St. Peter. Ex.: 17 places.

PETH *E.* from *pæth,* a path. Ex.: Mor-peth (Northum.), the moor path.

PETHERWIN *E.* from St. Patarnus or Badarn, a British bishop. Ex.: Petherwin (Devon).

PETROX, PETROS, *B.* from St. Petrox, who fl. A.D. 532. Ex.: St. Petrox (Devon); St. Petros (Pemb.).

PEVEN, PAVIS, PEWS *E.* from Peva or Peowa, probably the name of the lord. Ex.: Peowans-ey, now Pevensey (Suss.), Peowa's water; Pews-ey (Wilts), the same; Pavenham (Bedf.).

PHIL, *Cornish,* St. Felix.: Ex.: Phillock and Philleigh (Cornw.).

PICK, PIX *E.* perhaps from *pihtas,* the Picts, a memorial of their incursions into England. Ex.: 9 places, all in north and midland counties except Pickenham (Norf.), the Pict's home, and Pix-ley (Heref.), the Pict's place. [Mr. Nokes, in his Worcestershire 'Notes,' suggests that 'Pix' is a remnant of the fairy mythology, in which the 'pixies' played an important part; but I find no instances of parishes or towns being named from that mythology, and I apprehend that it would have seemed to our forefathers an act of great impiety to have given such names to ecclesiastical divisions of the country. That rocks, lonely dells, and woods may have retained their heathen superstitious names is, however, probable enough.]

PIDDING *E.* perhaps from *Peadan,* the property of king Peada, fl. A.D. 652. Ex.: Pidding-hoe (Suss.), Peada's hill.

* Anglo-Saxon Chronicle.

† Wakeman's Notes to Liber Landavensis.

D. Old Danish. *G.* Greek. *L.* Latin. *N. F.* Norman French. *N.* Norse. *qu. v.* which see.

PIDDLE *E.* the slowly running stream. Ex.: Piddle-hinton (Dorset), Hinton's land on the Piddle; Piddle-trent-hide (ditto), the hide or plough-land of Trant on the same stream.

PIL. *See* Peel, *supra.*

PILLETH *B.* from *pwll* and *llaith*, the pool of blood. Ex.: Pilleth (Radn.).

PIM, PIN *E.* from *pinu*, a pine. Ex.: Pim-fern (Dorset), pine-place; Pine-hoe (Devon), pine hill; Pinner (Midd.), the pine-trees.

PINCH, PUNC, PUNCH *E.* from *pinca*, a finch. Finchley (Midd.), was anciently called Pincan-hal, *i. e.* Finch's hall, from the lord's name. Ex.: Pinch-beck (Linc.), the finch's brook; Punc-knowl (Dorset), the finch's knoll.

PINNOCK, PINX *E.* from St. Pinnock. Ex.: St. Pinnock (Cornw.); Pinx-ton (Derb.), Pinnock's town.

PIPE, PIPA, from Pippa, the name of a saint who was a bishop of Lichfield. Ex.: Pipe (Heref.), Pipa Minor (Staff.), the latter a prebend of Lichfield cathedral.

PIR, PUR, PYR *E.* from *pera*, a pear-tree. Ex.: Pirton, 3 places, pear-tree town; Pur-ley and Pur-leigh, pear-tree land; Pyr-ford (Surr.), the ford by the pear-tree.

PIS. *See* Pea, *supra.*

PISTYLL *B.* a small waterfall. Common in Wales. A large water-fall is called Rhaiadr, *qu. v.*

PIT *E.* from *pyt*, a pit; probably marking either a deep valley or a place where pitfalls were made to catch wild animals. Ex.: 8 places; Pit-minstre (Som.), the monastery in the deep valley.

PITCH, PYTCH *E.* a small hill, still used commonly with that meaning in Herefordshire. Ex.: Pitch-cot (Bucks), the cottage on the small hill; Pytch-ley (Northam.), the meadow by the pitch.

PLAIT *E.* a plat or small piece of land. Ex.: Plait-ford (Wilts).

PLAS *B.* a palace or mansion. Common in Wales. Place in England has a like meaning. Ex.: Cumnor Place (Oxf.).

PLAY, PLEAS *E.* from *plega*, a battle, or from *place*, an open place, street, or mansion. Ex.: Play-ford (Suff.); Please-ley (Notts).

PLESH *E.* from *pleach* or *plash*, to form a hedge. Ex.: Plesh-ey (Ess.), the hedged place near the water, or the enclosed water.

B. British. *C.* Celtic. *E.* The Old English, commonly known as Anglo-Saxon.

PLINLIMMON *B.* from Pum-lummon, the hill of the five standards, perhaps indicating that five clans assembled there in time of war.

PLUM, PLUMB *E.* the plum-tree. Ex.: Plumb-land (Cumb.); Plum-stead, 4 places (Norf.), plum stations.

PLUMP E. a clump or cluster. Ex.: Plump-ton (Northam. and Suss.), the town of the clump of trees, or the enclosed cluster of houses.

PLYM *B.* a river in Devonshire, perhaps from *plwm*, lead, with reference to the hue of its waters or to the lead mines. Ex.: Plymouth, the mouth of the Plym; Plym-ton, the town by the same river.

POL, Cornish form of *pwll* (*B.*), a pool. Ex.: Pol-perro, St. Piran's pool.

POLES, POLING, POLE *E.* from *pol*, a pole, afterwards adopted as a personal name. Ex.: Poles-worth (Warw.), Pole's estate; Pol-ing, Pole's meadow; Pole-brook (Northam.), Pole's brook.

PONT *B.* from the Latin *pons*, a bridge. Ex.: Pont-faen (Pemb.), stone bridge; Ponte-fract (Yorks.), broken bridge, so called from the bridge breaking down when William Archbishop of York was passing over, *temp.* Stephen; Pontes-bury (Ches.), bridge-town.

POOLE, PUL, PWLL, from *pwll* (*B.*), a pool. Ex.: Poole (Dorset), Pul-borough (Suss.), pool town; Pwll-meurig (Monm.), King Meurig's pool, the site of his victory over the Saxons.

POOLHALLOCK *B.* perhaps from *pwll halawg*, the polluted pool, from some deed of blood perpetrated there. Ex.: Pool-hallock (Heref.).

POR, PORT, PORTIS, PORTH *B*, from *porth*, a harbour. Ex.: Porloca,* now Porlock (Som.), the enclosed port; Por-chester (Hants), the port camp; Portsmouth (Hants), the mouth of the port; Portis-head (Som.), the head of the port; Porth-kerry (Glam.), the rocky port.

PORKINGTON *B.* anciently Brogyntin, the *din* or fortress of Brogyn. Ex.: Porking-ton (Salop).

POSLING, POSTLE *E.* perhaps from the church being dedicated to an Apostle. Ex.: Posling-ford (Suff.), the Apostle's ford; Postl-ing (Kent).

* Portus claustrum.—*Saxon Chronicle.*

D. Old Danish. *G.* Greek. *L.* Latin. *N.F.* Norman French. *N.* Norse. *qu. v.* which see.

Post *B.* the post of a door-way, hence a house. Ex.: Post-wick (Norf.), a collection of houses.

Pots, Potter *E.* from the trade of potter. Ex.: Pots-grove (Bedf.), the potter's grove; Potter (Norf.).

Pough, perhaps from the Brit. *buwch,* a cow. Ex.: Pough-ill (Devon), cow hill.

Poul. *See* Paul, *supra.*

Pound *E.* an enclosure. Ex.: Pound-stock (Cornw.), the pound station.

Powys *B.* perhaps a corruption of Pwyth, 'the purchased place,' or Pwll-ys, 'below the pool,' the capital being situated lower down the Severn than Pwll, now called Welshpool. The place where Julius Cæsar landed is said to have been known to the Britons as Pwyth Mein-las,* 'the green place of the purchase.' Ex.: Powys (Salop and Kent).

Preen *B.* from *prain,* the house or palace of a prince. Ex.: Preen (Salop).

Prees *B.* from Ap Rhys, the chief's name. Ex.: Prees (Salop).

Prendergast *B.* from *pren,* tree, *dwr,* water, and *gwest,* an inn or lodging-place. Ex.: Prendergast (Pemb.), the inn by the tree near the water.

Pres, Prest, Pris *E.* from *presbyter,* a priest,† indicating a living which did not belong to either a monastery or a bishop, 38 places. Ex.: Pres-hute (Wilts), priest's hut; Prest-bury (Ches.), the priest's fortified town; Pris-ton (Som.), Prestre-tun, now Pres-ton (Heref.), priest's town.

Pridd *B.* earth. Ex.: Ty-pridd, earth house.

Princes *E.* belonging to a prince. Ex.: Prince's Risborough (Bucks), so called from Edward the Black Prince, who resided there.

Prior *L.* first in rank in a priory, which ranked next to a monastery; indicating a place belonging to a prior. Ex.: Prior's Marston (Warw.), thus distinguished from the other 15 Marstons.

Pucking *E.* from Pucca, and *incga.* Ex.: Pucking-ton (Som.), the town of Pucca's descendants.

Puckle, Pockling *E.* from Pucca or Pocca, the lord's name. Ex.: Puck-lege-circ, now Pucklechurch (Glouc.), the church

* Richards, in Welsh Dictionary.

† Pres-ton (Monm.) belonged to Abraham the priest.—*Domesday Book.*

in Pucca's meadow; Pock-len-ton, now Pockling-ton (Yorks.), the town on Pucca's *len, i. e.* land held on fee-farm.

PUD, PUT, PUTN, *E.* from Pudda, Pot, or Putta, a man's name, still preserved in the names Potts and Potter. Among the first bishops of Hereford, fl. seventh and eighth centuries, were men of these names. Ex.: Puds-ey (Yorks.), Pudda's water; Poteslepe,* now Put-ley (Heref.), Putta's leap; Puts-ton (ditto), Putta's town; Puttan-heath, now Putney (Surr.), Putta's heath or land. *See* Hartlip, *supra.*

PUDDING *E.* from Pudda, and *incga.* Ex.: Pudding-ton (Bedf.), the town of Pudda's descendants.

PUL. *See* Poul, *supra.*

PULVERBATCH, from *pwll-fa* (*Brit.*), the place of a pool, and *bach* (*S.*), a path. Ex.: Pulverbach (Salop), the path by the pool.

PUNCH, *E.* from *pincan*, a pine-tree. Ex.: Pincanes-tun, now Punchestown (Pemb.), the town of the pine-trees.

PUR, PYR. *See* Pir, *supra.*

PURSLOW *E.* perhaps Perry's hlaew, the hilly district through which the river Perry flows. Ex.: Purslow (Salop).

PURY *E.* from *burh*, a fortified place; occurs only in 4 instances. Ex.: Paulers-pury (Northam.), Hart-pury (Glouc.).

PUT. *See* Pud, *supra.*

PWLL *B.* a pool. *See* Pool, *supra.*

PY, PYE *B.* from *beu* (pron. by), an abode. Ex.: Py-worth-ey (Devon), the British station, which afterwards became a Saxon *wyrth*, or well-watered estate.

PYLE, PYLLE. *See* Pill, *supra.*

PYON *E.* from Peowan, belonging to Peowa, an Anglian chief. Ex.: Pyon (Heref.).

PYTCH. *See* Pitch, *supra.*

* Domesday Book.

Q

Not to be found in either British or English names, save where they have been corrupted by the introduction of Norman French or Latin. The sound is expressed in British by *chw*, as in *chwart*, a quart; and in Saxon by *cw*, as in *cwen*, a companion.

QUADING *E.* perhaps from *hwata*, omens, and *ing*, a meadow. Ex.: Quading (Linc.), the meadow of omens, or the place of divination.

QUAIN *E.* from *cwen*, a companion, and also a queen. Ex.: Quainton (Bucks), the queen's town.

QUANTOCK, QUANTOX *E.* perhaps from the British *gwaun*, a mountain meadow, or down, and *taeawg*, a tenant in villenage. Ex.: Qnantock hills (Som.), the mountain meadow of the tenants in villenage; Quantox-head (Som.), the head or end of the Quantock range of hills.

QUAR, QUARN, QUARREN, QUARRING, QUORN *E.* from *cwearn*, a mill. Ex.: Quar-lege, now Quarley (Hants), the mill meadow; Quarn-don (Derb.), Quarren-don (Bucks), mill hill; Quering-don, now Quarring-ton (Linc.), mill hill; Quorn (Leices.), the mill.

QUATT *E.* from the British *gwadn*, the base or foundation. Ex.: Quatt-moel-hafren, now Quatt Malvern (Salop), the base of the bare hill by the Severn; Quat's-ford, the ford near Quatt.

QUEEN, QUEENI, QUEN, QUIN *E.* from *cwen*, a companion, and also a queen. Ex.: Queen-borough * (Kent), and Queeniborough (Leic.), the queen's fortified town; Quen-don (Ess.), the queen's hill; Quin-ton (Glouc.), the queen's town.

QUENING *E.* from *cwen* and *incga*. Ex.: Quening-ton (Glouc.), the town of the descendants of the companion of the king. (*Cwen* is masculine as well as feminine.)

* So named from Philippa, Queen of Edward III.

QUERN *E.* from *cwearn*, a mill. Ex.: Quern-moor (Lanc.), mill moor.

QUIDDEN, from the British *gwydden*, a tree or shrub ; hence *with*, a willow. Ex.: Quidden-ham (Norf.), the home among the trees.

QUIN. *See* Quen, *supra*.

QUORN. *See* Quar, *supra*.

R

RAC, RACK, *E.* from Wracca, the owner's name. Ex.: Rack-heath (Norf.).

RAD, RADDING, RADN, RAT, RATTER, RED *E.* from *red* or *read*, red, the colour of the soil or rock upon which the town is placed. Rad occurs in 16 instances, all on the red sandstone formations. Ex.: Rad-ford (Notts), the ford by the red rock; Radenelau,* now Radlow (Heref.), the red hill; Radding-ton (Som.), the red town; Radn-or, the red district; Rat-cliff (Notts), the red cliff; Ratter-ey (Devon), the red water; Red-cliff (Glouc.), etc.

RADYR *B.* from *rhann*, a portion, and *dir*, land. Ex.: Rhann-dir, now Radyr (Glam.).

RAG *E.* seems to mean rugged or rocky. Ex.: Rag-dale (Leic.); Rowley rag, the rock at Rowley Regis (Staff.).

RAGLAN *B.* perhaps from *rhagor llan*, the supreme or excellent church. Ex.: Raglan (Monm.).

RAIN, perhaps *B.* from *rhên*, a lord, or from *rhann*, a portion or share. Ex.: Rain-ham (Kent and Norf.); Rain-hill (Lanc.), and Rain-ton (Dur.).

RAITH, REETH *D.* from *raad*, counsel. Ex.: Raith-by (Linc.), the seat of counsel or place of consultation; Reeth (Yorks.).

RAM, RAMP, RAMPIS, RAMS, REM, REMPIS *E.* or *D.* from *ram*, a male sheep, probably adopted as a chief's name. Ex.: Ram-ey (Cornw.), the pool of the ram; Ramp-ton and Remps-ton (Notts), ram's town; Remen-ham (Berks), Reming-ton (Yorks.), and Rampis-ham (Dorset), ram's home; Rams-ey (Ess.), etc. By monastic writers this last place is termed *insula arietum*, ram's island.

RAN, RAND, REN, REND, *D.* from Randa or Randal, a chief's name. Ex.: Ran-moor (Yorks.), Randa's moor; Rand and Rand-by (Linc.), Randa's dwelling; Rand-wick (Glouc.), Randa's village or abode; Ren-hold (Bedf.), Randa's fortress or holt, *i. e.* wood; Rendles-ham and Rend-ham (Suff.), Randal's home; Raunds (Northam.), Randa's property.

* Domesday Book.

RAPE *N.* from *hrep*, a division of country, still in use in Iceland, where an 'amt' or province is divided into *hreps*. Ex.: the Rapes of Sussex.

RASEN *E.* from the *Rase*, a river in Lincolnshire, whose name is probably derived from *ree*, the Saxon word for a stream. Ex.: Market Rasen, the market town on the Rase.

RAT. *See* Rad, *supra.*

RATLINGHOPE, from *Hratlan* (Saxon), belonging to Hratla, or Hridla,* now Riddell, a man's name, and *hwpp, B.*, a sloping plain between hills. Ex.: Ratlinghope (Salop), Hratla's hope.

RAUCE *D.* from Hrolf, name of several noted Norse chiefs. Ex.: Rauce-by (Linc.), Hrolf's abode.

RAVE, REVES *E.* from *gerefa*, a reeve or bailiff. Hence *scyre-gerefa*, sheriff, etc. Ex.: Refa-lege, now Raveley (Hunts), the rèeve's place; Reves-by (Linc.), the reeve's abode.

RAVEN *D.* from *hraefn*, a raven, the Danish standard, and probably an indication of the abode of a Dane. Ex.: 8 instances, all within the Danelagh, or Danish England; and one Raven-seech, Raven's edge or hill, in Herefordshire, which the Danes several times invaded.

RAW, ROUGH, ROW *E.* from *hreog*, or *ruh*, rough; German, *roh*. Ex.: Raw-marsh (Yorks), the rough marshy place; Rough-ham (Norf.), the rough home; Row-ley (Staff.), the rough land.

RAY, REA, REI, REIGH, REY *E.* from *ree*, a stream. Ex.: Ray-leigh (Essex), the place at the stream; the river Rea (Warwicks.); Rei-gate (Surr.), the gate or fortification at the stream; Reighton (Yorks.), the town at the stream; Rey-don (Suff.), the hill at the stream.

READING *E.* from *hreod*, a reed, and *ing*, a meadow. Ex.: Rad-ing,* now Reading (Berks).

RECULVER *E.* from the Latin name of the place, Regulbium, which seems to be an adaptation of the British *Rhagolwgbeu*, a conspicuous dwelling-place.

RED, REED *E.* from *hreod*, a reed. Ex.: 20 places; Hreod-bricge,† now Redbridge (Hants), the bridge at the reedy spot; Reed-ness (Yorks.), the reedy promontory or headland.

REDRUTH *B.* anciently Tref-derwydd, the druids' town. Ex.: Redruth (Cornw.).

* So spelt on the common seal of the borough. † Bede.

D. Old Danish. *G.* Greek. *L.* Latin. *N. F.* Norman French. *N.* Norse. *qu. v.* which see.

REETH *E.* from *rith*, a small stream. Ex.: Reeth (Yorks.).

REI. *See* Ray, *supra.*

RENDLESHAM *E.* from Rendle, a man's name, and *hám*, home. "Rendle's ham, that is, Rendle's mansion," says Bede. Ex.: Rendlesham (Suff.).

REP *E.* from Hreopa, the lord's name. Ex.: Hreopandun, now Repton (Derb.), Hreopa's town or hill; Rep-ham (Norf.), Hreopa's home.

RES. *See* Ray, *supra.*

RET *E.* perhaps from *rith*, a small stream. Ex.: Ret-ford (Notts), Rettan-don (Essex), the hill by the stream.

RHAGLETT *B.* from *rhagor lid*, conspicuous tract or district. Ex.: the Rhaglett range of hills (Salop).

RHAYADER *B.* from *rhaiadr*, a waterfall. Ex.: Rhaiadr-ar-Gwy, now Rhayader (Radnors.), the falls of the Wye.

RHIW *B.* an ascending path. Ex.: Rhiw-abon (Denb.), St. Mabon's ascending path.

RHOS *B.* a moist meadow or plain. Ex.: Rhos-collen (Angl.), the moist meadow of the hazle-tree.

RHUDD *B.* red. Ex.: Rhudd-lan (Flints), red church, probably from its being built of red sandstone; Rhuddre (Glam.), red town.

RHYD *B.* a ford. Ex.: Rhyd-y-meirch (Monm.), the ford of the stallions.

RHYDDERCH *B.* a king's name. Ex.: Llanddewi Rhydderch (Monm.), the church of St. David, built or founded by Rhydderch, one of "the three generous princes of Britain."*

RHYDDLAD *B.* a saint's name. Ex.: Llan-Rhyddlad (Angl.), St. Rhyddlad's church.

RHYDIAN *B.* a saint's name. Ex.: Llan-Rhydian (Glam.), St. Rhydian's church.

RHŶN *B.* a promontory; ῥὶν (Gr.), a nose; *ness*, *S.* Ex.: Penrhŷn (Cornw.), the head of the promontory.

RHYSTUD *B.* a saint's name. Ex.: Llan-Rhystud (Card.), St. Rhystud's church.

RIB, RIBBES, RIBS *E.* from Hreoba, or Hreopa, the lord's name. Ex.: Rib-chester (Lanc.), Hreoba's camp; Ribbes-ford (Worc.), Hreoba's ford; Ribs-ton (Yorks.), Hreoba's town.

RIC, RICH, RICK *E.* from *ric*, rule or lordship. Ex.: Ricc-all

* British Triads, t. 30.

(Yorks.), the hall of the lord; Good-rich (Heref.), Godu's rule; Rast-rick (Yorks.), Hrosta's rule; Ricking-hall (Suff.), the hall of the lord or ruler.

RICHMOND *N. F.* from Rich, the Norman lord to whom William the Conqueror gave the land, and *mont*, a hill. Ex.: Richmond (Yorks. and Surrey).

RICKMANS *E.* from *ric*, and *man*, the man who rules; afterwards a proper name. Ex.: Rickmans-worth (Herts), Rickman's watered estate.

RID, RIDDLE *E.* from Hretla or Hridla, a Danish chief. Ex.: Rid-ley (Kent), Hridla's land; Hridlan-ton, now Riddlington (Norf.), Hridla's town; Hridlas-worth, now Riddles-worth (Norf.), Hridla's estate.

RIDING *E.* the *thridding* or third part of the county of York; incorrectly applied to the *two* divisions of the Irish county of Tipperary. Not used in any other county.

RIMING. *See* Ram, *supra.*

RING *E.* from the name of the British tribe called by the Romans the Regni.* Ex.: Ring-wood, anciently Rini-wold (Hants), the forest of the Regni; Rings-wold (Kent), the same. Or rather, as I think, from the Norse king Ringe, from whom a district in Norway is still called Ringerige, *i. e.* Ringe's kingdom.

RIPON *L.* anciently (*see* Bede) 'Inrhypum,' *quasi in ripa*, with the Saxon *ham* added, *i. e.* the home on the river's bank. Ex.: Ripon (Yorks.).

RIPPLE, RIPPING *E.* from Hreopa, the lord's name. Ex.: Hreopanaelh, now Rippingale (Linc.), Hreopa's hall; Hreop-lege, now Ripple (Kent), Hreopa's land.

RIS, RISING, RISH, RISSING *E.* from *arisan*, an elevated position. Ex.: Ris-bury (Heref.), the elevated camp; Rise-ley (Bedf.), the elevated place; Rish-ton (Lancas.), the elevated town: Rising Castle (Norf.), the castle on the elevated site; Rissington (Glouc.), the elevated town.

RISCA *B.* ? from *rhisg*, bark. Ex.: Risca (Monm.), perhaps meaning a village of huts constructed of bark; or from *yr-hesygae*, the sedgy field.

RIX. *See* Ric, *supra.*

* Bosworth's Anglo-Saxon Dictionary.

D. Old Danish. *G.* Greek. *L.* Latin. *N. F.* Norman French. *N.* Norse. *qu. v.* which see.

Ro *E.* from *hrof*, a roof. Ex.: Hrof-cestre, now Rochester (Kent), 'so called from one that was formerly the chief man of it, called Rhof'*; Ro-cester (Staff.), the same.

Roade, Roath *B.* from *rhwth*, an open place or clearing. Ex.: Roade (Northam.); Roath (Glouc.).

Roch *N. F.* a rock. Ex.: Roch Abbey (Yorks.), the abbey near the rock.

Rock, Roke, Rox from *roche*, a rock. Ex.: Rock-bourn (Hants), rock brook; Roke-by (Yorks.), rock dwelling; Rox-ton (Bedf.), the town of a chief who bore the word rock as a name.

Rod, Rodd *B.* from *rhwth*. Ex.: Rod-borough (Glouc.), the fortified town on the open land or clearing; Rodd-nash (Radnors.), the promontory of open land.

Rodmers, Rodmar *E.* from Hrodmer, the lord's name. Ex.: Rodmeres-ham (Kent), Hrodmer's home, Rodmar-ton (Glouc.), Hrodmer's town.

Rogers, from Roger, the Norman lord. Ex.: Rogers-ton (Monm.), Roger's town.

Roke. *See* Rock, *supra*.

Rolles, Rolls, Rouls, Rowls, from Rowland, the Norman lord. Ex.: Rolles-ton (Notts), Rowls-ton (Heref.), Rowland's town; Roll-ric, now Rollright (Oxf.), Rowland's rule or possession; Rouls-ton (Linc.).

Rom, Romans, Romn, Roms *E.* pointing out a Roman station. Ex.: Rom-ford (Essex), Roman ford; Romans-leigh (Devon), Roman's land; Romn-ey † (Kent), Roman station by the water; Roms-ey (Hants), the same.

Roothing *B.* from *rhwth*, open, and *ing, E.*, a meadow. Ex.: 8 places, all in Essex.

Rop, Rops, *E.* from Hreopa, the lord's name. *See* Rip, *supra*.

Rose, Ross, either from *ross* (Norse), a headland, or *rhôs*, (Brit.), a moist plain or meadow. Ex.: Rose-ash (Devon), the ash meadow; Ross (Heref.), etc.

Roth from *rhwth* (*B.*), open. Ex.: Roth-bury (North.), the fortress on the open land.

* Bede, iii. 73.

† Maluit Baxterus scripsisse Roman-ey, *i. e.* Romanorum insula.—*Bosworth.*

ROTHER *B.* from *yr odar*, the boundary.* Ex.: rivers in Sussex, Kent, and Yorkshire, the last-mentioned being the northern boundary of Mercia; Rother-was (Heref.), the water boundary of Mercia towards Wales.

ROTTING *E.* from Hrotan, the lord's name. Ex.: Rotting-dean, anciently Rothington (Suss.), Hrotan's hollow.

ROUGH, Row *E.* from *ruh*, rugged or uncultivated. Ex.: Rough-ham (Norf.), the home on the uncultivated land; Row-byryg, now Rowberrow (Som.), the camp on the uncultivated land.

ROX. *See* Rock, *supra.*

ROY *E.* from *hry*, plural *hrygas*, a thorn. Ex.: Roy-don (Ess.), thorn hill.

ROYD *E.* a road cut in a wood, or land ridden over; the allusion being to the traditionary grants of as much land as the grantee could ride round in a day. Ex.: Hunt-royd and Mytholm-royd (Yorks.), the name Boothroyd, etc. The people of south-west Yorkshire still pronounce *coat* and *throat* as *coyt* and *throyt.*

ROYS *N.F.* from Roysa, a female name. Ex.: Roys-ton (Camb.), the town of Roysa, Countess of Norfolk, who founded it, temp. William the Conqueror.

RUAN, *Cornish*, from St. Ruman. Ex.: 3 places.

RUAR *B.* from *rhiw-ar*, sloping-path field. Ex.: Ruar-dean (Glouc.), the hollow of the sloping-path field.

RUCK. *See* Rug, *infra.*

RUD *B.* from *rhudd*, *S. rude*, red, referring to the colour of the rock. Ex.: Rud-ford (Glouc.), the red ford.

RUG, RUGE *E.* from *rug*, rough or rugged. Ex.: Rug-by (Warw.), the Danish town on the rough site; Ruge-ley (Staff.), the rough land; Ruck-ing (Kent), rough meadow.

RUMBOLD *E.* St. Rumbold. Ex.: Rumbold's wick (Suss.), Rumbold's dwelling.

RUN, RUNNING, RUNNY *E.* from *rune*, counsel. Ex: Run-hall (Norf.), the hall of counsel; Runen-tun, now Runnington (Som.), the town of counsel; Runen-mæd, now Runnymede (Berks), the meadow of counsel.

* The Kentish Rother was called by the Romans *limen*, thus suggesting that the river was the boundary of some of the native tribes, and that the Romans translated the word for a boundary which they heard applied to the river.

RUNCORN *E.* from Rum-cofan, the ancient name, meaning the wide cove or inlet.

RUS, RUSH, RUSK *E.* from *risc*, a rush. Ex.: Rus-comb (Berks), the rushy valley; Rush-den (Herts), the same; Riscan-tun, now Ruskington (Linc.), the rush-town. Hence the surname Risk.

RUSHOPE *B.* in Domesday Book styled Ruiscope, Rua's hill-top. Ex.: Rushope (Heref.). *See* Cop, *supra.*

RUT *E.* from *rot*, red. This being the favourite colour with the Northmen, they used the word to signify splendid or beautiful. Ex.: Rut-land, anciently Rota-land, the splendid or beautiful district.

RUTHIN *B.* from *rhûdd-yn*, red place. Ex.: Ruthin (Denb.).

RUY *E.* from *hry*, a thorn. Ex.: Ruy-ton (Salop), thorn town. Or it may be from *rhiw-wy* (*B.*), the sloping path by the water.

RY *E.* from *rih*, rough. Ex.: Ri-haela,* now Ryhall (Rutl.), the hall in the rough place.

RYS *E.* from *risc*, a rush. Ex.: Rys-ton (Norf.), rush town.

* Saxon Chronicle.

S.

Sa *E.* from *secg*, sedge, called *seg* or *sag* in the northern counties; the guttural being, as usual, dropped before a word beginning with a letter of the same organ. Ex.: Sa-comb (Herts), sedge valley; Sa-ham (Norf.), the home among the sedges.

Sadding, Sed *E.* probably from *sæd*, seed, indicating an arable farm. Ex.: Sadding-ton (Leic.), the town of the arable farm; Sed-bury, now Sedbergh (Yorks.), the fortified town of the same.

Saddle *E.* probably from Sedla, the lord's name. Ex.: Saddle-worth (Yorks.), Sedla's watered estate.

Saffron *E.* the crocus, designating the place where that plant was cultivated for the dye obtained from its stamens. Ex.: Saffron Walden (Ess.), the saffron farm on the wild land.

Saint *B.* and *E.* a saint. Ex.: Saint-bury (Glouc.), the saint's fortified town.

Sal, Sale, Saul *E.* from *salh*, a willow, still called *sally* in Heref. and *sough* in Scotland. Ex.: Sal-ford (Lanc.), willow ford; Sale-hurst (Suss.), the willow wood or copse; Saul (Glouc.).

Salisbury *E.* from Searesbyryg, Sarum's fortified place, the site to which the population of Old Sarum removed, *temp.* Edward II.

Salt *E.* from *sealt*, salt, indicating a site near the sea or on a river where its waters are salt. Ex.: Saltfleet-by (Linc.), the harbour-town at the sea. Salt-hill (Berks) derives its name from the Eton College boys there demanding money under the cant name of 'salt.'

Sam, Samp. *See* Sand, *infra.*

Sand, Sound *E.* from *sond*, sand of the sea, or a sandy soil inland. Ex.: Sand-all (Yorks.), the hall on the sandy site; Sandon (Norf.), sand hill; San-ton (Norf.), sand town; Sound-by (Notts), sand abode.

Sander, Saunders *E.* from Sander, a contraction of Alexander, still used in Scotland. Ex.: Sander-sted (Surr.), Alexander's station; Saunders-foot (Pemb.), Alexander's place at the foot of a hill.

D. Old Danish. *G.* Greek. *L.* Latin. *N. F.* Norman French. *N.* Norse. *qu. v.* which see.

SARN, SARNS *B.* a causeway or Roman road. Ex.: Sarn Helen, the road made by order of the Empress Helena, mother of Constantine; Sarns-field (Heref.), the field of the sarn.

SARRAT *E.* anciently Sceargeat,* from *scear*, a share or division and *geat*, a gate. Ex.: Sarrat (Herts).

SATTER, *E.* from Seater, the supposed god from whom Saturday was named. Ex.: Satter-thwaite (Cumb.), Seater's clearing.

SAUL. *See* Sal, *supra*.

SAVIOUR *N. F.* from *Sauveur*, our Saviour. Ex.: St. Saviour, 4 places. The Saxon word was Hælend, which does not occur as the name of a place. Saxon names seem to have been given in most cases while the people were yet heathen.

SAX, from *seax*, a short sword worn by one division of the invaders, who were thence called Saxons. Ex.: Sax-by (Linc.), the Saxon abode among the Danes; Saxmund-ham (Suff.), the home in the Saxon entrenchment.

SAXILBY *D.* probably from Saxwulf, the owner, and *by*, abode. There was a Saxwulf, a missionary to the Mercians, A.D. 674.† Ex.: Saxilby (Linc.).

SAXLING *S.* the possession of Saxons. Ex.: Saxling-ham (Norf.), the home of the Saxon possession.

SCAL, SCALD, SCALE, SCAW, *N.* from *scald*, a bard. Ex.: Scal-by (Yorks.), the scald's abode; Scald-well (Northam.), the scald's well; Scale-by (Cumb.), the scald's abode; Scaw-ton (Yorks.), scald's town.

SCAM, SCAMBLE, SCAMP *D.* from Scamble, the owner's name. Ex.: Scambles-by, and Scamp-ton (Linc.), the abode and the town of Scamble.

SCAR, SCAUR, SCOR, SCARIS *E.* a precipitous rock. Ex.: Scar-cliff (Derb.), the precipitous cliff; Nash Scaur (Heref.), the precipitous rock of the *næsse*, or promontory; Scar-borough (Yorks.), the fortified town of the precipitous rock; Scor-ton (Yorks.), the same; Scaris-burh, now Scarisbrick (Yorks.), the fortified town of the scaur.

SCENFRITH *B.* from *hês ga ffridd*, the sedgy place in the wood. Ex.: Scenfrith (Monm.).

SCETHROG *B.* from King Brochwel Ysgythrog. Ex.: Scethrog (Brec.).

* Saxon Chronicle. † Bede.

SCOT *E.* from *Scota*, a Scotchman, indicating the abode of some rover from Scotland who joined the crowd of Northmen. In Yorkshire a Scotchman is still colloquially styled a 'Scottie.' Ex.: Scot-ærn, now Scothern (Linc.), the Scot's place; Scot-hoe, now Scottow (Norf.), the Scot's hill; Scota, now Scotter (Linc.).

SCOUL, SCUL *E.* from *sceole*, a shoal, or a multitude of fish. Ex.: Scoul-ton (Norf.), Scul-coates (Yorks.), the town and the huts near shallow water.

SCRA, SCRAYING, SCREM *D.* probably from *scra*, the sea-swallow, and *incga* children, the name of the bird being given to the ship in which the adventurers arrived; or it may have been the name of their ancestor or chief. Ex.: Scra-field (Linc.), Scranby, now Scremby (Linc.); Scray-ingham (Yorks.), the home of the children of the sea-swallow, or of Scra.

SCREV, SCRIVALS, SCRIVAN *E.* probably from Scrival or Scriva, the lord's name. Ex.: Screvs-ton (Notts), Scriva's town; Scrivals-by (Linc.), Scrival's abode; Scriva-ærn, now Scriven (Yorks.), Scriva's place.

SCROO, SCROOP, SCROP, SCRU *E.* or *D.* from Scroop, the lord's name. Ex.: Scroo-by (Notts), Scroop's abode; Scrop-ton (Derb.), Scru-ton (Yorks.), Scroop's town.

SCWD *B.* a corruption of *ysgwd*, a jet or shoot; as in *melin ysgwd*, a mill-race. Ex.: Scwd-hen-rhyd (Brec.), the mill-race at the old ford.

SEA *E.* when the termination of a name, is the possessive *s* ending the owner's name, joined with *ea* or *ey*, water. Ex.: Alders-ey (Ches.), Aldred's water; Batters-ea (Midd.), Batta's water.

SEA *E.* the sea. Ex.: Sea-ham (Durh.), the home by the sea.

SEAL *B.* from *sel*, a seal of office. Ex.: Part-y-seal (Monm.), the *parth* or piece of land held by grant under the king's seal.*

SEAL *E.* from *sælig*, holy. Ex.: Seal (Leic.).

SEAR *E.* from *sær*, a battle. Ex.: Sear-by (Linc.), the battle abode or place.

SEASON, SEIZIN, CISSAN, SIS, *E.* from Cissa, king of West Saxons. Season or Seizin-cote (Glouc.), Cissa's hut or cot; Cissan-cestre, now Cirencester, and Chichester, Cissa's fortified town; Sis-ton, Cissa's town; Sis-land (Norf.), Cissa's *len*. *See* Len.

* A common tenure in Brit. times.—See Rees' 'Lives of Welsh Saints.'

D. Old Danish. *G.* Greek. *L.* Latin. *N.F.* Norman French. *N.* Norse. *qu. v.* which see.

SEASALT *N.* probably from *syssel,* the name of a subdivision of country. Iceland is thus divided into amts, hreps, and syssels, something like our province, shire, and hundred. Ex.: Seasalters (Kent), the capital of the syssel.

SEAT, SET, SETT, *E.* from *setu,* the seat of a tribe. Occurs always as a suffix. Ex.: Dorset, Somerset, Stepleset;* Wetheringsett (Suff.), Forn-seat (Norf.), Wood-setts (Derb.).

SEATON *E.* sea town, afterwards assumed by the owner as a personal name, and then transferred to his abode. Ex.: Seaton Carew, S. Delaval, and S. Ross, all which seem to have been once the property of the Seatons, and named from them; but to have afterwards fallen to the Carews, Delavals, and Rosses.

SEAVING. *See* Seven, *infra.*

SECK *E.* from *secg,* a sedge. Ex.: Secgan-tun, now Seckington (Warw.), town among the sedges.

SEDBERGHAM *E.* from the owner's name. Ex.: Sedberga's home.

SEDGE *E.* from *secg,* a sedge. Ex.: Secg-byryg, now Sedgeberrow (Worc.), the fortified town among the sedges, *i. e.* in a watery site.

SEIGH *E.* from *secg,* a sedge, still called *seg* in Yorkshire. Ex. Seigh-ford (Staff.), the sedgy ford.

SEL, SELLY *E.* from *sælig,* holy. Ex.: Sel-by (Yorks.), holy abode; Selly-oak (Worc.) holy oak. Or it may be from *sel,* gnat. Ex.: Sel-wudu, now Selwood (Som.), the gnat wood.†

SELLACK *B.* from *sel,* a seal, and *llech,* a broad flat stone. Ex. Sellack (Heref.), the stone or altar of the seal, *i. e.* the stone upon which the king's seal was publicly affixed to some grant of land.

SELSEY *E.* seals' island. Ex.: Selsey (Suff.), so styled from the seals resorting thither.‡

SEPULCHRE, from the Holy Sepulchre, a trace of the Crusades, as indicating a church then built or rebuilt. Ex.: St. Sepulchre (Kent).

SETTERINGTON *E.* from Seater, the god, and *incgatun.* Ex.: Setterington (Yorks.), the town of Seater's children. *See* Satter, *supra.*

* Domesday Book.

† Bosworth's Anglo-Saxon Dictionary.

‡ In Selsey, that is, the island of the sea-calf.—*Bede.*

B. British. *C.* Celtic. *E.* The Old English, commonly known as Anglo-Saxon.

SETTLE *E.* from *setl*, a seat or throne, episcopal or regal. Ex.: Settle (Yorks.).

SEVEN, SEVING, SEAVING, SHEVING, SHABBING *N.* from Sebba, the owner's name. Ex.: Sebban-ham-tun, now Sevenhampton (Glouc.), Sebba's home town; Sevin-cote (Glouc.), Sebba's sheepcot; Seving-ton (Kent), Seaving-ton (Som.), Sheving-ton (Lanc.), Shabbing-ton (Bucks), Sebba's town.

SHABBING. *See* Seven, *supra*.

SHACKER *E.* from *sacu*, a battle. Ex.: Saccu-tun, now Shackerton (Leices.), battle town.

SHAD, SHADDING *E.* from *scead*, the fish now called shad, and *incga*, children. Ex.: Shadding-field (Suff.), the field of the children of a chief who took that fish as his cognizance; Shad-well (Midd.), Shad's well.

SHAFTES *E.* from *sceaft*, the peak or point of a hill. Ex.: Shaftes-bury (Dorset), the fortified town of the peak. Or the name may be a corruption of the British Caer Septon,* whence Septon-burh, Sefton-burh, Shaftes-burh.

SHAL, SHEL *E.* from *sceol*, a shallow place. Ex.: Shal-fleot (Hants), shallow harbour; Shel-ey (Essex), shallow water; Sceolwick,† now Shelwick (Heref.), abode in the shallow.

SHAP, SHEP, SHIP, SHIPPER, SKIP *E.* from *sceap*, sheep. Ex.: Shap-wick (Dorset), sheep village; Shap-fells (Cumb.), sheep ridge; Shep-ey (Kent), sheep water or island; Ship-ton, 8 places, and Skip-ton (Yorks.), sheep-town—the latter form of the word marking the presence of the Danes.

SHARD, SHARES, SHARN, SHARRING, SHERN, SHERRING *E.* from *scearn*, a share or division. Ex.: Shard-low (Derb.), the separated hill site; Shares-hill (Staff.), the same; Sharn-ford (Leices.), the dividing ford; Scear-ingaton, now Sharring-ton (Norf.), the town of the children of the division; Sher-ring-ton (Bucks), the same; Shern-born (Norf.), dividing brook.

SHAUGH, SHAW, SHOE *E.* from *scua*, a small wood. Ex.: Shaugh-prior (Devon), the prior's wood; Shaw-bury (Salop), the fortified town in the wood; Shoe-bury (Essex), the same.

SHEEN, SHEIN, SHEN, SHENING, SHIN *E.* from *scene* or *scen*, bright. Ex.: Sheen (Staff. and Surrey), Shein-ton (Salop), Shenfield (Essex), Shin-field (Berks), the bright field.

* Galfridus Monm. † Domesday Book.

SHEER. *See* Shard, *supra.*

SHEF, SHIFF *E.* from *sceaf*, a sheaf. Ex.: Shef-ford (Berks), sheaf ford; Shef-field (Yorks.), sheaf field; Shiff-nal, anciently Sceafan-aelh (Salop), sheaf hall.

SHEL. *See* Shal, *supra.*

SHELDS, SHIELDS *E.* from *scyld*, a shield. Ex.: Sheld-wick (Kent), shield village; Sheld-don (Devon), shield hill; Shields (Northum.).

SHELF, SHELVE *E.* from *scylf*, a terrace or flat piece of land on a hill. Ex.: Shelf (Yorks.), Shelve (Salop).

SHEP. *See* Shap, *supra.*

SHENINGTON *E.* from *scen*, bright, adopted as a name, and *incga*, descendants. Ex.: Scen-ingaton, now Shenington (Oxf.), the town of Scen's descendants.

SHERBOURN *E. scire-bourn*, *i. e.* clear brook. Ex.: Sher-bourn, now Sherborne (Dorset), called by the monks Fons Clarus, a translation of the Saxon name.

SHERWOOD *E.* from *scyre*, a shire, and *wood.* Ex.: Sher-wood (Notts), under an oak in which the shire-motes were held.

SHIFF. *See* Shef, *supra*

SHIL, SHILLING. *See* Shal, *supra.*

SHERSTON *E.* anciently *scyre-stán*, the division-rock, or boundary stone. Ex.: Shers-ton (Wilts).

SHIN, SHING. *See* Sheen, *supra.*

SHIP, SHIPPER. *See* Shap, *supra.*

SHIRE *E.* from *scyre*, a shire. Ex.: Shire-newton (Monm.), the new town of the shire.

SHOB, *B.* from *siob*, a tassel, or a round hill. Ex.: Shob-don (Heref.), *i. e.* Siob-din, the camp of the round hill.

SHOCK, SHUCK *E.* a pile of sheaves, thence a farm, or a hill resembling a shock in shape. Ex.: Shock-latch (Ches.), the inclosed farm, or the inclosure on the shock-shaped hill; Shuckan-hill, now Shucknell (Heref.), the shock-shaped hill.

SHORE. SHORNE *E.* from *score*, a shore. Ex.: Shore-ham (Kent and Suss.), shore home; Shorne (Kent).

SHOT, SHOTS, SHOTTES, SHOTT, SHUTT *E* from *sceotan*, to shoot, indicating an off-shoot from a larger hill or range of hills. Ex.: Shot-by (Suff.), Shots-well (Warw.), Shottes-ham

(Norf.), Shottis-ham (Suff.); Cock-shott (Yorks.), and Cock-shutt (Heref.), little shoot; Shute (Devon).

SHRAW, SHREW, SHROP *E.* from *scearu*, a share or division. Ex.: Shrawardin (Salop), *i. e. scearu din*, the British camp of the Saxon division; Shrews-bury, anciently Scyrobbes-burh, the fortified town of the division or district; Scyrobbes-scyre, now Shropshire, the shire of the Scyrobbes-byryg.

SHRIVEN. *See* Scriven, *supra.*

SHUCK. *See* Shock, *supra.*

SIB, SIBBER, SIBBERTS *E.* from Sigbert, illustrious warrior, a man's name. Ex.: Sibber-toft (Northam.), Sigbert's grove; Sib-berts-wold (Kent), Sigbert's wold or wild land; Sib-thorp (Notts), Sigbert's farm.

SID *B.* perhaps from *ys*, low-lying, and *yd*, corn-land. Ex.: Sid (Devon), the river flowing through corn-land; Sid-mouth (Devon), the mouth of the Sid.

SIDDING, SITHING *E.* from *Sida*, spacious, adopted as a name, and *incga*, children. Ex.: Sidd-ington (Glouc.), the town of the children of Sida; Sitting-bourn (Kent), the brook of the same.

SIDE *E.* spacious. Ex.: Side (Glouc.), Side-strand (Norf.), the spacious street or the strand of Sida. *See* Sidding.

SIDMON *E.* from *Sidamund*, the large protection, a man's name. Ex.: Sidmon-ton (Hants), Sidamund's town.

SIG, SIGGLES *E.* from *sig*, war, and *sigla*, a warrior. Ex.: Sigs-ton (Yorks.); Siggles-thorn (Yorks.), the warrior's thorn-tree.

SIL *E.* from *sel*, a seat or station. Ex.: Sele-tun, now Sil-ton (Yorks.), station town.

SILCHESTER *E.* from Silicus-cestre, the flint fortification, so-called from its being partly constructed of flints.* Ex.: Silchester (Hants).

SILE, SILO, SILS, SILVERS *B.* from St. Silas, or Silvanus. Ex.: Sile-by (Leices.), St. Silas's place, afterwards seized by the Danes; Llan-silo (Monm.), St. Silas's church; Sils-oe (Bedf.), Silas's *hoe*, the Danish word for hill; Silvers-ton (Northam.), Silvanus's town.

SILK *E.* from *seolc*, silk, which appears to have been adopted as a man's name, perhaps in reference to his wearing a silken robe,

* Archæologia.

D. Old Danish. *G.* Greek. *L.* Latin. *N.F.* Norman French. *N.* Norse. *qu. v.* which see.

a rare and costly dress in Saxon times. Ex.: Silkston (Yorks.); Silk Willoughby (Linc.).

SILS. *See* Sile, *supra*.

SILVER *L.* when a suffix, is a corruption of *sylva*. Ex.: Monksilver (Som.), the monks' wood.

SIM, SIMON, SIMP, SYMONDS *E.* from St. Simon. Ex.: Simonbourn (Northam.), Simon's brook; Simps-ton, now Simpson (Bucks), Simon's town; Symonds-bury (Dorset), Simon's fortified town.

SIOR *B.* St. George. Ex.: Llan-sior (Denb.), St. George's church.

SIS. *See* Season, *supra*.

SITH *E.* a path. Ex.: Sithan-ey (Cornw.), the path by the water.

SITTING *S.* *See* Sidding.

SKEFFING, Danish form of *sceaf*, a sheaf, and afterwards a man's name, and *incga*, children. Ex.: Skeffing-ton (Leices.), the town of Skeff's children; Skeffling (Yorks.), from *sceaf* and *len*, Skeff's land, which he granted to a tenant.

SKEG, the Danish form of *shaugh* or *scua*, a small wood. Ex.: Skeg-by (Notts), the abode in the small wood; Skeg-ness (Linc.), the promontory of the small wood.

SKEL *N.* from *skeal*, a drinking hall. Ex.: Skel-ton (Yorks.), the town of the drinking hall.

SKEL, SKELLING, a Danish form of *sceol*, a shallow or low place. Ex.: Skel-ton (Cumb.), Skelling-thorp (Linc.), the low town and farm.

SKENDLEBY *D.* from Skandla, the chief's name. Ex.: Skendle-by (Linc.), Skendla's abode.

SKER, SKERNE, SKIR, Danish form of *scear*, a share. Ex.: Skerton (Lanc.); Skerne (Yorks.), *quasi scear-aern*, the place of the share, *i. e.* the town of the division; Skir-coat (Yorks.), share cot.

SKETHROG *B.* from Brochwel Ysgithrog, *i. e.* Brochwel the Long-toothed, a British king, A.D. 617. *See* Scethrog.

SKID *B.* from *ysgwyd*, a shield, hence Skid-mawr (corrupted to Scudamore), the great shield. Ex.: Skid-by (Yorks.), the abode of the shield-bearer.

SKIDDAW *B.* and *D.* probably from *ysgwyd*, a shield, and *hoe*, a hill. Ex.: Skiddaw (Cumb.), the hill of shields, probably from some conflict. Cumberland contains many British names of places, pure and mixed, as might be expected in Cymryland, the land of the Britons.

SKILLING. *See* Skel, *supra.*

SKIP *D.* form of *sceap*, sheep. Ex.: Skips-ea (Yorks.), sheep's pool; Skip-ton, sheep's town; Skip-with (Yorks.), sheep's willow.

SKIRBECK *D.* from *skir*, a share or division, and *beck*, a stream. Ex.: Skir-beck (Yorks.), the dividing stream, probably separating two jurisdictions.

SLAID, SLAI, SLAY, SLED *E.* from *slæd*, a plain or open country. Ex.: Slaid-bourn (Yorks.), open site by the brook; Slaithwaite (Yorks.), the cleared plain; Slay-ley (Northam.), the open meadow; Sled-mere (Yorks.), the pool in the open plain.

SLAP *E.* perhaps from *slope.* Ex.: Slap-ton (Bucks, Devon, Northam.), slope-town.

SLAUGHTER *E.* from *slogan*, to slay, indicating the scene of some battle or massacre. Ex.: Slaughter (Glouc.); Slaughterford (Wilts).

SLEAFORD *E.* anciently Sliowa-ford, perhaps from *sliu* (*S.*), a tench. Ex.: Sleaford (Linc.).

SLID. *See* Slaid, *supra.*

SLIM *E.* from *slim*, slime or mud. Ex.: Slim-bridge (Glouc.), the bridge over the slimy or muddy stream.

SLIN *B.* from *llyn*, a pool. Ex.: Slin-don (Suss.), pool hill; Slin-fold (Suss.), pool sheep-fold.

SLINGS *D.* probably from a chief named Slinga. Ex.: Slings-by (Yorks.), Slinga's abode.

SLIP *E.* perhaps from *slope.* Ex.: Slip-ton (Northam.), slope-town.

SLO, SLAUGH, SLAWS, SLOUGH *E.* from *slog*, a slough. Ex.: Slo-by (Norf.), slough place; Slough (Bucks); Slaws-ton (Leic.), slough town; Slaugh-ham (Suss.), the home in the slough or marsh, such places being often chosen as more easily defended.

SMALL *E.* from *smal*, small. Ex.: Small-burgh (Norf.), small fortified town; Small-ey (Derb.), small pool or stream.

SMAR *E.* perhaps from *mere*, a pool. Ex.: Smar-den (Kent), mere hollow.

SMEA, SMEETH, SMITH *E.* from *smethe*, smooth. Ex.: Smea-ton

(Yorks.), the town in the smooth place; Smeeth (Kent), the same; Smith-field (Midd.), the smooth field.

SMETH, SMITHY *E.* from smith, still pronounced *smeth* in Scotland. Ex.: Smeth-wick (Staff.), the smith's village; Smithy Bullock (Lanc.).

SNAITH *E.* from *snæd*, a piece separated from a manor. Ex.: Snaith (Yorks.).

SNAPE *D.* from *snibbe*, a check or stoppage, perhaps indicating a place where war was stopped by a treaty. Ex.: Snape (Suff.).

SNAR, SNARES, SNORE *N.* from Snorri, name of a Norse chief. Ex.: Snar-ford (Linc.), Snorri's ford; Snares-ton (Leices.), Snorri's town; Snare-ham (Ess.), Snarri's home.

SNEA, SNEAD, SNEYD, SNAD, SNEN, SNOD *E.* from *snæd*, a piece of land separated from a manor. Ex.: Snea-ton (Yorks.), the town of the piece of land so separated; Snead (Mont.); Sneyd (Staff.), Snad-lands,* (Suss.); Snædan-tun, now Snenton (Notts), the same as Sneaton; Snod-land (Kent), Snodhill (Heref.).

SNEL *E.* from *snel*, active, afterwards a man's name, and still a surname. Ex.: Snel-land (Linc.), Snel's *len*; Snels-ton (Derb.), Snel's town. *See* Len, *supra.*

SNETTER, SNETTIS, SNITTER *E.* from *snitan*, to cut or excavate, whether to form caves, or to make trenches. Ex.: Snetterton (Norf.), the town of the excavation; Snettis-ham (Norf.), the home of the same; Snitter-by (Linc.), the abode of the same.

SNITTER. *See* Snetter.

SNOD. *See* Snea.

SNOR *D.* from Snorra, the chief's name. Ex.: Snorran, now Snoring (Norf.), Snorra's possession. *See* Snar, *supra.*

SOCK *E.* from *soc*, privilege or jurisdiction. Ex.: Sock-bourn (Durham), the privileged place at the brook, indicating a place which had a court of its own, and was exempt from the jurisdiction of the scyre-gerefa, or (in Norman times) of the feudal lord.

SOD *E.* turf. Ex.: Sod-bury (Glouc.), the town fortified with a sod or earthen rampart.

* Bosworth's Anglo-Saxon Dictionary.

B. British. *C.* Celtic. *E.* The Old English, commonly known as Anglo-Saxon.

SOHAM, SOHO, perhaps from *saugh*, a willow. Ex.: So-ham (Camb.), willow home; So-ho (Midd.), willow *hoe*, *i. e.* hill.

SOLI *E.* corrupted from *sel* or *sil*, a seat or station. Ex.: Sel-hill, now Solihull (Warw.), hill station. [It is still pronounced Silhill by the common people, who seem to have in this as in other cases preserved the true name.]

SOLLARS, the name of the owner. Ex.: Sollar's-hope (Heref.), Sollar's slope or ascent between hills. The word Sollars became a territorial name, taken from a place called Salowe * (Heref.), which word means the place of willows, from *salix* (Latin).

SOM *E.* from *som*, union or concord. Ex.: Som-bourn (Hants), the brook of union, perhaps from some treaty being made there.

SOMER, SOMERS *E.* from *sumor*, summer. Ex.: Somer-setu, now Somerset, the Summer tribe-station; Somer-ton (Som.), the chief town of Somersetshire, which it anciently was.

SOND *E.* sand. *See* Sam, *supra.*

SOT, SOTHER, SOTTER *E.* perhaps from Seater, a Saxon deity from whom Saturday is named. *See* Satter, *supra.*

SOUND *E.* from *sund*, a shallow sea; still used.

SOUL, SOULD *E.* from *salh*, a willow. Ex.: Soul-bury (Bucks), willow camp; Sould-ern (Oxf.), willow place. See Saul, *supra.*

SOUTH, SUD, SUDE *E.* from *suth*, the south. Ex.: South-fleot, now Southfleet (Kent), southern harbour; Sud-bury (Suff.), southern fortified town, answering to Nor-wich, northern abode; Sude-ley (Glouc.), southern place; South-wark, anciently Sud-weord (Surr.), southern fortress.

SOW, SOWER, SOUR *E.* from *sawan*, to sow. Ex.: Sow-ea, now Sowe (Warw.), the sower's pool; Sower-by (Yorks.), the sower's abode; Sour-ton (Devon), the sower's town.

SPALD, SPELD, SPELS *D.* probably from Spalda, the chief's name. Ex.: Spaldan, now Spalding (Linc.), Spalda's possession; Spald-wick (Hunts), Spalda's dwelling or village; Speld-hurst (Kent), Spels-bury (Oxf.).

SPAR, SPARS *D.* from *spar*, the bar of a gate, taken to mean a dwelling. Ex.: Spar-ham (Norf.), the barred home; Spars-holt (Berks), the dwelling in the holt or wood.

SPAX, SPEECH, SPEKE, SPEX, SPIX *E.* from *spæc*, speech, indicating the place where public meetings, such as shire-motes,

* Salowe, or Willowford, Rhyd-yr-helig.—*Sylcester Giraldus.*

hundred courts, leets, etc., were held. Ex.: Spax-ton (Som.), speech-town; Spæce, now Speke (Lanc.); Speech-house (Glouc.), anciently Spæce-hus; Spæces-alh, now Spexhall (Suff.), speech-hall; Spix-worth (Norf.), the estate on which meetings were held.

Speen *L.* from *spinæ*, the thorns, the Roman name of the place. Ex.: Speen (Berks).

Spernall *E.* from *spurnere*, a fuller of cloth, and *alh*, a hall. Ex.: Spernall (Warw.), the fuller's hall.

Spetch, Spettis, probably corruptions of *hospitium*, a hospital. Ex.: Spetch-ley (Worces.), hospital place; Spettisbury (Dorset), hospital town.

Spital, Spittle *N. F.* a hospital. Ex.: Spital-fields (Midd.), hospital fields; Spittle-gate (Linc.).

Spoff, Spot *E.* perhaps from Spot,* a man's name. Ex.: Spotford, now Spofforth (Yorks.), and Spot-len, now Spotland (Lanc.), the ford and fee-farm land of Spot.

Spon, Spoon *E.* from *spóna*, a chip or splinter of wood. The word is applied by Bede † to the fragments of the 'true cross,' and hence probably points out places where these relics were deposited. Ex.: Spon-don or Spoon-don (Derb.), relic hill.

Sprat, Sprey, Sproat, Sprot, Sprough, Sprows *E.* from *spreot*, a spear, or from *sprot*, a sprig or sprout, afterwards a man's name. Ex.: Sprat-ton (Northam.); Sprey-ton (Devon), Sproat-ley (Yorks.); Sprot-borough (Yorks.); Sprough-ton (Suff.); Sprows-ton (Norf.).

Spring *E.* a spring of water. Ex.: Spring-thorp (Linc.), the farm of the spring.

Spyddid *B.* *See* Spytty.

Spytty *B.* from the Latin *hospitium*, a hospital. Ex.: Spytty or Yspytty Ystwith (Card.), the hospital by the river Ystwyth; Llan-spyddid (Brecons.), the church of the hospital.

Stad, Stead *E.* from *stede*, a station. Ex.: Stad-ham-ton (Oxf.), the town of the home station, or the village which afterwards became a town; Beces-stede, now Boxtead (Ess.), the station of the beech-trees; Stead-ham (Suss.).

* The name Spottiswood is well known.

† 'Of ham treowe, thæs halgan Cristis mæles sponas,' etc.

B. British. *C.* Celtic. *E.* The Old English, commonly known as Anglo-Saxon.

STAFF, STAVE, STAVER *E.* from *stæf*, a staff. Ex.: Stæf-ford,* now Stafford; Stave-ley (Derb.), staff-meadow; Staver-ton (Devon), *i. e.* Staef-ford-tun, staff-ford town. The allusion may be to a staff or pole fixed in the water to show the spot where it was fordable.

STAG *E.* a stag. Ex.: Stag-batch (Heref.), the stag's path; Stag's-den (Bedf.), the stag's hollow.

STAIN, STAM, STAN, STAUN, STEAN, STEYN, STONE *E.* from *stéan*, a stone, sometimes a boundary-stone. Ex.: Stain-by (Linc.), stone abode; Staines (Midd.) †; Stam-ford, anciently Stean-ford (Linc.), the ford of the stepping-stones; Stan-ton, 19 places, stone town; Staun-ton, corrupt spelling of ditto; Stean (Northam.); Steyn-ton (Pemb.), the same; Stone (Staff.); Stone-henge, the hanging stones. At the end of a word, *stone* is generally a corrupt spelling of *ton*, town, the *s* being the mark of the possessive case of the owner's name. Ex.: Barnardis-tone (Suff.), Barnard's town.

STAITHES, STATH, STAT *E.* from *stath*, a bank or shore. Ex.: Staithes (Cumb.); Stath-ern (Leices.), the place of the bank; Stat-fold (Staff.), the sheep-fold on the bank.

STAL *E.* from *stæl*, a stall or station. Ex.: Stal-bridge (Dorset).

STANWICK *E.* anciently Stanweg (*see* Saxon Chronicle, A.D. 1137), the stone way, perhaps from a Roman military station near which the town was built. Ex.: Stanwick (Northam.).

STAPLE *E.* from *stapul*, a stake, meaning the site of a market fixed by law, where the king's custom-duty on wool, skins, or leather, was received. Ex.: 24 places, in which staple is a prefix, as Staple-ford (8 places), the ford where the market was held. As a suffix it is sometimes corrupted into *stable*, as in Whit-stable, white market town, Dun-stable, hill market town, etc.

STARS, START *E.* from *steort*, a tail or a promontory. Ex.: Stars-ton (Norf.), promontory town; Start Point (Devon).

STAUGH, STOUGH, perhaps corrupt forms of *stoc*, the trunk of a tree. Ex.: Staugh-ton (Bedf.); Stough-ton (Suss.).

STAVE. *See* Staff, *supra*.

* Bosworth.

† So-called from the boundary stone of the jurisdiction of the city of London.—*Camden.*

D. Old Danish. *G.* Greek. *L.* Latin. *N.F.* Norman French. *N.* Norse. *qu. v.* which see.

STAW. *See* Stow, *infra.*

STEBB, STEP, STEEPING, STIBBING, STIB *E. stib*, the bole or trunk of a tree, from *stipes*, Latin. Ex.: Stebb-ing (Essex), bole meadow; Stepn-ey (Midd.), the pool or water by the bole; Steep-ing (Linc.), bole meadow; Stibbard (Norf.), Stibbing-ton (Hants).

STEEPING. *See* Stebb, *supra.*

STEEPLE *E.* from *stypel*, a steeple, distinguishing a village which possessed a church. Ex.: 5 places in Dorset, Essex, Bucks, and Camb.

STEPHEN, STEVEN, STEVING, STIVICH, ST. STEPHEN. Ex.: Ste-phen (Cornw.), 3 places; Steven-age (Herts), Stephen's edge or hill; Steving-ton (Bedf.), Stephen's town; Stivich-all (Warw.), Stephen's hall.

STEYN. *See* Stan, *supra.*

STICK, STIX *E.* from *stig*, a way. Ex.: Stigan-ey, now Stickney (Linc.), the pool by the way; Stiges-wold, now Stixwould (Linc.), the way across the wold or wild land.

STIFF *E.* from *stæf*, a staff. Ex.: Stiff-key (Norf.), *quasi* Stæf-ig, staff-pool. *See* Staff.

STIL, STILLING *E. stæl*, a stall or station, also a man's name, and *incga*, children. Ex.: Stil-ton (Hunts), Stæl's town; Still-ing-fleet, the harbour station of Stæl's children.

STINSFORD *E.* St. Stephen's ford. Ex.: Stinsford (Dorset).

STISTED *E.* St. Stephen's *stede*, or place. Ex.: Stisted (Ess.).

STIVICH. *See* Stephen, *supra.*

STIX. *See* Stick, *supra.*

STOCK, STOG, STOKE *E.* from *stoc*, or *stocce*, the stem or main part of a tree. When a prefix, indicating the chief town of a dis-trict; when a suffix, usually pointing out a town founded by the person whose name precedes it. Ex.: Stock-ton, 8 places; Grey-stoke (Cumb.), Grey's stoke; Stocces-ey, now Stogus-sey (Som.), the water stoke. Where the Saxon town became the seat of a Norman lord, his name is usually appended thus —Stoke Say (Salop); Stoke D'Abernon (Surr.), etc. Stock occurs as a prefix in 24 places; Stoke as a prefix in 65 places.

STONE *S.* from *stean* or *stán*, a stone. *See* Stan.

STOT, STOTTES *E. stot*, a young bullock. Ex.: Stot-fold (Bedf.), Stottes-den (Salop).

STOUGH. *See* Staugh, *supra.*

STOUR, STOWER, STUR, perhaps from the British *is* and *twr* or *tor*, under or at the foot of a hill, applied to several rivers in Kent, Worc., and Som., and afterwards designating towns on the banks of those rivers. Ex.: Stour-ton (Dorset); Stour-bridge (Worc.); Stur-minster (Dorset); Stour-mouth (Kent); Stower (Dorset).

STOW *E.* a form of *stoc, qu. v. supra.* Occurs as a prefix in 21 places, all in midland and eastern counties; and is frequent as a suffix.

STRAD, STRAF, STRAT, STREAT, STRET, STREET *E.* from *stræte*, a street or paved way, indicating a town on a Roman road. Ex.: Strad-sett (Norf.), the *setu* or tribal station on the street; Straf-forth (Yorks.), the ford on the line of the street; Strat-ford, 10 places, the same; Streat-ham (Surr.), the home by the street; Stret-ton,* 8 places, street town; Streat-hall (Ess.), the hall near the street. Strad occurs in 3 places; Straf in 1; Strat in 23; Streat in 3; Stret in 10; Street in 4; all as prefixes.

STRANG *E.* perhaps a corruption of *steng*, a pole. Ex.: Strang-ford (Heref.), the ford marked by a pole.

STRENS *E.* from *streone*, a watch-tower, also a name. Edric Streone was jarl of Northumbria, and took his second name from Streones-alh, called by the Danes Whitby. Bede translates *streone* by *sinus fari*, the bay of the watch-tower. Ex.: Strens-ham (Worc.), Streone's home.

STROUD, STROOD, STROWED probably from the *B. ystref-wŷdd*, a dwelling among trees. Ex.: Stroud (Glouc.), Strood (Kent), Strowed (Mont.).

STUB, STUBBING, said to be a corruption of St. Aubyn, a *N. F.* surname, as Sentlow is of St. Lo, and Sellinger is of St. Leger. I think it is rather from *stub*, *D.* for the stump of a tree, and *ing*, a meadow. Ex.: Stub-ton (Norf.). Probably, as in many other cases, the word *stub* was assumed as a man's name, in which case Stubbing would point out the abode of his *incga* or descendants.

STUD *E.* from *studu*, a post or pillar, thence a house. Ex.: Stud-

* Stretton Sugwas (Heref.) appears in Domesday Book as 'Stratone.'

D. Old Danish. *G.* Greek. *L.* Latin. *N. F.* Norman French. *N.* Norse. *qu. v.* which see.

ham (Herts), Stud-ley (Warw.), the home or the meadow marked with posts.

STUKELEY *E.* probably from *stig-lege*, path place, *i. e.* place beside the path. Ex.: Stuke-ley (Hunts).

STUR. *See* Stour, *supra.*

STUT, STUTCH, STUTTIS *E.* from *stuth*, a post or pillar, and thence a home. Ex.: Stut-ton (Suff.); Stutch-burh (Northam.), the town or the fortified place which grew up around the house of the thegn or lord.

SUCK *E.* from *soc*, a privilege. Ex.: Soc-lege, now Suckley (Worc.), the land held under privilege; Sock-bourn, etc.

SUD *E.* south. *See* South.

SUF *E.* south. Ex.: Suffolk, the folk who lived southward of the Northfolk.

SUFTON *E.* anciently Sifton, probably from Sifa or Sibba, the lord's name. Ex.: Sufton (Heref.), Sifa's town.

SUG *E.* from *secg*, the sedge. Ex.: Sug-was (Heref.), sedgy water or moist place of sedges.

SUL *E.* from *sul* or *syl*, a plough, and afterwards as much land as one plough could cultivate. Ex.: Sul-ham (Berks), the plough home; Sulan-tun, now Sallington (Suss.), the town of the plough.

SUN, SUNNING *E.* from *sunna*, the sun, and *incga*, children; probably indicating the scene of the worship of the sun-god. Ex.: Sun-bury (Midd.), the fortified town of the sun; Sunningwell (Berks), the well of the children of the sun-god.

SUNDER *E.* separate or privileged. Ex.: Sunder-land (Durham); Sunder-edge, now Sundridge (Kent), the privileged place on the ridge.

SURREY *E.* from *suth-rice*, southern kingdom.

SUS *E.* from *suth*, south. Ex.: Suth-stede (Norf.), south station; Sus-sex, the territory of the *Suth-seaxna*, or South Saxons.

SUT *E.* from *suth*, south. Ex.: Sut-ton,* 31 places, south-town, indicating that another town lay to the northward in the same district; Sutter-by (Linc.), southern abode of Danes; Sutcomb (Devon), southern valley.

SWA, SWAD *E.* from *swæth*, a path. Ex.: Swæth-by, now Swaby

* Sutton (Heref.) is styled in Domesday Book 'Sudtune.'

(Linc.), the Danish abode near the path; Swæth-len-cot, now Swadlingcot (Derb.), the cot on the *len* near the path. *See* Len, *supra.*

SWAFF, SWAVES, SWAY, SWEF *E.* from the owner's name. Ex.: Swaff-ham (Norf. and Camb.), Swaff-field (Camb.), Sway-field (Linc.), Swaves-ey (Camb.), the water, the field, and the home of Swaff; Swef-len, now Swefling (Suff.), the fee-farm land of the same.

SWAINS, SWAN, SWANS, SWANNING *E.* from the owner's name, perhaps Sweyn, king of Denmark, and conqueror of the Saxons in England, and *incga*, children. Ex.: Swains-thorp (Norf.), Sweyn's farm; Swan-ton (Norf.), Sweyn's town; Swans-ea (Glam.), Sweyn's water or harbour; Swann-ington (Norf.), the town of Sweyn's children.

SWAL, SWALE *E.* a vale or interval between hills. Ex.: Swale (Yorks.); Swal-cliff (Oxf.), etc.

SWARDER, SWARRA *E.* from *sweard*, sward or grass land. Ex.: Swarder-ton (Norf.), Swarra-ton (Hants), the town amid pastures; Swer-ford (Oxf.), grassy ford.

SWARKES, perhaps from Swark, the chief's name. Ex.: Swarkes-ton (Derb.)

SWAVES. *See* Swaff, *supra.*

SWEF. *See* Swaff, *supra.*

SWELL, SWILL, SWILLING *E.* from *swale*, a vale. Ex.: Swell (Glouc.), Swil-land (Suff.), the len, or fee-farm land in the vale; Swilling-ton (Yorks.), *i.e.*, Swalen-tun, the town of the vale.

SWER. *See* Sward, *supra.*

SWETTEN *E.* from *sweot*, a band. Ex.: Swetten-ham (Ches.), the home of the band, or the village whose men were associated in war.

SWIM, SWIN, SWINE *E.* from *swin*, swine, an animal kept in vast herds in the forests in old English times. Ex.: 20 places, of which Swin-bridge, now Swimbridge (Devon), Swin-brook (Oxf.), Swines-head (Linc.), mean respectively the bridge, the brook, and the hill of swine.

SWITH *E.* from *swæth*, a path. Ex.: Swith-land (Leices.).

SYCH *B.* dry. Ex.: Sych-nant, the brook whose channel was often dry.

D. Old Danish. *G.* Greek. *L.* Latin. *N. F.* Norman French. *N.* Norse. *qu. v.* which see.

SYDEN, SYDERS, from Sida, the chief's name. Ex.: Sydn-ope (Derb.), the sloping plain of Sida; Syden-ham (Oxf., Kent, and Devon), Sida's home; Syders-ton (Norf.), Sida's town. *See* Sidding, *supra.*

SYMONDS *E.* *See* Sim, *supra.*

T

TAB *E.* St. Ebbe. Ex.: Tab-ley (Ches.), St. Ebbe's land.

TACH, TACK, TACOLN, TAK *E.* from *tacen*, a standard. Ex.: Tach-brook (Warw.), the brook of the standard, *i. e.* of the rallying-place for the men of the tithing or hundred; Tack-ley (Oxf.), the place of the standard; Tacolns-ton (Norf.), the town of the standard; Takelly (Essex), standard place.

TAD, TEDDING, TEDS, from *tod*, a fox, adopted as a man's name, and still preserved in the name of Todd. Ex.: Tad-caster (Yorks.), the fox's camp; Tad-mere-tun, now Tad-marton (Oxf.), fox's pool town; Tedding-ton (Midd.), fox's town; Toddes-thorn,* now Tedstone (Heref.).

TAFF *B.* from *taf*, a river. Ex.: the river Taff (Glam.).

TAL *B.* the forehead, or the end of a causeway, or of a lake. Ex.: Tall-y-llychau (Carm.), the end of the lakes; Tal-sarn, the end of the Roman road: Llanfair Talhaiarn (Denb.), St. Mary's church, built by Talhaiarn.

TALERDDIG *B.* from *tal-yr-ddeg*, 'end of the ten,' or tithe-land. Ex.: Talerddig (Card.).

TALHAIARN *B.* iron brow, the name of a famous chief or bard.

TAM, TAMAR *B.* from *tam* or *taf*, a river, hence Teme and Thames. Ex.: Tam-worth (Warw.), the estate by the Teme; Tamar, Tamar-ton (Devon), the river and the town beside it.

TAN *B.* below. Ex.: Tan-y-bwlch (Card.), below the pass.

TAN, TANNING *E.* from *Tana* or *Dana*, the owner's name. Ex.: Tan-field (Durh.), Tana's field;† Tan-worth (Warw.), Tana's estate; Tann-ing-ton (Suff.), the town of the descendants of Tana.

TANG *B.* peace. Ex.: Tang-le (Hants), the place of peace, probably the place where a treaty was concluded.

TAP *E.* the top. Ex.: Tap-low (Bucks), the top of the hill.

TAR *B.* from *tor*, a tower or hill. Ex.: Tor-ffin, now Tarvin (Ches.), boundary tower or hill.

* Domesday Book.

† Donafelda is identified by Dr. Gale with Tanfield.

Tarn *N.* from *tiern,* still used in Iceland, a mountain lake.

Tarnam *B.* Ex.: Llan-tarnam (Monm.), either the church of Tarnam, or (Llan-tor-Nonn) the church of the hill of St. Nonn, the mother of St. David.

Tarporley *D.* and *E.* anciently *thorp-lege,* the place of the farmhouse. Ex.: Tarporley (Ches.).

Tarrant *B.* from *dwr-gwent,* bright water. Ex.: the river Tarrant (Dorset). *See* Dar, *supra.*

Tarren *B.* a knap or rocky tump. Ex.: Tarren-gower (Pemb.).

Tarring *B.* from Darren, a small hill. Ex: Tarring-ton (Heref.), the town of the small hill.

Tas *E.* a mow of corn. Ex.: Tas-ley (Salop), the place of corn.

Tat, Tath, Tats, Tatten, Tatter, Tattings *E.* from *teotha,* a tenth or a tithing, *i. e.* a group of ten farms. Ex.: Tat-ham (Lanc.), tithe or tithing village; Tath-well (Linc.), tithe or tithing well; Tats-field (Surrey); Tatten-hall (Ches.); Tattings-ton (Suff.), tithing town; Tatter-set (Norf.), tithing station; Tatters-hall (Linc.).

Taunton, anciently Tangwn-tun, from St. Tangwn,* a British saint, mentioned in Rees' 'Lives of Cambro-British Saints,' as having lived there. Probably the river Tone is named from the same personage.

Taver *E.* from *tawer,* a leader. Ex.: Taver-ham (Norf.), the leader's home.

Tavi, Tavy *B.* from *taf,* a river. Ex.: Tavi-stock (Devon), the stockade near the Tavy river.

Taw *B.* from *taf.* Ex.: the river Taw (Devon); Taw-ton, the town by the Taw.

Tayn, Tean *B.* apparently from *tân,* the sacred fire, which was kindled on May 20, which day is still called in Scotland Beltane, Bel's fire. Ex.: Tayn-ton (Glouc.), the town on the site where the sacred fire was kindled; Tean (Staff.).

Teal, Tellis *E.* perhaps from *tillan,* to till or cultivate. Ex.: Teal-by (Linc.), the tiller's abode; Tellis-ford (Som.).

Tean. *See* Tayn, *supra.*

Ted, Teds, Teff *E.* from *tod,* a fox. Ex.: Ted-bourn (Devon), the fox's brook; Tef-font (Wilts), the fox's fountain or well. *See* Tad, *supra.*

* The local pronunciation 'Tanton,' still preserves the first syllable of the saint's name.

TEG *B.* fair. Ex.: Pant-teg (Mon.), the fair valley.

TEIGH *E.* from *teag*, an enclosure. Ex.: Teigh (Rutl.).

TEIGN *B.* from *tân*, the sacred fire of the Druids. Teignton 'a Danis crematum,' says a Saxon author. Ex.: Teign river, and Teign-grace (Devon). *See* Tayn, *supra.*

TEL. *See* Teal, *supra.*

TEME *B.* from *tam*, a river. Ex.: the rivers Teme (Warw. and Salop).

TEMPLE, TEMPS *N. F.* pointing out the property of the Knights Templars. Ex.: 8 places; Temps-ford (Bedf.).

TENBURY, anciently Temen-burh, the fortified place on the river Teme. *See* Tam and Tavy, *supra.*

TENBY *B.* corrupted from Din-bychan, little camp. Ex.: Tenby (Pemb.).

TENDRING *S.* from *thegn*, a nobleman, and *incga*, children. Ex.: Tendring (Essex).

TENTERDEN *E.* from *thegn* and *denu.* Ex.: Tenter-den (Kent), the nobleman's hollow.

TER. *See* Dar, *supra.*

TERRING. *See* Darren, *supra.*

TET, TETTEN *E.* from Theoda or Tetta, the chief's name. Ex.: Tet-bury (Glouc.), Tetta's fortified town; Tets-worth (Oxf.), Tetta's watered estate; Tettan-ey, now Tetney (Linc.), Tetta's pool; Tetten-hall (Staff.), Tetta's hall.

TEVERS *E.* from *tawer*, a leader. Ex.: Tevers-all (Notts), the leader's hall.

TEW *E.* from Tiw or Tuisco, a Saxon deity, from whom Tiwes-daeg, now Tuesday, is named. Ex.: Tew (Oxf.); Tewin (Herts).

TEWKESBURY *E.* anciently Theoca's-burh, *i. e.* Theoca's fortified town. Ex.: Tewkesbury (Glouc.).

TEY *E.* perhaps a corruption from *tŷ* (*B.*), a house. Ex.: 3 places in Essex.

TEYN. *See* Teign, *supra.*

THAKE, THATCH, THAX *E.* from *thac*, thatch; hence *thecen*, a roof. Ex.: Thake-ham (Sussex), the thatched village; Thatch-am (Berks), the same; Thax-ted (Essex), the thatched station.

THAME, THAMES. *See* Tam, *supra.*

THANINGTON *E.* from *thegn*, a nobleman, *incga*, children, and *tun*, a town. Ex.: Than-incgatun, now Thanington (Kent), the town of the nobleman's children.

D. Old Danish. *G.* Greek. *L.* Latin. *N. F.* Norman French. *N.* Norse. *qu. v.* which see.

THEDDING, THEDDLE *D.* from Theod, or Thode, still a name used in Denmark. Ex.: Theoden-wyrth, now Theddingworth (Leices.); Theoda-thorp, now Theddlethorp (Linc.), Theod's farm. A famous witch named Thioda made a great sensation in Germany in A.D. 847.—Bergmann *On Icelandic Poetry.*

THEL *E.* from *thel,* an upper story. Ex: Thel-wall (Ches.), the walled building of two stories.*

THEMEL, THIMBLE *D.* from Themel, the owner's name. Ex.: Themel-thorp (Norf.), Thimble-by (Linc.).

THET, from *theote,* a pipe or conduit. Ex.: the river Thet (Norf.), Thet-ford (Suff.).

THIMBLE. *See* Themel, *supra.*

THINGE *N.* from *tinga,* an assembly. Ex.: Tinge-hele, or Tinge-halle, now Thinge-hill (Heref.), the hall of assembly, probably the place of meeting for the hundred.

THIRKLE *D.* from Torkil, the owner's name. Ex.: Thirkle-by (Yorks.), Torkil's abode.

THIRSK *B.* from *tref-ysg,* town by the water.† Ex.: Thirsk (Yorks.).

THISTLE *E.* from *thistel,* a thistle. Ex.: Thistle-ton (Rutl.).

THOR, THORES, THORING, THUR, THURS, THURSTA, THURSTON *E.* from Thor, the thunder-god. Ex.: Thor-ley (Hants), Thor's land; Thores-by (Linc.), Thor's Danish abode; Thor-ington (Suff.), the town of Thor's children; Thor-man-by (Yorks.), Thor's man's abode; Thur-low (Suff.), Thor's hill; Thurs-by (Cumb.), Thor's abode; Thurstas-ton (Ches.), the town of Thurston, or of Thor's rock; Thurston-land (Yorks.), the fee-farm land, or farm let out, of Thurston.

THORN, THURN *E.* the hawthorn. Ex.: 44 places, 16 being Thorn-ton, thorn town; Thurn-ing (Norf.), thorn meadow.

THORO *E.* from Thorold, the owner's name. Ex.: Thoro-ton (Yorks.), Thorold's town.

THORP *E.* from *thorp,* a farm-house. Ex.: 28 places as a prefix, and 281 as a suffix.

THORRING. *See* Thor, *supra.*

THRAPS, THREP, THROAP *E.* from *throp,* the meeting of cross roads. Ex.: Thraps-ton (Northam.), Throap-ham (Yorks.), the town and the village built at the *throp*; Ægle's threp, now Aylesford.‡

* Bosworth *in voce.*

† Lewis's Top. Dict. *in voce.*

‡ Anglo-Saxon Chronicle, year 455.

Threcking, Threx, Throcking *E.* from Threcca, a man's name, and *incga*, children. Ex.: Threcking-ham (Linc.), the home of the children of Threcca; Threx-ton (Norf.), the town of Threcca; Throcking (Herts), the meadow of the same.

Threp, Thrip *E.* from *throp*. *See* Thraps, *supra*.

Throcking. *See* Threcking, *supra*.

Throgmorton *E.* Throgga's or Throcca's town by the pool.

Throw *E.* from *thræw*, crooked. Ex.: Throw-leigh (Devon), Throw-ley (Kent), the crooked place.

Thrump *E.* from *thrym*, a meeting-place, or a heap. Ex.: Thrump-ton (Notts).

Thrux *E.* from Throcca, a man's name. Ex.: Thrux-ton (Heref.).

Thry *E.* three. Ex.: Thry-burh, now Thrybergh (Yorks.), three fortified places or camps.

Thunders *E.* from the thunder-god, Thor, and probably indicating the site of his temple or altar. Ex.: Thunders-by (Ess.), Thundridge (Herts).

Thur. *See* Thor, *supra*.

Thurcas, Thurgar, Torkard, Torks *E.* from Thurca or Torca, the chief's name, meaning the car of the thunder-god. Ex.: Thurcas-ton (Leic.), Thurgar-ton (Norf.), Torkard Hucknall (Notts); Torks-ey, Torca's pool.

Thurl *E.* from *thyrl*, an opening or door, or from Thurloc or Thurla, the owner's name. Ex.: Thurlas-ton (Leic.), Thurleston (Yorks.), Thurloxton (Som.), Thurl-ton (Norf.).

Thurn *E.* from *thyrn*, a thorn. Ex.: Thurn-scoe (Yorks.), thorn-shaw, or wood.

Thurrock *E.* from *thurruc*, a boat. Ex.: Thurrock (Ess.).

Thwaite *D.* an open place or clearing. Ex.: 3 places (Norf. and Suff.), as a prefix; and 30 places where it is a suffix.

Thwing, Thong, Tong *E.* from *thwang*, a thong or a narrow strip of land. Ex.: Thwing and Thong (Yorks.); Tong, 4 places.

Tib, Tibber, Tiber, Tiver *E.* from *tiber*, holy, or place of sacrifice. Ex.: Tib-shelf (Derb.), the holy place on the shelf of the hills; Tibrintin-tun,* now Tiberton (Heref.), holy town; Tibberton (Glouc.); Tiben-ham (Norf.); Tiverton (Devon).

Tice, Ticken, Tickn, Titch *E.* from *thecen*, a roof, or *tice*, a beam, indicating a house. Ex.: Tice-hurst (Suss.), Ticken-cote

* Domesday Book.

D. Old Danish. *G.* Greek. *L.* Latin. *N. F.* Norman French. *N.* Norse. *qu. v.* which see.

(Rutl.), Ticken-hall (Staff.), Tickn-all (Derb.), Tick-hill (Yorks.); Tices-well, now Titchwell (Herts).

TID, TIDEN, TIDES, TYD *E.* from *tid*, tide or stream. Ex.: Tid-comb (Wilts), stream dingle; Tiden-ham (Glouc.), the village by the stream; Tides-well (Derb.), the tides' well, from the celebrated ebbing and flowing well there; Tydd (Camb.).

TIL, TILE *E.* from *til*, good, or *tille*, a station. Ex.: Tilla-burh,* now Tilbury (Ess.), Tile-hurst (Berks), Tillington (Heref.).

TIMBER *E.* from *tymbre*, wood. Tymbre land was land given for the sustentation of churches, etc.† Ex.: Timbers-comb (Som.), the tymbre-land in the dingle; Timber-land (Linc.).

TIN *B.* from *din*, a fortification. Ex.: Tin-tagel (Cornw.), St. Degla's fortification; Tin-tern (Monm.), the fortification of the *teyrn*, or prince.

TING *N.* from *ding*, a council. Ex.: Tinge-wick (Bucks), council village; Ting-rith (Bedf.), council brook.

TIR *B.* land. *See* Dir, *supra.*

TIR *E.* a form of Thor, or Tirr, the thunder-god. The only example is Tir-ley (Glouc.), Thor's land.

TITCH. *See* Tice, *supra.*

TIT. *See* Tet, *supra.*

TIVER *E.* from *tifer*, a form of *tiber*, a place of sacrifices. Ex.: Tiverton (Devon).

TITTERSTONE *E.* traditionally said to be a corruption of Totter-stone, from a tottering or loggin stone on the summit of the hill, which has now disappeared. Ex.: Titterstone (Salop).

TOCKEN *E.* from *thecen*, a roof. Ex.: Tocken-ham (Wilts), the roofed home or village.

TOD *E.* from *tod*, a fox. Ex.: Toden-ham (Glouc.), the fox's home; Tod-mor-den (Lanc.), the hollow of the fox's pool; Tod-wick (Yorks.), the fox's village.

TOFT *D.* from *tofte*, a grove, or the grounds of a house.‡ Ex.: 8 places in which it is a prefix, and 22 in which it is a suffix.

TOL *E.* from *toll*, indicating a market or place where toll was levied. Ex.: Tolland (Som.); Tolles-hunt and Tolles-bury (Ess.).

TONG. *See* Thwing.

* Bede. † Terra data ad ædificia reparanda, etc.—*Mon. Ang.*

‡ Prof. Munch.

TOOTING *E.* probably from *teotha*, a tenth or a tithing. Ex.: Tooting (Surr.); or from *tohta*, a leader.

TOP, TOPPING *E.* a hill. Ex.: Topcroft (Norf.), the field on the hill; Roseberry Topping; Topsham (Devon), the hill village.

TOR *B.* a hill. The word is frequent in Devon, Cornw., and Derb.

TORKSEY, Torkil's pool. *See* Thirkle, *supra.*

TORRINGTON, corrupted from Tori-ton, hill town. Ex.: Torrington (Devon. and Linc.).

TOSTOCK *E.* from Tostig, the owner's name. Ex.: Tostock (Suff.), or from Thores-stock, Thor's station. *See* Thor.

TOT, TOTTEN, TOTTER, TOTTING *E.* from *teotha*, a tenth or a tithing. *See* Tat, *supra.*

TOW *N.* from *to*, a grass-plot.* Ex.: Tow-ton (Yorks.), the town of the grass-plot.

TOWCESTER *E.* from *Tove*, name of the river, and *cestre*, camp. Ex.: Tow-cester (Northam.), the town and camp of the river Tove.

TOWEDNACK, from St. Dewednack. Ex.: Towednack (Cornw.).

TOWYN, TOYN *B.* from *twyn*, a curved hillock or bank. Ex.: Towyn (Merion.); Toyn-ton, 4 places (Linc.).

TRAETH *B.* the sea-shore. *See* Draeth, *supra.*

TRALLWNG *B*, a quagmire in a road. Ex.: Trallwng (Brecons.).

TRAWS *B.* opposite. Ex.: Traws-fynydd (Merion.), opposite the well.

TRE *B.* from *tref*, a town originally a single house. Ex.: Tre-ago, anciently Tref-y-goll (Monm.), hazel town; Tre-neglos (Cornw.), church town.

TREBOROUGH, TREE *E.* from *treow*, a tree, the fortified place of or at the tree. Ex.: Treborough (Som.); Tree-ton (Yorks.).

TREDING *E.* from *trything*, now corrupted into *riding*, the third part of a county, as in the ridings of Yorkshire. Ex.: Treding-ton (Glouc. and Worc.), the town of the trything.

TREF *B.* the form of *tre*, when the following word begins with a vowel or a liquid. Ex.: Tref-eglwys (Mont.), church town; Tref-lys (Carnarv.), palace town.

TRENT (doubtful), said by Bosworth to have been anciently called Drouent 'a flexu sive ambitu sui curcus,' therefore, the winding stream. Ex.: the river Trent.

* Prof. Munch.

TRENTIS-HOE *D.* Tranta's hill. (The name Trant still survives as a surname.) Ex.: Trentishoe (Devon).

TREVETHIN *B.* a corruption of Tref-y-ddin, camp town. Ex.: Trevethin (Monm.).

TRIM, TRIMING *E.* from *thrym*, a heap or mass, also a name. Ex.: Trim-don (Durham); Trim-ingham (Norf.), the home of Trim's children.

TRING *B.* from *draen*, a thorn. Ex. Tring (Herts).

TROED *B.* the foot. Ex.: Troed-y-aur (Card.), the foot of the golden hill, probably pointing out one of the places where the precious metal was obtained in British times.

TROS *B.* above or over. Ex.: Tros-tre (Monm.), higher town.

TROTHY *B.* a slow, trickling stream. Ex.; the river so named; Blaen-trothy, the source of that river (Mon.).

TROWBRIDGE *E.* anciently Trutha-burh, the faithful town. Ex.: Trowbridge (Wilts).

TROY *B.* from tre-wy, the town by the Wye. Ex.: Troy (Monm.).

TRUM *B.* from *drum*, the back of an animal, or a ridge resembling it in shape. Ex.: common in Scotland and in Ireland.

TRURO *B.* from *tre-rhiw*, the town of the sloping path. Ex.: Truro (Cornw.).

TRY *B.* from *tre*, town, the suffix to the name of many places. Ex.: Coven-try, Daven-try, etc.

TUDDEN, TUDE *E.* from *tod*, a fox. Ex.: Tudden-ham (Norf.), Tudeley (Kent), the fox's home and place.

TUDY *B.* from St. Tydaw. Ex.: St. Tudy (Cornw.).

TUF *D.* from *thufe*, a branch. Ex.: Tuf-ton (Hants).

TUMP *B.* from *twmp*, a small round hill, common in Heref.

TUN *E.* a town. Ex.: Tun-bridge (Kent), bridge town; Tun-stall (Yorks. and Suff.), town station.

TUP *E.* the male sheep. Ex.: Tup-ton (Derb.), Tups-ley (Heref.), probably named from some chief who assumed the pugnacious tup as his cognizance.

TURK *N.* from Torkil, the chief's name. Ex.: Turk-dean (Glouc.). Torkil's hollow.

TURNAS, TURNERS *N. F.* from the *tourn*, or feudal court, from attending which the tenant's deputy was styled an attorney. Ex.: Turnas-ton (Heref.), tourn town; Turners-puddle, (Dorset), the pool near which the tourn was held.

TURVEY, TURVILLE *E.* *turf-ey*, the grassy banked pool or stream.

Ex.: Turvey (Bedf.); Turville (Bucks), turf-town or village; Tur-weston (Bucks), turf Weston, in distinction from other Westons.

TUTBURY *E.* from Tot, or Thoth, or Tiw, the god of Tuesday, who is thought to have been worshipped on the spot now called Tutbury (Staff.).

TWER *E.* from *thweor*, crooked. Ex.: Twer-ton (Som.).

TWICKEN, TWITCHEN *E.* from *twy-cina*, two ways, the junction of two roads. Ex.: Twicken-ham (Midd.); Twitchen (Devon).

TWIN, TWINE *E.* from *twegen*, two. Ex.: Twin-berrow (Worc.), two fortifications; Twine-ham (Suss.), two homes.

TWISTLE *E.* from *twislung*, a receiving or store-house. Ex.: Oswal-twistle (Lanc.), Oswald's store-house; Hal-twistle (North.), store-house hall; Twisle-ton, store-house town.

TWITCHEN. *See* Twicken, *supra.*

TWLL *B.* a hole or cave. Ex.: Cae-fran-Twll (Glam.), the high field near the cave.

TWRCH *B.* a hog. Ex.: Pen-twrch, hog hill, and Cwm-twrch, hog's dingle (both in Glam.). Or, as neither place is far from a coast which bears many traces of the Norsemen, they may mean the hill and the dingle of Torchil, as in the case of Torchil's dean, now Turkdean (Glouc.).

TWY *E.* from *twegen*, two. Ex.: Twy-ford, 4 places, two fords. Or *B.* from *dwy ffordd*, two ways.

TWYN *B.* a curved or semicircular hillock or bank in the shape of the eyebrow. *See* Towyn.

TY *B.* a house. Ex.: Ty-gwyn (Monm.), white house; Ty-defailog (Carn.), Defailog's house.

TYLE *B.* the place where a house has been, or the ruins of a house. Ex.: Cwm-tyle (Monm.).

TYNE *B.* from *tain*, a river. Ex.: Tyne-ham (Dorset), the river Tyne (North.), Tynemouth, etc.

TYRS *E.* from Tir or Thor, the thunder-god. Ex.: Tyrs-ho, now Tyrsoe (Bedf.), Thor's hill.

TYTHER *E.* from *teotha*, a tenth or a tithing, *i. e.* the tenth part of the division called a hundred. Ex.: Tyther-ton (Wilts); Tythering-ton (Glouc.), tithing-town.

D. Old Danish. *G.* Greek. *L.* Latin. *N. F.* Norman French. *N.* Norse. *qu. v.* which see.

U

Ubbes, Ub *D.* from Ubba, or Hubba, a Danish river. Ex.: Ubbeston (Suff.), Ub-ley (Som.). *See* Hubbers, *supra.*

Uff *E.* from Uffa, name of a famous king of the East Angles, A.D. 575. Ex.: Uff-culme (Devon), Uffa's *cwm* or dingle; Ufford (Suff.), Uffa's ford; Uf-ton (Warw.), Uffa's town.

Uch *B.* higher or above. Ex.: Uchlawrcoed (Monm.), the plot of ground above the wood.

Uchel *B.* lofty.

Uchaf *B.* highest.

Uffington *E.* from Uffa, and *incgatun.* Ex.: Uffington (Berks, Linc., Salop), the town of the children of Uffa; probably the Anglian king of that name.

Ug *E.* from Ugga, the chief's name. Ex.: Ug-borough (Devon), Ugga's fortified town; Ugges-hall (Suff.), Ugga's hall, Ugley (Ess.), Ugga's place.

Ul, Ulce *D.* from Ulf, or Ulfa, the chief's name. Ex.: Ulce-by (Linc.), Ulf's abode; Ul-comb (Kent), Ulfa's dingle; Uldale (Cumb.).

Ulles *E.* from Ulla or Ella, an Anglian king. Ex.: Ulles-water (Westm.), Ulles-thorp (Leices.), Ulla's farm.

Ullin *E.* from Ulfwin, the chief's name. Ex.: Ullins-wick (Heref.), Ulfwin's village.

Ulvers *D.* from Ulfor, or Wulfhere. Ex.: Ulverston (Lanc.).

Umbers *E.* from Umba or Humber, the owner's name. Ex.: Umbers-lade (Warw.), Umba's brook; Humbers-ton (Leic.).

Under *E.* lower. Ex.: Under-mil-beck (Westm.), the lower mill brook; Under-skiddaw (Cumb.), below Skiddaw.

Up, Upper *E.* the higher of two places, or a high situation. Ex.: 44 places, of which 22 are Uptons.

Upton *E.* In the case of Upton-on-Severn the word is derived by Stukeley from Ypocessa, the name of a Roman station near that site.

Ur, *E.* from *ufa,* higher. Ex.: Ur-peth (Cumb.), higher path. *Ur,* in German, signifies the origin or spring of anything.

Urch *E.* from *urchin,* the hedgehog. Ex.: Urch-font (Wilts), the hedgehog's fountain, or the source of a stream called the Urch, or hedgehog's brook.

Usk *C.* water. Ex.: the Usk river (Mon.).

Utter, Uttox, perhaps from *Uthr,* wonderful, the name of a famous British king. Ex.: Utter-by (Linc.), Uthr's abode; Uttoxeter (Staff.), Uthr's *cestre* or camp.

Uwch *B.* higher. *See* Uch, *supra.*

Ux *E.* from ox. Ex.: Ux-bridge, anciently Ox-bridge (Midd.).

Uzmas *E.* from Osmund. *See* Osmas, *supra.*

V

VACHES *B.* from St. Maches. Ex.: Llan-vaches (Glam.), St. Maches' church.

VAINOR *B.* from *faen* or *maen*, a rock, and *or*, a boundary. Ex.: Faen-or, now Vainor (Brec.), the rock boundary.

VANS *B.* from *fannau*, plural of *ban*, high. Ex.: The Vans (Carmarth.), the high places.

VEDW *B.* corrupted from Fedw, *qu. v. supra.*

VENN *B.* from *wen* or *gwen*, fair or beautiful. Ex.: Venn Ottery (Devon), the beautiful place of the otter's pool.

VENNY *B.* from *fynydd*, mountains. Ex.: the Venny river (Mon.).

VERN *B.* from *gwern*, the alder-tree. Ex.: The Vern (Heref.), the alders.

VENTNOR, from *venta*, the Latin form of *Gwent* (bright or shining), adopted by the Saxons as the name of the district now called Hants, and *or*, a boundary. Ex.: Ventn-or, *i. e.* Ventan-or (Hants), the boundary of Hants.

VILLE *N. F.* a town or village. Ex.: Tur-ville (Bucks), Thor's village.

VIRGIN *E.* the Virgin Mary. Ex.: Virgin-stow (Devon), the Virgin Mary's station.

VOW *B.* perhaps from *ffau*, a wild beast's den. Ex.: Vow-church (Heref.). *See* Fown.

W

WAC, WAX *E.* weak or small, perhaps from the British *gwac*, vacant, or thinly peopled. Ex.: Gwac-ty, an uninhabited house; Wac-ton (Heref.), the small town; Wax-ham (Norf.), the small village.

WAD, WADDES, WADS, WADEN *E.* from Waddy, son of Woden, one of the mythic heroes from whom the kings of Northumbria (see *A. S. Chronicle*, A.D. 560) deduced their lineage. Ex.: Wad-hurst (Sussex), Waddy's wood; Waddes-don (Bucks), Waddy's hill; Wads-ley (Yorks.), Waddy's place; Waden-hoe (Northam.), Waddy's hill.

WADDING *E.* from King Waddy, son of Woden, and *incga*, descendants. *Ex.*: Waddingham (Linc.), and Waddington (Leices.), the home and the town of Waddy's descendants.

WADE *E.* from *wadan*, to wade. Ex.: Wade-bridge (Cornw.), the bridge by the ford.

WAFER, WAVER, WHAV *E.* from *waeg-faru*, a way by the water, afterwards a personal name.* Ex.: Wafer Hopton, Tedstone Wafer (Heref.), Wavertree (Lanc.), the town by the water way; Wavertun,† now Wharton (Heref.).

WAGHEN *E.* from *wæg*, a way. Ex.: Waghen, now Wawn (Yorks.).

WAIN *B.* corrupted from *waun*, or *gwaun*, a meadow or down. Ex.: Wain (Glam.).

WAIN *E.* from *wæg*, a way, plural *wægen*. Ex.: Wain-fleet (Linc.), the way by the harbour.

WAITH *E.* from *waad*, woad. Ex.: Waith (Linc.), probably a place where the woad plant (*Isatis tinctoria*) grew.

WAKE *E.* from *wæg*, a way. Ex.: Wake-field (Yorks.), the field by the wayside; Wake-ring (Essex), the way of the Regni, a British tribe. *See* Ring, *supra*.

* There was a Sir Robert de Wafre temp. Henry II.

† Domesday Book, and writ to Hugh, Abbot of Reading, temp. Henry I.

WALBER, WALBERS *E.* from Walbeof, the name of an English earl of Norwich, the son-in-law of William the Conqueror. Ex.: Walbers-wick (Suff.), Walbeof's village; Walber-ton (Suss.), Walbeof's town.

WALES *E.* perhaps from *wæl*, slaughter. Ex.: Wales (Yorks.), Wales-by (Linc.).

WALD *E.* from *walda*, a ruler, frequent in personal names. Ex.: Ethel-wald, the noble ruler; Oswald, the ruling hero, etc.

WALDEN, WALT, WEALDEN, WEALD, WOLD *E.* from *wæald*, wild or uncultivated land, hence wood. Ex.: Walden Saffron (Essex), the wild place, where saffron was afterwards cultivated; Walt-ham (Essex), Weald (Essex), Wealden (Kent), Wold (Linc. and Yorks.), Cottes-wold (Glouc.), etc.

WAL, WALL, WALLS *E.* from *gwal*, a wall, in most cases, if not in all, indicating a site on or near a Roman fortification. Ex.: Wal-ford (Heref.), the ford near Ariconium; Wal-ditch (Dorset), the entrenchment; Walls-end (Northum.), the end of the wall of Severus; Sutton-walls (Heref.), Sutton entrenchment, *i. e.* the palace of Offa; Wal-mer (Kent), the Roman fortification by the sea; Walton, 20 places.

WALK, WALKER, WALKING *E.* from *wealcere*, a fuller of cloth, and *incga*, children. Ex.: Walk-ern (Herts), the fuller's place; Walker-incgaham, now Walkeringham (Notts), the fuller's children's village; Walking-ton (Yorks.), the fuller's town.

WALLINGFORD *E.*, anciently Wealincgaford, from Weala, a stranger (*i. e.* a Briton), *incga*, children, and *ford*: the ford of the children of the stranger, or the ford of the Britons.

WALLOP *B.* from *wall*, a Roman fortification, and *hwpp* (Brit.) an ascent between hills. Ex.: Wallop (Hants), the ascent to the Roman camp.

WALSALL *E.* the hall near the Roman fortification. Ex.: Walsall (Staff.), anciently Wallas-hall.

WALSHAM *E.* the home near the Roman fortification. Ex.: Walsham (Heref.).

WALSINGHAM *E.* from *wells-incgaham*, the village of the children of the well, *i. e.* the wishing-well of St. Mary. Ex.: Walsing-ham (Norf.).

WALT *E.* from *weald*, wild or uncultivated land. Ex.: Weald-ham, now Waltham (Essex), and 10 other places in the eastern counties.

B. British. *C.* Celtic. *E.* The Old English, commonly known as Anglo-Saxon.

WALTERSTON *N. F.* from Walter, the Norman lord. Ex.: Walters-ton (Heref.), Walter's town.

WAN, WANS *E.* from Woden, the war-god. Ex: Wans-borough (Surrey), Wans-borough (Wilts), anciently Woden's beorh, *i. e.* Woden's fortification; Wans-ford (Northam.), Woden's ford.

WANDS *E.* from the river Wandle. Ex.: Wandles-worth, now Wandsworth (Surrey), the estate by the Wandle, *i. e.* the osier river. *See* Windle.

WANG *E.* from *wang* or *wong*, a piece or strip, still used as whang in Scotland.* Ex.: Wang-ford (Suff.), the strip of land near the ford.

WANT *E.* from Wanta or Wanda, the chief's name. Ex.: Want-age (Berks), Wanta's edge, being situated on the edge of a stream.

WAP, WAPPEN, WAPON *E.* from *wæpen*, a weapon, indicating the place of military exercise or weapon-show. Ex.: Wap-ley (Glouc.), the weapon field; Wappen-ham (Northam.), weapon village; Wapping (Midd.), the meadow of weapons; Wapontake, (Yorks.), a division of the county all the men in which mustered together.

WAR *E.* from *weare*, a weir or enclosure on a stream. Ex.: War-cop (Westm.), enclosed hill; War-den (Bedf.), enclosed hollow; War-grave (Bucks), the ditch enclosure; Weare-ham (Herts), now Warham, home near the weir.

WARB, WARBUR *E.* from St. Werburgha. Ex.: Warb-stow (Cornw.), St. Werburgha's station; Werburgha's wic, now War-brick (Lanc.), St. Werburgha's village; War-burton (Ches.), St. Werburgha's town; Warboys (Hunts), St. Werburgha's ooze or moist place.

WARD *E.* from *weardian*, to guard. Ex.: Ward-ley (Rutl.), the guarded land; Ward-hill, now Wardle-worth (Lanc.), the watered estate by the guarded hill.

WARE *E.* from *weare*, an enclosure on a stream. Ex.: Ware (Herts), from the enclosure or weir formed in the Lea by the Danes, to protect their fleet; Ware-ham (Dorset), Ware-ham (Kent), the home or village at the weir.

WARK *D.* a building or fort. Ex.: Wark-worth (Northum.), the

* 'Frae a new cheese they cut a whang.'—*Ballad of the Gaberlunzie Man.*

fort on the watered estate; New-wark (Notts), the new fort;* Ald-wark (Yorks.), the old ditto.

WARM *E.* from *weare-hám*, the village by the wear, also a name. Ex.: Warm-field (Yorks.); War-minster (Wilts), the minster at the wear village.

WARMING *E.* from *weare-hám* and *incga.* Ex.: Warm-inga-hurst (Suss.), now Warming-hurst, the village in the wood inhabited by the children of Weareham.

WARN, WARRING *E.* from *wering*, a fortification. Ex.: Warnborough (Hants), the fortified town; Warring-ton (Ches.), the same.

WARREN *E.* a preserve for rabbits. Ex.: Warren (Pemb.).

WARTON *E.* from *weort-tun*, an herb enclosure, or garden. Ex.: Warton (Lanc.).

WARWICK *B.* and *N.* from *gwawr*, a hero, and *wic*, a village. Its British name was Caergwawr, the fortress of the hero. The Saxons called it Wering-wic, fortress village.

WASH, WASHING, WESSING, WASING *E.* from *wæs*, water, indicating a moist site. Ex.: Wash-bourn (Glouc.), and Washbrook (Suff.), the brook of the moist place, *i. e.* the marshy brook; Washing-ton (Suss. and Dur.) the town of ditto; Wessing-ton (Derb.), the same; Wasing (Hants), moist meadow.

WAT *E.* from *watel*, a wattled fortification, *i. e.* a defence formed with trunks of trees interlaced with boughs, and plastered over with mud or lime. Ex.: Wat-ford, Watton (Herts), the ford and the town on the line of the Watling-street.

WATCHET *E.* anciently *weced-poort*, the watched or protected port. Ex.: Watchet (Som.).

WATER *E.* from *wæter*, the pronunciation still given to the word, as indicating a river, in South Scotland: 'water-water,' being river-water as distinguished from 'wall-water,' *i.e.* well-water. Ex.: 9 places in which, as a prefix, it indicates a site on a river bank.

WATH, *C.* a ford. Ex.: Wath-upon-Dearne (Yorks.), the ford of the stream so called.

WAULD *E.* from *wæald*, a wild or uncultivated place. Ex.: Wauldby (Yorks.), the Danish abode on the weald.

* So called by the Danes on their rebuilding the Sidnacestre of the Saxons.

B. British. *C.* Celtic. *E.* The Old English, commonly known as Anglo-Saxon.

WAUN *B.* from *gwaun,* a meadow or down. Ex.: Waun-helygen (Rad.), willow meadow.

WAWN, WAWEN *E.* from *wæg,* a way. *See* Waghen, *supra.*

WAVEN, WAVER *E.* from *wæg-faru,* a way by the water side. Ex.: Wavendon (Bucks), the hill by the water path; Waver-ton (Ches.), the town by the water path; Wafre-tun,* now Wharton (Heref.), the same.

WAX. *See* Wac, *supra.*

WAY *E.* from *wæg,* a way. Ex.: Way-ford (Som.), the ford on the way.

WEALD *E.* from *wealt* or *wæald,* a wild or uncultivated place. Ex.: Weald-Bassett (Essex), the weald belonging to the Norman lord Bassett.

WEAR *E.* from *weare,* an enclosed place on a river. Ex.: Weare (Som.); the Wear river (Durham), etc.

WEASEN *E.* from *wæs,* water. *See* Wash, *supra.*

WEAVER *E.* from *wæg-faru,* a path by the water. *See* Waver and Wafer, *supra.*

WEB, *E.* from *wiba,* a weaver, afterwards a man's name. Ex.: Web-heath, (Worc.), Wiba's or the weaver's heath; Web-tree (Heref.), Wiba's wooded district; Web-ton (Heref.), Wiba's town.

WED *E.* from *wet,* watery. Ex.: Wed-more (Som.), the wet moor.

WEDDING *E.* from *wed,* a pledge. Ex.: Wedding-ton (Warw.), pledge town.

WEDNES *E.* from Woden. Ex.: Wednes-bury and Wednes-field (Staff.), Woden's fortification and field.

WEE *E.* from *wæg,* a way. Ex.: Wee-ford (Staff.), Wee-don (Northam.), etc.

WEEK, WEEKS *E.* from *wic,* a dwelling or village. Ex.: Week (Cornw.), Weeke (Hants), Week-ley (Northam.). *See* Ley, *supra.*

WEET *E.* wet. Ex.: Weet-ing (Norf.), wet meadow.

WEETH *E.* from *withig,* a willow-tree. Ex.: Weeth-ley (Warw.), willow place.

WEIGH *E.* from *wæg,* a way. Ex.: Weigh-ton (Yorks.), way town.

WEL, WELL *E.* a well. Ex.: Wel-comb (Devon), well dingle; Well (Linc.).

* Domesday Book.

WEL, WELLES *E.* Where the word is followed by bourn or *ford*, it is probably from *wilig*, the willow. Ex.: Wel-ford, 3 places, willow ford; Wel-borne (Norf.), and Welles-bourn (Warw.), willow brook.

WELLAND *E.* from Weland or Welond, the Saxon Vulcan. Ex.: Welland (Worc.).

WELLING *E.* from Weland. Ex.: Welling-ore (Linc.), Weland's river bank; Walen-tun, now Welling-ton, 5 places, Weland's town.

WELLOW *E.* and *D.* from *well*, and *hoe*. Ex.: Wellow, 4 places, well hill.

WELSH *E.* from *wealas*, strangers, indicating a place inhabited by the Britons in the neighbourhood of Saxon or Anglian settlements. Ex.: Welsh Bicknor (Glouc.), the Welsh town among the beech-trees, in distinction from English Bicknor; Welsh-pool (Mont.), in distinction from Poole in Dorset.

WEM, WEMB *E.* from *wamb*, the womb, indicating a cave or a town near a cave, or sometimes a bay. Ex.: Wem (Salop); Wemb-don (Som.), cave hill; Wem-worthy (Devon), the estate near the cave or bay.

WEMBURY *E.* anciently *wicgan-beorh*, the warrior's town.* Ex.: Wembury (Devon).

WEN, WENN, WENNING, WENS, name of a saint, and *incga*, children. Ex.: Wen-loca, now Wenlock (Salop), St. Wenn's enclosure; St. Wenn's (Cornw.); Wenning-ton (Ess.), the town of St. Wenn's children; Wens-ley (Yorks.), St. Wenn's land.

WEN *B.* from *gwen*, fair.

WENOL *B.* the swallow. Ex.: Rhaiadr-y-wenol (Denbighs.), the swallow's waterfall.

WENT *B.* from *gwent*, the fair or bright land. Ex.: Nether-went and Over-went (Monm.), the lower and higher Gwent.

WENTLOOG *B.* anciently Gwynll-wg, from King Gwynlliw, sixth century. Ex.: Wentloog (Monm.), Gwynlliw's territory.

WENTWORTH *E.* probably from Wanta or Wanda, the chief's name, and *wyrth*. Ex.: Went-worth (Yorks. and Camb.), Wanta's estate; Wentn-or (Salop), Wanta's boundary or river bank.

WENVOE *B.* from St. Gwenfo. Ex.: Wenvoe (Glam.).

WEOBLEY *E.* from Wiba, the name of the owner. Ex.: Wibelai,†

* Asser.

† Domesday Book.

now Weobley (Heref.), Wiba's place; Wiba-treowes, now Webtree (ditto), Wiba's wooded district.

WEONARD *B.* from St. Wonno, a British saint. Ex.: St. Weonards (Heref.). *See* Wonas, *infra.*

WERE *E.* from *weare,* an enclosure in a river. Ex.: Were-ham (Norf.).

WERGINS *E.* anciently Wythingas, from *withiges,* willows. Ex.: Wergins (Heref.).

WERRING *E.* from *wering,* a fortification, originally one made of piles or stakes. Ex.: Werring-ton (Devon).

WERN *B.* the alder-tree. Ex.: Wern-eth (Ches.), the alders; Llan-y-wern (Brec.), the church among the alders.

WERYDD *B.* from St. Gwerydd. Ex.: Llan-werydd, St. Gwerydd's church; Caer-werydd (now Lancaster), Gwerydd's fortification.

WESSING. *See* Wash, *supra.*

WEST *E.* the west, answering to some 'East' in the neighbourhood, or indicating a site to the westward of the principal town. Ex.: West-bourn (Suss.), answering to East-bourn; West-minster, so called from lying westward of London; West-wood (Wilts), answering to East-wood.

WESTON *E.* in one case (Weston, Heref.) a contraction of Wer-estan, 'the rock of the *wer,*' or penalty of manslaughter, but in most instances derived from waest-town, *i. e.* a town built on land previously waste or uncultivated. Ex.: 34 places, all south of Trent.

WET, WITTER *E.* from *wetter,* water. Ex.: Wet-ton (Staff.), the town on a moist site; Wet-wong (Yorks.), the wet open place; Witter-ing (Suss.), the same.

WETHER, WETHERING *E.* from *weder,* a band, and *incga,* children. Ex.: Wether-al (Cumb.), the hall of the band; Wethering-sett (Suff.) the *setu* or station of the tribe called the children of the band.

WEX *B.* from *gwac,* vacant, or thinly-peopled. Ex.: Wex-ham (Bucks), thinly-peopled village.

WEY, *B.* from *wy,* water. Ex.: the river Wey (Sussex), Wey-mouth (Dorset).

WHAD *E.* from *waad,* a wood, or from *wadan,* to wade. *See* Wad.

WHAL *E.* from *wheal,* a wall. Ex.: Whal-ley (Lanc.), walled place; Whal-ey (Ches.), the same.

WHAP *E.* *See* Wap, *supra.*

WHAR *E.* from *wæg-faru,* a way by the water. *See* Wafer, *supra.*

WHARFE *E.* from *hweorf,* a whirl or eddy. Ex.: the river Wharfe (Yorks.).

WHARTON *E.* cor. from Wavretun, the town by the water's edge. Ex.: Whar-ton (Heref.).

WHEAT, WHAT *E.* from *hwæt,* wheat, indicating the place where that grain was cultivated. Ex.: 9 instances; Wheat-acre (Norf.), the wheat field; Wheaten-hurst (Glouc.), the wheat field in or near the wood; Whets-ton (Leic.), the wheat town.

WHEE *E.* *See* Wee, *supra.*

WHER *E.* from *weare,* an enclosure. Ex.: Wher-well (Hants), enclosure well.

WHET. *See* Wheat, *supra.*

WHICH *E.* from *wicca,* a witch. Ex.: Which-ford (Warw.), the witch's ford; Which-ham (Cumb.), the witch's village.

WHICK *E.* from *wicca,* a witch. Ex.: Whick-ham (Durham).

WHIL. *See* Welt, *infra.*

WHIM, WHIN *B.* from *chwynn,* a weed, meaning the gorse (*Ulex* of botany). Ex.: Whim-ple (Devon), the pool among the whins; Whin-bergh (Norf.), the fortification among the whins.

WHIPS, WHIPPING *E.* from Wibba, the lord's name, and *incga,* children. Ex.: Whip-snade (Bedf.), Wibba's snead, *i. e.* separate piece of ground; Whipp-ingaham (Hants), the home of Wibba's descendants.

WHISSEN, WHISSON, WISSETT *E.* from Whis, the Saxon word for the river now called the Vistula, and probably indicating the settlements of a Sclavonian tribe. Ex.: Whissen-dine (Rutl.), the camp of the Whis tribe; Whissen-setu and Wissetu, the stations of the same.

WHISTON, a local corruption of White's-town, having been the site of a convent of white nuns. Ex.: Whis-ton (Worc.).

WHIT, WIT *E.* from *hwit,* white. Ex.: Whit-acre (Staff.), the white farm or land; Whit-burn (Durham), Whit-bourne (Heref.), Whit-beck (Cumb.), the white brook: Wit-ley (Surr.), white land or place.

WHITE'S *E.* probably from having been the property or site of a Cistercian monastery, the monks of that order wearing a white cassock. Ex.: St. White's (Glouc.), near the Cistercian abbeys of Flaxley and Tintern; White's-town, now Whitson (Monm.), ditto.

WHITTLE, WHITTLES *E.* perhaps from *wittol*, a man who knowingly permits his wife's unfaithfulness. Ex.: Whittle-bury (Northam.), Whittles-ey (Camb.).

WIB *E.* from *Wiba*, the owner's name. Ex.: Wibs-ey (Yorks.), Wiba's pool; Web-toft (Warw.), Wiba's grave; Wiba-tun, now Web-ton (Heref.), Wiba's town.

WICK *N.* from *wic* or *vic* a village, or place where people live. Ex.: Wick (Glouc.), Wick-war (ditto), fortified village; also frequent as a suffix, *e. g.* North-wick, north village; Ber-wick, boundary village. *See* Gwic, *supra.*

WICKEN *E.* from *wigcyng* or *wiking*, war-king or pirate leader. Ex.: Wicken, 3 places; Wicken-by (Linc.), the Danish pirate's abode.

WICKERS *E.* or *N.* from *wicca*, a witch. Ex.: Wickers-ley (Yorks.), the witch's land.

WID, WIDE *E.* from *wid*, wide. Ex.: Wid-ford, 3 places, the wide ford: Wide-comb (Devon), the wide dingle.

WIDDING *E.* from *withig*, a willow, and *incga*, descendants. Ex.: Widdring-ton (Lanc.), the town of the children of the willow, or of a chief named Withig.

WIG, WIGGEN, WIGGING *E.* war, or an idol. Ex: Wig-borough (Essex), war town or idol town; Wiggen-hall, 4 places; Wigging-ton, 3 places; Wiggen-holt (Sussex), war or idol wood. The idols were probably carried in war.

WIGAN, *E.* anciently Wibiggin, the building by the water. Ex.: Wigan (Lanc.).

WIGGLES *E.* Wiglaf's, probably from Wiglaf, king of Mercia, A.D. 782. Ex.: Wiggles-worth (Leices.), Wiglaf's estate.

WIGHT, derived by Whitaker from '*guith* or *guict*, Brit., separated;' but no such words can be found except in his statement. *Gwydd* means hedged up, or overgrown with brambles. Probably the true etymon is *gwac*, vacant, or thinly peopled, which word the Romans Latinised as *vectis*, and the Saxons altered into *wight*.

WIGHTON *E.* from *wig*, war, or an idol, and *tun*, a town. Ex.: Wigh-ton (Norf.).

WIGMORE *E.* anciently *Wigcynga-mere,** the war king, or the pool of victory.

WIL, WILLES, WILLERS, WILLING, WILS *E.* from *wil,* a willow. Ex.: Wil-crick (Monm.), willow craig or rock; Willes-den (Midd.), willow hollow; Willaveslege, now Willers-ley (Heref.), willow place; Willing-ale (Essex), willow hall; Wils-den (Yorks.), willow hollow.

WILBAR, WILBER, WILBRA, WILBUR *E.* from Wilburgha, or Wilbera, the name of the chief. Ex.: Wilbars-ton (Northam.), the town of Wilbera; Wilber-foss (Yorks.), the ditch or the force (waterfall) of Wilbera; Wilbra-ham (Camb.), the home of Wilbera; Wilbur-ton (ditto), the town of the same.

WILD. *See* Weald, *supra.*

WILDBOAR, *E.* from Wilbera. Ex.: Wildboar-clough (Ches.), Wilbera's valley.

WILKS. *See* Walk, *supra.*

WILLENHALL *E.* anciently Win-heala, victory hall. Ex.: Willenhall (Staff.).

WILLEY, WILYE, *E.* from *wil-ey,* willow pool. Ex.: Wilye (Wilts); Will-ey (Salop).

WILLOUGH *E.* from *wil,* a willow. Ex.: Willough-by, 4 places, willow abode; Willough-ton (Linc.), willow town. Willoughby was anciently called Wil-byrig, willow fortification, and Wile-bei, willow abode.

WILM, WILMING *E.* from William, the owner's name, and *incga,* children. Ex.: Wilms-low (Ches.), William's hall; Wilmington (Suss.), the town of William's children.

WILT *E.* perhaps from the Wylte or Wilt, a tribe which settled in Germany in the sixth and seventh centuries,† and some members of which may have come to England. Ex.: Wiltshire, anciently spelt Wyltescyre and Wylshire.‡

WILYE *E.* *See* Willey, *supra.*

WIM, *E.* from *win,* victory. Ex.: Wim-borne (Dorset), victory brook; Wim-bach, now Wimbush (Essex), victory path; Wimes-wold (Leices.), the wood or wild place of victory.

WIMBLEDON *E.* anciently Wibban-dun, Wibba's hill.

* Lye, Camden, etc.

† Bede. Eccl. Hist. anno 696.

‡ Halle's History of England.

B. British. *C.* Celtic. *E.* The Old English, commonly known as Anglo-Saxon.

WIMBOTS *B.* perhaps from *win* and *bot*, booty, together forming the owner's name. Ex.: Wimbots-ham (Norf.), the home of Wimbot, or of the winner of booty.

WIN, WINS *E.* victory; frequent in personal names, as Ead-win, happy victory; God-win, God's victory, etc. Ex.: Win-ford (Somers.), victory ford; Win-grave (Bucks), victory entrenchment; Win-la-ton (Durham), victory meadow town; Winnall (Hants), victory hall; Wins-low (Bucks), victory's hill; Wins-treow, now Winster (Derb.), victory's trees.

WINCANTON *E.* anciently Wynd-cale-tun, the town on the bend of the river Cale. Ex.: Wincanton (Som.).

WINCE, WINCH, WINCHEL, WINCHEN *E.* from *wincel*, a corner or nook. Ex.: Wince-by (Linc.), nook abode; Winch-comb (Glouc.), nook dingle; Winchelsea (Suss.), the nook by the water; Winchen-don (Bucks), corner hill or camp.

WINCHESTRE *E.* from Venta-cestre, called by the Romans Venta Belgarum, an adaptation of *Went* or *Gwent*, the British name of the district, whence also come *Hants* and Hantun-scyre, now Hampshire. *See* Gwent.

WINDLE, WINDLES *E.* from *wendel*, the tree from which baskets were woven, *i. e.* the osier. Ex.: Windle (Glouc.); Windles-ham (Surr.), osier village; Windles-ora, now Windsor (Berks), osier shore.

WINE. *See* Win, *supra.*

WINFOR *E.* from Widferd, the Saxon lord. Ex.: Widferdes-tun* now Winforton (Heref.), Widferd's town.

WINFRITH *E.* St. Gwynifor or Winifred. Ex.: Winfrith Newburgh (Dorset), Winifred's new fortified town.

WING *E.* from *wang*, a separate piece of land or a meadow. Ex.: Wing-field (Derb.), separated meadow; Wing-ham (Kent), village on the separated meadow.

WINK *E.* from *wincel*, a corner. Ex.: Wink-field (Wilts), corner field; Wink-leigh (Devon), corner land.

WINTER *E.* occurs in 20 out of 24 instances in the southern counties; by the Britons called Gwent, and by the Romans Venta, which would be naturally Saxonised into Winter. Ex.: Winterbourne (20 places in Dorset, Wilts, and Glouc.), meaning Venta brook.

WINTER-TON (Norf. and Linc.) and WINTERING-HAM (Linc.), are

* Domesday Book.

D. Old Danish. *G.* Greek. *L.* Latin. *N.F.* Norman French. *N.* Norse. *qu. v.* which see.

perhaps from some Norse chief named Gunter, and indicate his town and the home of his descendants respectively.

WIRKSWORTH *E.* the estate upon which mine-works were carried on. Ex.: Wirks-worth (Derb.), the seat of lead mining in Roman and Saxon times as well as now.

WIRRALL, anciently Wir-hall, from *gwyrdd* (*B.*), green, or grass-colour, and *haela* (*E.*), a hall. Ex.: Wirrall (Ches.), the hall on the grassy site.

WIS, WISE, WISH *E.* from *wæs*, moisture. Ex.: Wis-beach (Camb.), moist beach; Wis-borough (Sussex), the fortification in the moist place; Wise-ley (Surrey), moist place; Wishaw, *i. e.* Waes-scua (Warw.), moist wood; Wish-ford (Wilts), the ford in the marshy spot.

WISSING. *See* Wessing, *supra*.

WISTAN, WISTAS *E.* corrupted from Stephen's.* Ex.: Wistan-stow (Salop), Stephen's palisaded fortifications; Wistas-ton (Heref. and Ches.), Stephen's town.

WIT *E.* from *hwit*, white or fair. Ex.: Wit-ley (Surrey), white place; Wit-ton, 7 places.

WITCH *E.* from *wicca*, a witch. Ex.: 6 places; Witching-ham, *i. e.* Wiccan-ham (Norf.), the witch's village, or the village near some (supposed) bewitched tree.

WITH, WITHAM *E.* from *withig*, a willow. Ex.: With-ham, now Witham, 4 places, willow village; With-ern (Linc.), willow place; Withers-field (Suff.), *i. e.* withiges-field, the field of the willows; Withing-ton, 6 places, willow town.

WITHER, WITHERS, WITHING, WITHY *E.* from *withig*, a willow, frequent as both prefix and suffix. Ex.: Withy-brook (Warw.); Withing-ton (Heref.); Hoar-withy (Heref.), the gray willow; Wither-ley (Leices.); Withers-field (Suff.).

WITHIEL *B.* from Gwyddel, an Irishman. Earl Withiel was the lord of Lostwithiel in Saxon times. *See* Lost, *supra*. Ex.: Withiel (Som. and Cornw.).

WITN, WITTEN *E.* from *witan*, the national assembly. Ex.: Witn-ey (Oxf.), the witan's island or water; Witten-ham (Berks), the witan's village.

* Camden.

B. British. *C.* Celtic. *E.* The Old English, commonly known as Anglo-Saxon.

WITTER *E.* from *wetter*, water. *See* Wet, *supra.*

WIVE, WIVEN *E.* from Wyfa, or Wyva, name of the owner. Ex.: Wive-ton (Norf.), Wyva's town; Wiven-hoe (Ess.), Wyva's hill.

WIVELIS, WIVELS *E.* from *wifel*, a weevil. Ex.: Wivelis-comb (Som.), the weevil's valley; Wivels-field (Suss.), the weevil's field. Or perhaps from Wig-bold, the daring warrior, name of the chief.

WIX *E.* from *wicca*, a witch. Ex.: Wix, *i. e.* wicca's (Essex), the witch's place; Wix-ford (Warw.), the witch's ford.

WO, WOO *E.* from *woh*, a turning. Ex.: Wo-burn (Bedf.), Woo-burn (Bucks), the bend of the brook.

WOKING *E.* from *woh*, a turning, and *cina*, a way. Ex.: Woking (Surrey), the turning of the way; Woking-ham (Berks), the village at the turning of the way.

WOL, WOLD *E.* from *wold*, uncultivated land. Wol-borough (Devon), the fortification on the wold; Wolding-ham (Surr.), the village on the wold; Wol-ford (Warw.), wold ford.

WOLF *E.* from Ulf, the name of the owner. Ex.: Wolf-ham-cote (Warw.), the sheep-cote of Ulf's home.

WOLFER *E.* from Wulfhere, king of Mercia, A.D. 656. Ex.: Wolfer-low, Wolfer-ton (Heref.), Wulfhere's hill and town.

WOLS, WOLLAS, WOOLAS *E.* from St. Woolas. Ex.: Wols-ton (Warw.), Wollas-ton (Worces.), Woolas-ton (Glouc.), St. Woolas (Monm.).

WOLSTAN *E.* from St. Wulstan. Ex.: Wolstan-ton (Staff.). Wolf-stan or Wulstan means the wolf's rock.

WOOD *E.* from *wuda*, a wood. Ex: Wood-setts (Derb.), the tribe-station in the wood.

WOOD *E.* from *wuda*, a wood. Ex.: 40 places in which it is a prefix, and frequently a suffix.

WOLVER, WOLVES, WOLVEY *E.* from Wulfhere. Ex.: Wolver-ton, 4 places; Wolver-hampton (Staff.); Wolves-newton *i. e.* Wulfhere's new town (Monm.); Wolv-ey (Warw.), Wulf-here's water or pool.

WOM *E.* probably from Wan, a contraction of Woden, the name of the war-god. Ex.: Wom-bourn and Wom-bridge (Staff.), Woden's brook and bridge; Womb-well (Yorks.), Woden's well.

WOMENSWOULD, WOMERS *E.* from Wymond or Wigmond, the

warlike protector, and *wold*, uncultivated land. Ex.: Womens would (Kent), Wymond's wold; Womers-ley (Yorks.), Wymond's land.

WON *E.* from *waning*, a dwelling. Ex.: Won-ersh (Surr.), perhaps the dwelling in the marsh.

WONAS, WEONARDS, WONNO *B.* from St. Wonno. Ex.: Wonas-stow (Monm.), St. Wonno's station; St. Wonnard's or Weonard's (Heref.); Llan-wonno (Glam.), St. Wonno's church.

WOOL *E.* from *wold*, uncultivated land. Ex.: Wool-beding (Suss.), the low place on the wold.

WOOLAS, WOOLOS. *See* Wols, *supra.*

WOOLFARDIS *E.* from Wulfhere. Ex.: Woolfardis-worthy (Devon), Wulfere's estate.

WOOLHOPE *B.* and *E.*, anciently Hope Woolith, from *hwpp*, a slope, *wold*, uncultivated, and *ith* (doubtful, but may be cognate with *ytyng*, a way). Ex.: Woolhope (Herf.), the way of the uncultivated slope.

WOOLSTOS, WOOLSTON, St. Wulstan's. *See* Wolstan, *supra.*

WOOLVER. *See* Wolver, *supra.*

WOOT. *See* Wood, *supra.* Wootton occurs in 19 places.

WOR *E.* perhaps from *wære*, a weir or enclosure on a stream. Ex.: Wor-field (Salop), weir field; Wor-stead (Norf.), Worsthorne (Lanc.).

WORCESTER *E.* anciently Wigera-ceastre. The people of Worcestershire (anciently Wigera-ceastre-scyr) were called Hwycce: a word of uncertain derivation, but which may mean the people of the windings of the Severn. 'Wych' is a local word meaning a bend or turning,* and Wigera seems to be from Hwycce. Bede calls the people 'Wiccii.'

WORLA, WORLA *E.* from Worla, the owner's name, from whence comes Worling, the property of Worla. Ex.: Worla-by (Linc.), Worla's abode; Worling-ham (Devon), the village belonging to Worla; Worle (Som.), Worla-ham, now World-ham (Hants).

WORLDSEND *E.* the end of the world, *i. e.* the last cultivated spot at the edge of a waste or forest. Ex.: frequent in Mercian counties.

WORLOD *B.* from *gweirglôdd*, a meadow. Ex.: Pen-y-worlod (Rad.), head of the meadow.

* Edwin Lees, F.S.A.

B. British. *C.* Celtic. *E.* The Old English, commonly known as Anglo-Saxon.

WORM *E.* perhaps from *ormr*, Norse, the serpent or dragon, a warlike symbol or banner used by both Britons and Angles. In some cases, probably, it refers to the monsters so frequently mentioned in legends and ballads. Ex.: Worm river, Wormelow, and Worm-bridge (Herf.), Worming-ton (Glouc.), Worm-hill (Derb.), etc.

WORT, WORD from *wyrt*, a herb; whence *wyrt-tun*, a garden. Ex.: Wort-ley (Yorks.), Word-well (Suff.), Wort-well (Norf.).

WORTH, WORTHEN, WORTHIN, WORTHING, WORTING, WORTHY *E.* from *wyrth*, an estate or manor, usually one well watered. Ex.: Worth (Kent), Worthen-bury (Flints.), Worthing (Mont.), Worthing, anciently Worthung (Suss.), Worthy (Hants), Worting (Hants). As a suffix frequent in S. W. Yorkshire.

WOT. *See* Woot, *supra*.

WOUGH *E.* from *woh*, a turning. Ex.: Wough-ton (Bucks).

WOULD. *See* Wold, *supra*.

WRACH *B.* from *gwrach*, an old woman, probably indicating lands belonging to a dowager. Ex.: Pwll-y-wrach (Glam.), the old woman's pool.

WRAG, WRAX, WREAK, (doubtful), but probably from the same root with the Danish *vrag*, a wreck, and the Saxon *wræccan*, to avenge or destroy. Ex.: Wrag-by (Yorks. and Linc.), the abode of the Danish destroyer; Wrax-hall (Dorset), the destroyer's hall; Wreak-dale (Leices.), the destroyer's dale.

WRAT, WRET, WROT *E.* probably the same as *rate*, aquatic herbage. Ex.: Wrat-ting (Norf.), the *ing* or meadow near a stream full of rate; Wret-ton (Norf.), Wrot-ham (Kent).

WRAY, WREY, WRAN, WROUGH *E.* perhaps from the same root as *awry*, crooked; *B. gwragen*, a bow. Ex.: Wray (Lanc.), Wran-by (Linc.), the crooked town or village; Wrough-ton (Wilts), the same; Wrey river (Devon).

WRDA *B.* a saint's name. Ex.: Llan-wrda (Carmar.), St. Wrda's church.

WREN, WRENT *E.* perhaps from *wrenna*, a wren, adopted as the cognisance and thence as the name of the owner. Ex.: Wrenbury (Ches.), Wrent-ham (Suff.).

WRENNING, from Wrenna and *incga*. Ex.: Wrenning-ham (Norf.), the home of the children of Wrenna, which name still survives as Wren.

WREX, WROCK, WROX, probably identical with the first syllable in Uriconium, the Latin name of Wroxeter. *Wr* seems to be the British word *gwr*, a man, and may have been the name of the British tribe who inhabited the district of Salop and Denbighshire, in which only the names Wrexham, Wrockwardine, and Wroxeter occur. A parallel instance is found in the case of the ancient Germans, who called themselves Alemanni, or 'all men.'

WRING *E.* from *wringan*, to twist. Ex.: Wring-ton, and the Cheese-wring (Som.), the town of the stone twisted into the shape of a cheese, a trace of the ancient belief that huge stones owed their strange shapes to the agency of supernatural beings.

WROCK. *See* Wrex.

WROT. *See* Wrat.

WROX. *See* Wrex.

WY, WYE *B.* from *gwy*, water. Ex.: Wy-cliff (Yorks.), the cliff by the water; Wye (Kent); the river Wye (Derb. and Heref.).

WYKE *N.* from *wic* or *vic*, a village. Ex.: Wyke-ham (Yorks.), village home; Wyken (Warw.), the villages; Wyke Regis (Dorset), the king's village.

WYMER, WYMES, WYMING, WYMOND, WYND *E.* from Wigmund, protection in war, the name of the owner. Ex.: Wymer-ing (Hants), Wigmund's meadow; Wymes-wold (Leices.), Wigmund's place on the wold; Wyming-ton (Bedf.), Wigmund's town; Wymund-ham or Wyndham (Norf.), Wigmund's home.

WYN *B.* from *gwyn*, white or fair. Ex.: Ber-wyn (Mont.), the white boundary.

WYNDAF *B.* from St. Gwyndaf. Ex.: Llan-wyndaf (Glam.) St. Gwyndaf's church.

WYNNO *B.* from St. Gwynno. Ex.: Llan-wynno (Glam.), St. Gwynno's church.

WYT. *See* Wit.

WYVERS, WYVILLE. *See* Wivel.

Y.

Y, *B.* of the. Ex.: Pen-y-bont (Radn.), head of the bridge.

YALDING *E.* from *eald,* old. Ex.: Yald-ing (Kent), the old place in the meadow.

YAP *E.* perhaps from Eappa, a Saxon priest so named, one of the first missionaries to Sussex and the Isle of Wight, A.D. 681.* Ex.: Yap-ton (Suss.), Eappa's town.

YAR *B.* the river Yare. Ex.: Yarmouth (Norf. and Hants), the mouth of the Yare.

YARD *E.* from *geard,* an enclosure. Ex.: Yard-ley, 4 places, enclosed land; Brom-yard (Heref.), the broomy enclosure; Yard-borough, now Yarborough (Linc.), the fortified enclosure.

YARE *B.* from *iâr,* an ancient word for a river.† Ex.: the river Yare (Norf.); the Yar (Isle of Wight).

YARKHILL *E.* or *D.* anciently ‡ Archel, from Orchil, the chief's name. Ex.: Yarkhill (Heref.).

YARLINGTON *E.* probably from *eorling,* the possession of a jarl or pirate leader, whence our title *earl.* Ex.: Yarling-ton (Som.), the town of the earl's possession.

YARM, *B., S.* from *iâr,* river, and *ham,* a dwelling. Ex.: Yar-ham now Yarm (Yorks.), the dwelling near the river.

YARN *B.* from *garn,* a monumental heap of stones. Ex.: Yarnscomb (Devon), the dingle of the monumental heap; Yarnton (Oxf.).

YARPOLE *B.* from *iâr,* river, and *pwll,* a pool. Ex.: Yar-pole (Heref.), river pool.

YAT, YATTES, YATTEN *E.* perhaps from Eata, the name of a Saxon bishop of Lindisfarne, consecrated A. D. 681, very famous in his day, and often mentioned by Bede in his Eccl. Hist. Ex. Yat-ton (Heref.), Eata's town; Yate's-burh, now Yatesbury (Wilts), Eata's fortified town; Yatten-den (Berks), Eata's hill.

YATE *B.* from *iat,* a gate. Ex.: Yate (Glouc.), the gate.

* Bede. † Richards' Welsh Dictionary. ‡ Domesday Book.

YAVER *E.* from *efe*, the brink of a stream. Ex.: Yaverland (Hants), the land on the brink of a stream.

YAX *E.* from *æc*, an oak, or *æcse*, an axe, indicating a clearing in the forest. Ex.: Yax-ham (Norf.); Yax-ley (Suff. and Hants).

YAZOR, *E.* from *eás*, possessive case of *ea*, water, and *or*, a boundary. Ex.: Yazor (Heref.), water boundary.

YEA *E. ea*, water. Ex.: Yea-don (Yorks.), the hill by the water.

YEDDING *E.* from Edwin or Eadwin, king of Northumbria. Ex.: Yedding-ham (Yorks.), Edwin's home.

YEL, YELD, YELL *E.* from *yeldo*, a crane, probably the cognizance and afterwards the name of the owner. Ex.: Yel-don (Bedf.), crane's hill; Yeld-ham (Ess.), owner's village; The Yeld (Heref.); Yell-ing (Hunts), crane's meadow.

YELVER *E.* from *Ælfric*, the fairy ruler, name of the owner. Ex.: Yelver-ton (Norf.), Ælfric's town; Yelver-toft (Northamp.), Ælfric's grove.

YEO *E.* from *ea*, water. Ex.: Yeo-vil (Som.), the vill or town near the water called Yeo.

YET *E.* from *yth*, water. Ex.: Yet-minster (Som.), the monastic church by the water.

YN *B.* a place. Ex.: Dilwyn (Heref.), the idol's place, *qu. v. supra.*

YNYS *B.* an island. Ex.: Ynys-cynhaiarn (Carnarv.), Cynhaiarn's island; Allt-yr-ynys (Heref.), the steep place of the island.

YORK *L.* from Eboracum, the Roman name of the city, corrupted to Eoracum, and thence to Eorc.

YOUL *E.* perhaps from *geal*, bright, when also *gealcf* (*S.*), yellow, and afterwards a personal name still in use in Scotland as Youill, Youll, etc. Ex.: Youl-grave (Derb.), the entrenched house of Youl.

YOX. *See* Yax, *supra.*

YR *B.* the. Ex.: Dan-yr-allt, below the steep place.

YS *B.* below. Ex.: Ys-ceifiog (Flints.), below the Ceifiog, or the hunting-ground.

YSPYTTY *B.* from *hospitium*, a hospital. Ex.: Yspytty-ystwyth (Card.), the hospital on the bank of the Ystwyth.

YSTERN *B.* corrupted from *ystrin*, strife or contention. Ex.: Llanfihangel-ystrin-llewyrn (Mon.), St. Michael's church at the battle-field of the will-o'-the-wisp. The tradition is that a prince, having been guided out of a bog by a meteor of the kind mentioned, built a church on the spot.

Ystref, Ystry *B.* a village.

Ystrad *B.* a vale. Ex.: Ystrad-tywy (Carm.), the vale of the Tywy river.

Ystwyth *B.* flexible or winding. Ex.: the river Ystwyth (Card.).

Yw *B.* a yew tree. Ex.: Ystrad-yw (now Crick-howell), yew valley.

D. Old Danish. *G.* Greek. *L.* Latin. *N.F.* Norman French. *N.* Norse. *qu. v.* which see.

Z.

ZEAL. *See* Seal, *supra.*

ZENNOR, from St. Sennor or Sannor, a British saint. Ex.: Zennor (Cornw.).

APPENDIX.

Forgotten Names.—p. 49.

THE changes which time has brought about, in substituting names altogether new for those which were formerly in use, are most evident on a comparison of the designations of the hundreds as given in 'Domesday Book' with those by which they are now known. So completely are the old names obliterated in many instances, that it is only by reference to the places named as situated in particular hundreds that we can form a guess as to the parts of the country which were included; no precise idea of the boundaries of the ancient hundreds is obtainable in any way, nor can we even ascertain when the change took place. As, however, the present names all belong to the English of the pre-Conquest period, it is evident that the change must have taken place at a time when Norman-French had ceased to be the official language. In some cases, the change must have occurred even as late as the sixteenth century. For example, 'Domesday Book' describes 'Ewias' as in the hundred of 'Wrmelau,' yet the Act of Henry VIII. annexes the castlery of Ewias with other districts adjoining to the county of Hereford, and we now find them forming a hundred by themselves under the title of Ewias Lacy. The county of Hereford, indeed, may be taken as an example of the great changes which have been made, we know not when, in both the names and the number of the hundreds. As given in Domesday Book they are as follows:—

Bromesash, Bremesc, Bromesce, all evidently meaning the same hundred
Plegeliet
Dodintret
Nusse
Hazetrev, or Hagetrev
Dvnre
Stradford, or Stratford
Thorneleu, or Tcrnelau
Wimondestrev
Cutethorne, or Cutestorne
Stapel, or Stepleset
Elsedune
Vlfei, or Vlfagie
Wigmore
Greitrewes, or Gretrewe

The present hundreds are:—

Wigmore
Stretford
Huntington
Grimsworth
Webtree
Ewias Lacy
Wormelow
Greytree
Radley
Broxash
Wolphy

It is thus to be noted that there are now only eleven hundreds instead of the fifteen which existed in the eleventh century, and if we bear in mind the addition made to the county in the time of Henry VIII. (as already noticed), it will be observed that six of the ancient hundreds have been obliterated. As the number of villages has been but very slightly increased since Domesday survey, the few fresh ones being nearly counterbalanced by those which are now no longer discoverable, while others which were then villages are now mere farms or hamlets—it is fair to infer that, first, the hundreds were smaller in the eleventh century than at present, and next that that part of the *scyre* organisation was not subject to any special law or fixed rule, but followed the fortunes of war. The hundred of Greitrewes then included the city of Hereford, but now does not approach within seven or eight miles of that city. The boundaries of the shires, we find, did vary in like manner. Domesday Book includes in Herefordshire the manor of 'Monemude,' in which it is easy to recognise Monmouth, and also 'Raddrenore,' and several other places, which are now in Radnorshire, but seem to have been conquered by the Anglians and settled at some time before 1086.

A comparison of the lists shows that of the fifteen hundreds named in Domesday Book only four now remain, while seven fresh names have been introduced. The roots out of which they have been formed will be found in the Vocabulary *singulatim*; but it may be noted here that they are all compounded from names of villages or places in the hundreds themselves, with certain variations which show that the framers thought in the Old English language, whatever may have been the official language at the time. Thus Wormelow means the *hlaew*, or hilly tract in which the river Worm rises. Radlow, in like manner, is 'the red hills,' a name which shows that the namers had eyes for physical characteristics; the red sandstone and the deep red soil which lies upon it being striking features of the district. The syllable *rad* occurs also in the name of the adjoining county of 'Radnor,' the red boundary district. The hundred of Huntington is evidently named from the village of Huntington, which is situated at its extreme limit westward. Grimsworth and Broxash are names entirely fresh to the border counties, and seem to belong to the period of the Saxon conquest of Mercia under Æthelstan and his successors. Broxash, meaning the badger's ash-trees, suggests a familiarity with West Saxon modes of speech: the ash-tree forming the distinctive word in many names of places in Wessex. Grimsworth, on the other hand, is a trace of the Angle; Grim or Grime being a name which is found elsewhere only in the Anglian districts of south-west Yorkshire and north Lincolnshire; while *worth*, meaning a well-watered estate, is very rare beyond the boundaries of the same Anglian districts. The name Webtree seems to have been constructed on the model of Greytree, the name of the adjoining hundred, the framer taking the first part of the name 'Webton' as the distinctive syllable. The 'Greitrewes' of Domesday Book, and the 'Greytree' of the present day are shown to be the same by the names of several of the places mentioned in the former hundred; and the name is curious as suggesting the great antiquity of the family of Grey in the 'Trewes,' a forest district which then included most of the south-east part of Herefordshire. As Greys of Wilton, they remained lords of part of their vast ancestral domain down to the time of Charles II. Ewias Lacy in like manner recals the memory of the great baronial house of Lacy, whose earldom of Shrewsbury seems to have included a very large part of Herefordshire. Their greatness, however, was but brief; they soon died out or fell from the baronial rank, and the persistence of their name as the distinctive designation of so many places in Herefordshire is all the more remarkable when we consider the very short time in which they were lords of the soil, and the many changes of ownership which have occurred in the seven centuries which have passed since their fall.

The designation 'Norse.'—p. 8, *et seq.*

By Norse, I mean the Danske Tunge, the ancient tongue spoken over Scandinavia, which is now preserved to a remarkable extent in the Icelandic.—Johnes' *Philological Proofs of the Unity of the Human Race.*

'*Aber.*'—p. 121.

Aber, Celtic, from *ab*, water, and *ber*, effervescence.—*Ibid.*

'*Stock.*'—p. 261.

Generally this word means a place, but it seems to have originally meant—first, a post or stake, then an idol, and afterwards a place protected by a fortification of stakes. Its second stage is shown by a passage in Bishop Ælfric's translation of the Bible:

'Ge heornath stoccum und stanum.'—Deut. xxxviii. 36, 64.

This use of the word is illustrated by the habit of the New Zealanders of the present day, who carve into grotesqne figures of their gods the heads of the stakes of which their fortifications are composed. A New Zealander's 'pah,' indeed, seems to be very similar in most respects to the *stoke* or *stow* of the Angles and Saxons. Possibly they in like manner ornamented the heads of their *stoccum* with rude figures of Thor, or Baldur, or Woden; and so the same word came naturally to mean both the *stoc* and the idol carved upon it.

'*The Strid.*'—p. 116.

Derived by some from *stryth*, a contest, alluding to the tumultuous rush of waters; but I think rather from *strid*, a contracted form of the past participle of *gestrídan* (S.), to stride or step over anything.

LONDON: PRINTED BY
SPOTTISWOODE AND CO., NEW-STREET SQUARE
AND PARLIAMENT STREET

www.ingramcontent.com/pod-product-compliance
Lightning Source LLC
Chambersburg PA
CBHW021219270326
41929CB00010B/1192